Doing African Philosophy

Bloomsbury Introductions to World Philosophies

Series Editor:
Monika Kirloskar-Steinbach
Assistant Series Editor:
Leah Kalmanson
Regional Editors:
Nader El-Bizri, James Madaio, Ann A. Pang-White, Takeshi Morisato, Pascah Mungwini, Mickaella Perina, Omar Rivera and Georgina Stewart

Bloomsbury Introductions to World Philosophies delivers primers reflecting exciting new developments in the trajectory of world philosophies. Instead of privileging a single philosophical approach as the basis of comparison, the series provides a platform for diverse philosophical perspectives to accommodate the different dimensions of cross-cultural philosophizing. While introducing thinkers, texts and themes emanating from different world philosophies, each book, in an imaginative and path-breaking way, makes clear how it departs from a conventional treatment of the subject matter.

Titles in the Series:

A Practical Guide to World Philosophies, by Monika Kirloskar-Steinbach and Leah Kalmanson
Daya Krishna and Twentieth-Century Indian Philosophy, by Daniel Raveh
Māori Philosophy, by Georgina Tuari Stewart
Philosophy of Science and The Kyoto School, by Dean Anthony Brink
Tanabe Hajime and the Kyoto School, by Takeshi Morisato
African Philosophy, by Pascah Mungwini
The Zen Buddhist Philosophy of D. T. Suzuki, by Rossa Ó Muireartaigh
Sikh Philosophy, by Arvind-Pal Singh Mandair
The Philosophy of the Brahma-sūtra, by Aleksandar Uskokov
The Philosophy of the Yogasūtra, by Karen O'Brien-Kop
The Life and Thought of H. Odera Oruka, by Gail M. Presbey

Mexican Philosophy for the 21st Century, by Carlos Alberto Sánchez
Buddhist Ethics and the Bodhisattva Path, by Stephen Harris
Contextualizing Angela Davis, by Joy James
Yorùbá Art and Aesthetics, by Barry Hallen
Phenomenology of Tea, by Adam Loughnane

Doing African Philosophy

Beyond Textuality and Individual Authorship

Elvis Imafidon

BLOOMSBURY ACADEMIC
LONDON • NEW YORK • OXFORD • NEW DELHI • SYDNEY

BLOOMSBURY ACADEMIC

Bloomsbury Publishing Plc, 50 Bedford Square, London, WC1B 3DP, UK
Bloomsbury Publishing Inc, 1359 Broadway, New York, NY 10018, USA
Bloomsbury Publishing Ireland, 29 Earlsfort Terrace, Dublin 2, D02 AY28, Ireland

BLOOMSBURY, BLOOMSBURY ACADEMIC and the Diana logo are trademarks of Bloomsbury Publishing Plc

First published in Great Britain 2026

Copyright © Elvis Imafidon, 2026

Elvis Imafidon has asserted his right under the Copyright, Designs and Patents Act, 1988, to be identified as Author of this work.

For legal purposes the Acknowledgements on p. xi constitute an extension of this copyright page.

Series design by Louise Dugdale
Cover image: Fokasu Art/Adobe Stock

All rights reserved. No part of this publication may be: i) reproduced or transmitted in any form, electronic or mechanical, including photocopying, recording or by means of any information storage or retrieval system without prior permission in writing from the publishers; or ii) used or reproduced in any way for the training, development or operation of artificial intelligence (AI) technologies, including generative AI technologies. The rights holders expressly reserve this publication from the text and data mining exception as per Article 4(3) of the Digital Single Market Directive (EU) 2019/790.

Bloomsbury Publishing Plc does not have any control over, or responsibility for, any third-party websites referred to or in this book. All internet addresses given in this book were correct at the time of going to press. The author and publisher regret any inconvenience caused if addresses have changed or sites have ceased to exist, but can accept no responsibility for any such changes.

A catalogue record for this book is available from the British Library.

A catalog record for this book is available from the Library of Congress.

ISBN:	HB:	978-1-3504-6427-8
	PB:	978-1-3504-6423-0
	ePDF:	978-1-3504-6424-7
	eBook:	978-1-3504-6425-4

Typeset by RefineCatch Limited, Bungay, Suffolk
Printed and bound in Great Britain

For product safety related questions contact productsafety@bloomsbury.com.

To find out more about our authors and books visit www.bloomsbury.com and sign up for our newsletters.

*To my soulmate and anchor, Sandra
And in fond memory of my first educators and
loving parents, Marcus and Alice Imafidon*

Contents

Acknowledgements		xi
Series Editor Preface		xiii
Foreword		xiv
Preliminaries: Doing African Philosophy		1
Doing Philosophy		1
The African Way		5
Reimagining Identity		10
1	Redefining a Philosophical Tradition	17
	The Dominant Understanding of a Philosophical Tradition	18
	Contesting Individual Authorship	26
	Contesting Textuality	33
	Contesting the Politics of Naming and Transgenerational Coherency	40
	Contesting Whiteness and Literacy	43
	What is a Philosophical Tradition?	47
2	The Orality of African Philosophy	51
	Oral Repositories of Philosophy	52
	Orality, Transgenerationality and Epistemic Reliability	61
	Language, Orality and Truth	67
	Names and the Philosophy of Human Existence	71
	Oralizing Relationality	74
3	Symbolism and African Philosophy	81
	Problematizing the Aesthetic Hermeneutical Encounter	82
	Creating, Performing and Curating Philosophy	87
	Symbolizing Ontological Commitments	92
	Symbolizing Individuality in Relationality	96
	Symbolizing Knowing and Learning	101

4	The Textuality of African Philosophy	109
	Legacies	110
	Resistance	116
	Defence	123
	Mirroring	127
	Doing	131
5	Trans-textuality and Collaborative Strategies	137
	Trans-textuality and the Crisis of Relevance	139
	Afro-communitarianism as Method toward Ecocentric Intellectuality	144
	Relationality, Fluidity and Difference	149
	Collaborative Research and Pedagogies	154
	On Polemics and Enigmatics	158
6	Contemporaneities and Futures: On Street Philosophy	165
	Acknowledging Contemporaneity: Philosophy in the Streets	167
	Japa, Sapa and the Philosophy of Migration	172
	'School na Scam': Critiquing Education	175
	Reimagining Futures	181

References	187
Index	199

Acknowledgements

The problematizing of authorship as purely emerging from subjective intellectuality quickly becomes apparent from the pages of this book. It follows, therefore, that although I am clearly acknowledged as the author of this book, my authoring has benefitted from, depended largely on, and is indebted to intersubjective, co-embodied, and co-positioned intellectualities and collaborations.

I am, first and foremost, indebted to the many indigenous African communities for the oral, symbolic and textual repositories of philosophical knowledge that I have heavily relied upon in drafting this book. This book would not exist without the presence and availability of the carefully and painstakingly preserved textual and non-textual knowledge forms, such as names, proverbs, stories, adages, parables and other enigmatic sayings, as well as disruptive texts and symbols in African traditions. I am also grateful to all those who, throughout my life and particularly during my research for this book, have exposed me to African ways of doing philosophy and producing philosophical knowledge.

I would like to express my sincere gratitude to the institutions and individuals who, in one way or another, have provided the opportunity and enabling environment to draft and curate this work. In particular, I am thankful to the British Academy for awarding me the 2024–2025 Mid-Career Fellowship grant, which allowed me time away from my usual academic and administrative duties to primarily focus on writing this book. Additionally, I am grateful to several institutions in Ghana and Nigeria that granted me access to their rich collections of African arts and symbols during my research for this book, including the National Museum of Ghana, the Museum of Archaeology at the University of Ghana, the National Museum in Lagos, Nigeria, the Nike Art Gallery in Lagos, Nigeria, and the National Museum in Benin City, Nigeria. Many of my colleagues, students and friends have also been incredibly helpful through formal and informal discussions, a display of care and collegiality, as well as suggestions and recommendations. Notable among them are Ana Nenadovic, Richard King, Isaac Ukpokolo, Ayman Shihadeh, Polycarp Ikuenobe, Kenneth Uyi Abudu, Austine Iyare, Richmond Kwesi, Chika Mba, Stefania Travagnin, Amanda Suzzane Evans, Sunday Alabi and Momoh Yunusa Ahmed. I cannot overlook the indispensable role played by my Research and Knowledge Exchange colleagues at SOAS University of London, both past and present, including Christopher Machell and Tameka Thompson, in securing the British Academy grant and successfully carrying out this research, as well as the support received from the Bloomsbury Introductions to World Philosophies Series team including Monika Kirloskar-Steinbach, Colleen Coalter and Aimee Brown.

My family has always been a source of support and provided me with a relaxing and enabling environment to carry out my research and writing. I am very much indebted to my wife, Sandra, and my children, Evelyn, Ellen, Elliott and Emilia, for being supportive, patient, caring and genuinely concerned about the progress of this work, creating as much space and time as possible for me to work on it. I am also grateful to my siblings, Collins, Felix, Kester, Rita, Itohan and Ivie, for their support, love and care. Above all, I am indebted to the Nonpareil Being for leading and guiding me through the paths of life.

Series Editor's Preface

Bloomsbury Introductions to World Philosophies offers plural, hitherto unexplored pathways into the study of world philosophies. Instead of privileging a single philosophical approach as the basis of comparison, the series provides a platform for diverse philosophical perspectives to accommodate the many different dimensions of cross-cultural philosophizing. While the choice of terms used by the individual volumes may indeed carry a local inflection, they do not foreclose critical thinking about philosophical plurality. Each individual volume strikes a balance between locality and globality.

Doing African Philosophy dwells on the embodied and collaborative nature of philosophical activity in general, and African philosophy in particular. Zeroing in on the concept of Africa that is rich with meaning for sub-Saharan peoples and those associated with them beyond the African continent, Elvis Imafidon details how people in this specific place have utilized oral and symbolic repositories to think about different aspects of a lived philosophy, beginning from determining the subjects of interpretation to the viability of a philosophical method. Paying close attention to the manner in which the concept of African philosophy is embodied, collaborative and ecocentric in differently lived contexts, Imafidon carefully works out the concept of an African self and its specific way of being in the world, while performing what it means to belong to the African philosophical tradition here and now. Through such an unabashed acknowledgement of its philosophical identity, *Doing African Philosophy* showcases how to do academic philosophy today.

Monika Kirloskar-Steinbach

Foreword
Wisdom Has Feet: On Doing, Living, and Becoming African Philosophy

By
Michael Onyebuchi Eze

What does it mean to do African philosophy? Why African philosophy – and for whom? Whose voice speaks when we say 'Africa'? Should we speak of African philosophy, or of philosophies from Africa? And who gets to ask these questions – and why?[1] These are not idle musings. They are foundational questions, etched into the very tissue of Africa's intellectual history – questions that throb with urgency, legacy, and longing. To approach them is to enter a contested space: a space where the production of knowledge in Africa is never merely academic, but always historical, embodied, and insurgent. It is a space marked by contemporaneity – not merely the co-existence of now and then, but the braided presence of past, present, and possible futures. In this view, knowledge is not a possession to be owned or hoarded. It is a living inheritance – a flame that grows only when shared. It circulates not as transaction, but as tradition: performative, situated, breathing. It is both a gift and a task, diffused through storytelling, carved into symbols, carried in proverbs, and sung through generations. As Valentin Mudimbe reminds us, to do African philosophy then, is not only to think, but to remember. To share. To build. To live:

> Families reenact this discourse in their ordinary lives; mothers consciously transmit its rules to their children [. . .] and the community as a whole – through its procedures of initiation, schooling and socialization – will make sure it produces a citizen who has the 'feel' of

---

[1] See Eze, M.O. and T. Metz. 'Emergent Issues in African Philosophy: A Dialogue with Kwasi Wiredu', *Philosophia Africana*, 17 (2):75–87 (2015).

a tradition and who thus, as an adult, will act and react normally and correctly in everyday life.²

Mudimbe's observation is reminiscent of the Akan proverb: *'Wisdom is like a baobab tree; no one individual can embrace it.'* Being a baobab tree, African philosophy then is prefigured within a constant quest for knowing; negotiation, engaging, questioning and understanding that no one individual has monopoly of knowledge. Somewhere else, I have referred to this epistemic conditionality for knowledge acquisition as 'ontological turbulence', that is, a recognition that no system of knowing, or philosophy thus acquired is absolute; for philosophy is ever on a shaky ground, in a turbulence.³

Here, a lesson for us all as in this Kirundi proverb, *'ukura utabaza ugasaza utamenye'* which suggests that *'if one grows up without asking question, then they will die like an idiot'.* On this point, the community is not merely a place for knowledge production, but an interactive space for performativity which then induces a contemporaneous learning culture. Learning is not a destination but a lifelong unfolding – an ever-deepening act of becoming.⁴ And knowledge, like a flame, is not diminished when shared. As another Kirundi proverb reminds us: *'Ubwenge bukura iyo busangiwe'* – wisdom grows when it is shared. The more it is offered, the more it multiplies. This truth echoes across the continent. The Malian saying tells us: *'When an elder dies, a library burns to the ground.'* In that loss is more than memory – it is the silencing of lived insight, the closing of questions never asked, the vanishing of a world of experience not passed on. To share knowledge, then, is not merely an act of generosity – it is an ethical gesture of preservation, a weaving of continuity across generations. It is how we keep the library

---

² V.Y. Mudimbe, *The Idea of Africa* (James Currey, 1994), xiii
³ Eze, M.O. 'Interculturality as Dialogical Reciprocity in African and Comparative Philosophy' in Dutch philosophical journal *Philosophy and Practice* (Filosofie en Praktijk) special issue on African philosophy and interculturality, Filosofie & Praktijk 43 (2022) 3/4, p 43
⁴ Eze, M.O. 'Africana Philosophy and the Imperative for Moral Education' in *Essays in Honor of Ifeanyi Menkiti*, editors, Edwin Etieyibo and Polycarp Ikuenobe (New York: Rowman and Littlefield/- Lexington Books, 2020)

from burning. It is how we make the night shorter and the dawn more certain. It is how we become – through the otherness of the other, in their timeless differentiations. And so, one might dare to say: I know because you are. Not in the sense of *savoir* (*wissen* in German) – to possess or accumulate knowledge as abstract fact – but *connaître* (*kennen* in German) – to know through relation, through encounter, through presence. I am because you are. And because you are, I am capable of knowing.

This book does not just ask questions in abstraction, nor does it rush to answer it with borrowed vocabularies or secondhand certainties. Instead, it lives the question. It lingers with it. It performs it. And in so doing, we are invited into a remarkable journey – across time, across systems, across cultures, peoples, voices and spaces – through which African philosophy becomes not merely an object of study, but a living practice: oral, symbolic, dialogic, collaborative, embodied, insurgent.

Doing African Philosophy is a deeply original, elegantly written, and methodologically bold contribution to contemporary African thought. It arrives at a critical moment, when African philosophy is asserting itself not only as a counterpoint to the Western canon but as a site of epistemic innovation and metaphysical depth. Yet, this book does not content itself with critique alone. It builds without exclusion. It affirms without essentializing. It reimagines without unanimity; it reclaims without hierarchy; it restores agency without otherness denunciation! There is a shift from the understanding of African philosophy as merely a residual epistemology, racial protest, anti-racist declaration or as an epistemic location of permanent resistance in constant contestation for recognition – to a new understanding of philosophy as a creative cultural infusion and epistemic adaptations.

This work is not merely sequence of arguments, it is instead a genealogical composition – a curation of divergent philosophical worlds from Africa that rejects coloniality, ontological rigidity and epistemic enclosures. Within the pages of this magisterial manuscript, the author illuminates African ways of knowing that have long been misread or ignored – oral traditions, symbolic forms, street expressions, performative rituals, collaborative epistemologies – recasting them as not only philosophically legitimate but deeply generative, cumulative and transformative. The book refuses to treat African philosophy as something that must conform to Eurocentric norms of textuality and individual authorship, but it does so without denouncing other traditions. African philosophy thus tells its own story; not just as an epistemic footnote, calling to mind Chinua Achebe's famous epigram:

> There is a great proverb – that until the lions have their own historians, the history of the hunt will always glorify the hunter. That did not come to me until much later. Once I realized that, I had to be a writer. I had to be that historian. It's not one man's job. It's not one persons' job. But it is something we have to do, so that the very story of the hunt will also reflect the agony, the travail – the bravery, even, of the lions.[5]

African philosophy displaces those norms of epistemic alienation or hierarchically infused pedagogy. It shows, with clarity and grace, that philosophy is also what happens in the symbolic carving of an Ukhure staff, in the sonic power of Afrobeat lyrics, in the enigmatic depths of naming rituals, in the laughter of street dialogue, in the rhythm of call and response, in the performative speech of the palaver tree. African philosophy is like a mother, calling her children home, provoking a literary convergence with the likes of Gabriel Okara (1953) in the *The Call of The River Nun* and with Okara it affirms a motivated response:

> .... I hear your call!
> I hear it from faraway
> I hear it break the circle
> Of these crouching hills ...
> I want to view your face again and feel your cold embrace ...[6]

---

[5] Achebe, C. 'Chinua Achebe, The Art of Fiction No. 139.' Interviewed by Jerome Brooks. *The Paris Review*, no.133 (1994).
[6] Gabriel Okara, *The Call of the River Nun*. Nigerian Festival of Art Award, 1953.

African philosophy is a mother – ancient, knowing, and deep – calling her children home. She does not shout; she sings. She hums through riverbeds and rustling leaves, through ancestral breath and the silence between words. Like the River Nun she flows with memory, beckoning us to return – to take refuge in her warmth, to drink from her wisdom, to remember that we are never far from her epistemic embrace.

There is something radically humanizing in the way this book restores meaning to African philosophical practice. The author does not seek to translate African thought into the languages of legitimacy defined by Western academia. Rather, he calls for a redefinition of philosophy itself – one that takes seriously the manifold forms through which wisdom is pursued, contested, transmitted, and lived in African communities. African philosophy here is not merely reactionary or derivative; it is formative, formative of persons, transformative of communities, and renewal of moral worlds. It is not a response to Western philosophy; it is a world in its own right, with its own criteria of truth, beauty, ethics, and personhood.

The author's concept of contemporaneity – a layered and compelling theme throughout the book – is especially important. It refers not only to the co-presence of the individual and the community, or of oral and textual modalities, but to the simultaneity of past, present, and future within African philosophical space. Contemporaneity means that ancestors and descendants are never entirely absent; that place is never merely a backdrop but a participant in the work of thought; that doing philosophy always occurs in situated time and embodied space.

In this sense, the book shares a moment of deep resonance with my own work on African communitarianism where I Introduced the idea of contemporaneity[7] and argued that the community and the individual exist in mutual co-constitution, and that our ethics must move beyond consensus toward what I have called a realist perspectivism – an

---

[7] Eze, M.O. 'What is African Communitarianism? Against Consensus as a Regulative Ideal', *South African Journal of Philosophy*, 2008, Vol. 27:4, pp 386–399.

intersubjective, dialogical, and perspectival mode of political and moral reasoning. Drawing on Ubuntu philosophy, I framed this pedagogical possibility as an invitation to ontological mobility. Rather than rehearsing the oft-cited Mbiti formulation – 'I am because we are' – I proposed an alternative: *I am because you are*.[8] This shift is not merely semantic. It insists that recognition must reach beyond sameness. It challenges us to see not only those who mirror our identities, our beliefs, our cultural codes or those who look like us – but also those who do not. It calls us to embrace the human and more-than-human: neighbours and strangers, ancestors and descendants, animals, trees, spirits, and even the unknowable. In this expansive vision, subjectivity is not confined by identity; it is opened through relation; relation and distance.[9] To be is to be in the presence of others, not just those we understand, but also those we do not yet know how to understand. And it is precisely this gesture – this ethical openness – that *Doing African Philosophy* embodies with such intellectual clarity and poetic force. Where I sought to trouble the hegemony of consensus in African political thought, *Doing African Philosophy* extends that project into new terrain: it troubles the hegemony of textuality, of abstraction, of disembodied reason, and it does so by reclaiming philosophy as it is lived – in dance, in symbols, in naming, in migration, in music, in ritual, in the streets.

The chapter on street philosophy – perhaps one of the most original contributions to the field in years – is a masterclass in seeing the philosophical in the everyday. Here, the author draws on Nigerian popular culture, youth language, meme aesthetics, Afrobeat music, and urban life to show how African peoples are theorizing their existence through the poetics of survival. Concepts like Japa and Sapa are treated not as slang but as ontological claims – expressions of suffering, mobility, aspiration, loss, and imagination. This is philosophy with its feet on the ground, with its ear to the street, and with its eyes on the horizon.

---

[8] Eze, M.O. 'Ubuntu/Botho: A Theory of Humanism in African Philosophy' In Chiara Robbiano and Sarah Flavel, (editors) *A Tool Kit for Philosophers: Key Concepts in World Philosophies* (Bloomsbury 2023)
[9] Eze, M.O. *Intellectual history in contemporary South Africa.* (New York: Palgrave Macmillan, 2010, 190–191

Likewise, the book's discussion of trans-textuality disrupts the tyranny of the printed word. It recognizes that philosophical thinking does not begin and end with peer-reviewed journals or tightly edited monographs. Herein, he engages with the ghost of Pauline Hountondji[10] but also transcends him. Trans-textuality begins in naming ceremonies and ends in funerals; it weaves through kente cloth and flares up in community debates beneath the shade of a tree; it survives in oral histories, in performance, in the ethics of healing, in the untranslatable symbols etched on ancestral objects. The author calls us not to abandon textuality, but to open it – to recognize it as one node in a constellation of epistemic practices that include but are not exhausted by the written word.

This expansive methodological vision is grounded in epistemic humility and historical responsibility. This work is neither a romanticization of the past, an epistemic adoration of a pristine unanimity, nor uncritical claim that all African traditions are pure or liberatory. Rather, it profoundly gives space for epistemic dialogue, the politics of recognition, and the collaborative nature of African philosophical work. In this, the work is marked by an ethic of gratitude: to the elders, to the ancestors, to the communities whose wisdoms philosophers' channel without appropriating.

The book is also politically courageous. It takes seriously the decolonial imperative – not as a fashionable posture but as a structural reckoning with the histories that have silenced African voices, marginalized non-textual knowledge systems, and elevated disembodied reason over embodied experience. Yet, unlike some decolonial discourse that stops at critique, this book builds, transcends and reclaims. It constructs an architecture of African philosophical practice rooted in place, relation, performance, and plurality. And it does so with care and craft. The scholarship is rigorous. The writing is clear. The insights are transformative.

What emerges from these pages is not only a reframing of African philosophy – it is a reframing of philosophy! For if philosophy is the

---

[10] Hountondji, Paulin, *African Philosophy: Myth or Reality* (Bloomington, Ind.: Indiana University Press, 1996)

love of wisdom, then wisdom must not be confined to what can be footnoted, peer-reviewed, or transcribed into syllogistic form. Indeed, the baobab metaphor is reminiscent at this point. Wisdom lives, too, in the trembling voice of a griot, in the tension of ritual silence, in the semiotics of textile, in the epistemic joy of shared laughter. Above all, it is neither organic nor essentialist, but performative, and constantly enduring. *Doing African Philosophy* is a gift. It is a reorientation. It is a summons. It is a future, a signifier of the present but also sensitive, at to the past, as we learn from the African saying, that '*the river that forgets its source will dry up!*'

For scholars of African philosophy, this book will become indispensable. For philosophers more broadly, it offers a bracing challenge: to do philosophy otherwise. For educators, it offers new pedagogies of embodiment and collaboration. For students, it opens the door to worlds they may have never been taught to recognize as philosophy – but which now, illuminated by this work, come into view as sources of profound insight. This book will reshape the field.

More than that, it will remind readers that the field of philosophy – when truly decolonized – is no longer a field. It is a forest, a forest of symbols, imagination, communities, humanities. But it is also a street as it is an *indaba*; a gathering under a tree as it is a carnival, it is a celebration; it is a circle of dancers. It is a whisper in the dusk. It is the naming of a child. It is the decision not to speak, and the speaking that follows. It is always becoming.

I am honored to write this foreword, not only in admiration of the scholarship here presented, but in solidarity with the vision that animates it. To all who pick up this book, I say: read it slowly for as the African saying goes, 'wisdom does not come overnight'. Let it question you. Let it move you. Let it teach us how to do again. Because *Doing African Philosophy* is not just a book. It is a quiet revolution – a call to life, to patience, to deep listening and deeper understanding. It teaches us, in the spirit of the African proverb, that '*no matter how long the night, the day is sure to come.*' And indeed, that day dawns the moment we realize that to know is not merely to think, but to live – to feel, to dance, to name, to mourn, to laugh. For knowledge, in its most luminous form, is not diminished when it is shared. As another candle is lit, the flame only multiplies.

And so, this book becomes a fire passed hand to hand – a constellation of lights in a world still learning how to see. Thus, as the fire is animated through this epistemic and subjective convergence, I invoke Okara once again, this time, in *The Fisherman's Invocation*:[11]

> The celebration is now ended
> But the echoes are all around
> Whirling like a harmattan . . .
> the drums lay quiet, silent waiting
> And the dancers disperse, walking
> with feet that have known many dances
> waiting for the next walking . . .
> . . . singing green lullabies which tingle our heads
> . . . we learn to sing half familiar half strange songs
> We learn to dance to half familiar, half strange . . .

Like the final tremor of a drum still reverberating through ancestral air, even as the celebration ends, this book, too, is such an echo – green with lullabies, strange with songs remembered in dreams, dancing in rhythms both ancient and newly born. Its wisdom lies not in finality, but in return, in dispersal with 'feet that have known many dances,' and in the silence that is not absence, but waiting. Let us walk on, then – half familiar, half strange – toward the next invocation.

That is all!

Africana Studies
California State University, Fresno
ante diem VII Kal. Aug., A.D. MMXXV
Beneath the fierce Californian sun, at the foot of the Sierra Nevada,
in reverence for the enduring genius of Africana wisdom –
sapientiae Africanae aeternae honorem tribuentes.

---

[11] Okara, Gabriel. *The Fisherman's Invocation*. Commonwealth Joint Poetry Award, 1979.

Bibliography

Achebe, Chinua. (1994). 'Chinua Achebe, The Art of Fiction No. 139.' Interview by Jerome Brooks. The Paris Review, no. 133.

Eze, Michael Onyebuchi. (2008). 'What is African Communitarianism? Against Consensus as a Regulative Ideal.' *South African Journal of Philosophy* 27 (4): 386–399.

Eze, Michael Onyebuchi. (2010). *Intellectual History in Contemporary South Africa*. New York: Palgrave Macmillan, 190–191.

Eze, Michael Onyebuchi. (2020). 'Africana Philosophy and the Imperative for Moral Education.' In *Essays in Honor of Ifeanyi Menkiti*, edited by Edwin Etieyibo and Polycarp Ikuenobe. New York: Rowman & Littlefield / Lexington Books.

Eze, Michael Onyebuchi. (2022). 'Interculturality as Dialogical Reciprocity in African and Comparative Philosophy.' *Filosofie en Praktijk* 43 (3/4): 43. Special issue on African Philosophy and Interculturality.

Eze, Michael Onyebuchi. (2023). 'Ubuntu/Botho: A Theory of Humanism in African Philosophy.' In *A Tool Kit for Philosophers: Key Concepts in World Philosophies*, edited by Chiara Robbiano and Sarah Flavel. London: Bloomsbury.

Eze, Michael Onyebuchi, and Thaddeus Metz. (2015). 'Emergent Issues in African Philosophy: A Dialogue with Kwasi Wiredu.' *Philosophia Africana* 17 (2): 75–87.

Hountondji, Paulin J. (1996). *African Philosophy: Myth or Reality?* Bloomington, IN: Indiana University Press.

Mudimbe, Valentin-Yves. (1994). *The Idea of Africa*. Oxford: James Currey.

Okara, Gabriel. (1953). *The Call of the River Nun*. Nigerian Festival of Art Award.

Okara, Gabriel (1979). *The Fisherman's Invocation*. Commonwealth Joint Poetry Award, 1979.

Preliminaries: Doing African Philosophy

Doing Philosophy

There is a sense of deliberateness in my use of 'doing' in relation to philosophy in general and African philosophy in particular throughout the pages of this book. The decision, after careful thought, to use the action verb 'doing' to set the stage for redefining the identity of African philosophy, emerged from the understanding that human enquiry cum meaning-making, philosophical or otherwise, is fundamentally a doing, a performative action geared toward understanding. As a doing or performative action, it implies that one has the power and agency to do so and so and that one is keen on fulfilling a hermeneutic ethical interest – the duty to interpret and understand one's experiences. The balance here between the political and ethical implications of doing as a form of performativity – the actual power to and act of doing something – makes it an important word for analysing the performance of philosophy in specific contexts, African or elsewhere. Such an analysis of the performance of philosophy raises questions, such as: What does it mean to do philosophy? What tools or methods are used in doing philosophy? Who or what does philosophy? How has philosophy been done in human history? How is philosophy done in mainstream academia today?

What does it mean to do philosophy? To rephrase etymologically, what does it mean to perform and to action deep love and fondness for, and strong affection and interest in, wisdom? The concept 'wisdom' (*Sophia*) or the state of being wise as contained in the concept of philosophy, signals the ability to discern or to draw general and fundamental conclusions from particular, observable experiential knowledge. It is not simply knowing but discerning and making sound judgements from the connections and disconnections that exist among what is known and what makes such knowledge forms possible. This explains why epistemology, for example, would not necessarily be concerned with specific knowledge claims, such as clouds are heavy, octopuses have three hearts and good relationships make us happy, but with discerning the very essence of knowledge, the general principles that make it possible to claim to know anything or to justify any form of knowledge claims. Similarly, when the Esan people of the Bini Kingdom of Southern Nigeria (a heritage that I come from) say 'Ai gu-unyibhin' ('No one has a mastery of existence'), they are projecting an existentialist philosophy that goes beyond specific existential experiences. It is the intense love and fondness for seeking such wisdom that emerges from deep solitary and collaborative reflections on the many facets of the human and non-human experiences that result in the doing and performing of philosophy. There ought to be a deep-seated and emotional investment in doing philosophy, for love is nothing without action, and it is this deliberate disposition to pursue and derive wisdom out of the manifold of experiences that has sustained the blurred and delicate divide between philosophy and other (scientific) forms of human enquiry.

If doing philosophy, then, consists of actively and critically reflecting on our lived experiences in a place of dwelling and producing wisdom in the process, one wonders how mainstream academic philosophy, often represented with the problematic category of Western philosophy, became involved in the quest for objectivity, infallibility and universality. If philosophy is performed in place by persons who are either within such place and experiencing it, or by persons who have topophilic affinity or even topophobic hostility to such place and experiences within it, is the philosophy produced not more subjective, intersubjective, fallible, relative and contextual than it is objective, infallible and universal? The trivialization of place and positioning as well as selves and bodies doing the philosophizing for the sake of highly prized objectivity and universality, finds bold and firm expressions in the tools and methods for doing philosophy that have been championed by those who have claimed ownership of the right to do philosophy, the West. These tools and methods are punctuated with emphasis on subjective intellectuality and disembodiment. To do philosophy as it is understood in mainstream academia is to do so intellectually (and, of course, this is why it is called an *intellectual* tradition) in ways that prioritize and elevate abstract, intellectual rationality over placial and embodied experiences and rationality. Here, reasoning and thinking are presented as processes that are somehow detached and removed from place and body. There exists the privileging of pure thinking as if the thinking somehow exists and happens outside of the body and place. Ideas of how to do philosophy from the intellect saturate the history of (Western) philosophy from Plato's divinization of the intellect to Cartesian *cogito* and the many transcendental methods after. In the conventional sense, therefore, doing philosophy comes with the expectation of disowning one's place and body and embracing the intellect, the abstract and the transcendental.

There are several reasons why we must critically interrogate this intellectual tradition of philosophy as we do in this book. The intellect with its functions of thinking and reasoning, by its very nature, is shaped by and cannot be detached from or done away from places and bodies and all that is wrapped up in them, such as language, culture, emotions and bodily experiences, without creating a hegemonic and colonized experience of the intellect. Any approach to philosophizing that de-positions and de-embodies the intellect is an approach that deliberately or non-deliberately privileges itself and, by implication, its place and corporeality, while oppressing, denying and imprisoning (suspending the freedom of) other places and corporealities. The denial of the place and geography of reason (the de-positioning of thought) (Gordon 2011; Gordon 2018) and of the embodiment of reason (the de-embodying of thought) have had dire consequences for Western philosophy, resulting in a philosophical tradition that is in many ways patriarchal, ableist, racist and colonialist. We see glaring evidence of this in the maleness of reason (Lloyd 1998; Moller 2002) and in the racialization of reason (Eze 1997; Freter 2018). Genevieve Lloyd (1998: 387) aptly captures, for example, the maleness of reason thus:

> The equation of maleness with superiority goes back at least as far as the Pythagoreans. What is valued – whether it be odd as against even numbers, 'aggressive' as against 'nurturing' skills and capacities, or Reason as against emotion – has been readily identified with maleness. Within the context of this association of maleness with preferred traits, it is not just incidental to the feminine that female traits have been construed as inferior – or, more subtly, as 'complementary' – to male norms of human excellence. Rationality has been conceived as transcendence of the feminine; and the 'feminine' itself has been partly constituted by its occurrence within this structure.

Lloyd aptly captures here the patriarchy of rationality that is so deeply embedded in intellectual traditions in general, and in philosophy in particular, that one wonders if the masculinity of nouns and pronouns in the past was not deliberate. When Voltaire (1901: 260), for example, writes that 'Nothing can be clearer than that *men*, enjoying the faculties of their common nature, are in a state of equality; they are equal when they perform their animal functions and exercise their understandings', was he innocently using '*men*' to refer to 'humans' or did he deliberately and specifically mean '*men*'? What is abundantly clear, however, from the writings of Voltaire and colleagues such as Immanuel Kant, David Hume and G. W. F. Hegel is the racialization of reason. While presenting the intellect, thinking and rationality as transcendental, de-embodied and universal, these and several other philosophers succeeded somehow in making these human features essentially of the white male body in European places, and succeeded in perpetuating on a grand scale the colonization of thought and epistemic racism against the non-Western, including the African.

Considering the harm that the de-positioning and de-embodying of the intellect can produce in the performance of philosophy, I will begin in the first chapter of this work by paying close and critical attention to the dominant understanding and features of a philosophical tradition with the aim of redefining it. This is important because the de-positioned and de-embodied understanding of what makes a philosophical tradition plays a key role in the denial and marginalization of African philosophy in the global philosophical empire. The chapter will examine, contest and critically analyse specific defining features that have been conventionally attributed to a philosophical tradition and employed to deny the ability of many traditions to perform or do philosophy. In contesting these features, the first chapter will focus on several debates and issues that are implied in these features, such as the problem of whiteness, the graphocentric-phonocentric debate, the problematic concept of literacy and the naming-owning debate. Based on these analyses, the chapter revisits the question of a philosophical tradition, showing that such a tradition is much more defined by its ability to do philosophy as etymologically intended and to produce philosophical concepts, arguments and thought in general than by its commitment to abstract and subjective intellectuality and de-embodied and de-positioned rationality, as well as to modes of storing up what it produces in its performance, such as in the form of individually authored texts. The first chapter will thus preface the others by showing that the performance and repositories of philosophical knowledge are largely defined by place, bodies and time.

The African Way

From cooking, fishing, gardening, pursuing leisure and making art to engaging in enquiries, there are different ways of actualizing specific human activities. It is difficult to argue for only one way of doing something or achieving a human activity without falling into the trap of methodological exclusionism and epistemic colonization. The acknowledgement and exploration of the different ways of doing a particular human activity enriches the understanding of that activity and humanizes the discourse of the activity, for it is a human ontic way of being to do things differently. Thus, the ways of doing things and pursuing human activities consist of a variety of processes and methods that humans in different places and times employ in carrying out specific human activities. Bearing these meta-methodological facts in mind, there are at least two things that are implied in, or can emerge from, the conceptualization and analysis of the African way of doing philosophy: first, it is an acknowledgement of the importance of place, in this case, an African place, in shaping how philosophy is done within such a place; and second, it is the quest to unravel and explore specific ways of doing philosophy or showing profound fondness for wisdom in African places. It is therefore important to say a few things about the relationship between place and philosophy specifically in connection to African philosophy.

Whenever we prefix the word 'philosophy' with a place, as we do with Chinese philosophy, European philosophy, Western philosophy, Mexican philosophy, Indian philosophy, Mayan philosophy, Africana philosophy and African philosophy, we position and situate philosophical knowledge in that place in order to show how relevant the place is in defining the kind of philosophizing that happens therein. Place is ontic for humans, philosophers included. We are thrown into a place of existence, a context of meaning and lived experiences that shape who we are and how we think and live, and more so, we also have the potential to shape these meanings and experiences in place as well. The failure of an enquirer to acknowledge ontic places and how they shape ideas, thinking and reflection (positionality and reflexivity) is the denial of the very way of being human, which results in epistemic and hermeneutical injustices. How then can we take place seriously in thinking about philosophy? Bruce Janz (2004: 103–5) provides eight fundamental questions that arise when thinking about philosophy in relation to place: 'Where does philosophy (best) come from? ... What is philosophy's place among the disciplines? ... Do the ethnic, racial or national (or for that matter the religions, political or ideological) commitments of the practitioners of philosophy affect the philosophy that is done? ... Is philosophical thought unaffected by the places in which it is practised? ... Can philosophy be conducted "in place"? ... Are there inhospitable places for philosophy? ... Is philosophy appropriate to all places? . . . Can philosophy attend to a place and still remain philosophical?' Janz's analysis of these questions reiterates much of what we have said in this introductory chapter already. Philosophy cannot be confined to a particular place as it has been the custom to restrict it to the Greek, European or Western place, nor can it be done away from the many places, geographical or otherwise, that it emerges from. In his words (2009: 6):

> The fact is, philosophy is not from nowhere. Philosophy always comes from a place, and that place is never completely covered over by abstraction. It is never irrelevant, even if it has been ignored. Not that there is some necessary causal connection or geographical determinism, as if by figuring out the place from which philosophy comes, we can encapsulate it, know it, and need not attend to its actual content. Place is a far more complex notion than what can be contained in geography. Philosophy is not reducible to place; there is no genetic fallacy or geographical determinism here. Philosophy remains a reflection on its place, geographically, culturally, disciplinarily, and intellectually.

Flowing from this background, we can now think more concretely about what the African place means for philosophy or what the African way of doing philosophy suggests. The discourse of the African way of doing philosophy or, in line with our etymology of philosophy above, the African way of showing love and profound fondness for wisdom, a task at the very heart of this work, must speak to and pay deliberate and careful attention to African methods and processes of philosophizing and the ontologies, epistemologies, ethics and related philosophical systems or taken-for-granted assumptions and ideologies that they are founded on. To be sure, methods emerge from and are deeply rooted in ontological, epistemological and ethical commitments. The primacy of sensory perception and observation in the scientific method, for example, cannot be divorced from commitments to a materialist, physicalist ontology, an empiricist epistemology and logical positivist (emotivist) ethics. Similarly, an essentially rationalist method of philosophizing is inseparable from commitments to an idealist and transcendental metaphysics. In the chapters of this book, we will see how the relational, collaborative, enigmatic and artistic ways of doing philosophy in African places are deeply rooted in the commitment to a holistic and relational ontology, epistemology and ethics.

I have proceeded thus far with conceptualizing what the discourse of the African way of doing philosophy would entail by presuming that we – you (the reader) and I (the author) enmeshed in this printed conversation – already share an understanding of this place in question, the African place, which is the subject of discourse here, but there is a strong possibility that I am mistaken. It is crucial, therefore, that I clarify and make more apt as succinctly as possible how and in what sense(s) I use the thick and loaded term 'African' when speaking about the African way of doing philosophy. I am not primarily concerned here about the genealogy of the concept 'African', how it has been invented and the extent to which it is politically, ethically or epistemologically correct. Much can be said about this and, indeed much has been said. I believe V. Y. Mudimbe has given us a manifold of treasures in *The Invention of Africa* (1988) to engage in this sort of genealogical analysis. I am proceeding with the most basic assumptions that 'African' is a concept that is useable and that it is a site of meaning-making and heritage of identity for the nearly two billion African and African Diasporic peoples. However, it is important to still explicate how and in what sense(s) I use it.

I use 'Africa' in two specific senses. In the first sense, I mean a geography of reason and meaning-making (Gordon 2011). And in this sense of place as geography, I am particularly interested in referring to, delimiting my focus and place of interest to and primarily drawing resources from, sub-Saharan Africa and the philosophizing that happens there and how it happens. Sub-Saharan Africa is a place booming with cultures and traditions, languages and philosophies. In exploring the philosophical traditions of the sub-Saharan African place, I am interested in unravelling and analysing connections and disconnections in the multifaceted and multilayered ways of being, knowing and acting in this place. Much of the similarities that can be found in the sub-Saharan African place, in the way philosophizing happens and with regard to the sort of philosophical knowledge produced, emerge fundamentally from shared ontological outlooks, commitments to a relational and holistic understanding of being, and commitments to non-textual and collaborative methods of performing or doing philosophy. Such ontological commitments and processes of philosophizing shape how reasoning happens in sub-Saharan African places and how wisdom is pursued, accessed and assessed. Therefore, the chapters of this book will pay close attention to such ontologies cum philosophies and processes of philosophizing, which will open up interesting sites of meaning, including attentiveness to language, oral, symbolic and artistic ways of philosophizing, and collaborative spaces of knowledge production.

However, this first sense of understanding the concept 'African' as we use it within the pages of this book, which delimits it to the sub-Saharan, is a necessary but still insufficient way of thinking about Africa in this context. Necessary because it acknowledges the place and geography of reason, meaning-making and wisdom production, but insufficient as it remains a narrowing down of the possibility of being African that not only depends on or emerges in place, but transcends and shapes experiences out of place. Place and the wisdom produced therein thus spills beyond the specific geography it begins from into other places and experiences, such as identity, memories, histories and meaning-making that transcend place but are very much still connected to, and rooted in place, as geography. This informs the second, much broader sense in which I use the concept 'African'. In the second sense, I explore the concept 'Africa' or 'African' as a site of shared experiences of peoples with a common heritage, with such experiences emerging from or happening because of their connections to place as geography, and with such experiences resulting from or producing specific kinds of philosophy or modes of philosophizing or performing philosophy. (Sub-Saharan) African and Africana (African Diasporic) peoples may not be in one geographical place but their connection to the African geography of place, their heritage, and the philosophies and philosophizing therein, have significantly shaped their lived experiences, response to such experiences, philosophical commitments and ways of doing philosophy. For example, the experience of the effects of colonization and slavery, racism and the denial of philosophy, is shared and collectively felt by African and Africana peoples, perhaps in varying degrees and intensity based on specific locales. Also, music and art as oral and symbolic ways of philosophizing respectively permeate African and African Diasporic communities (Skitolsky 2020) even though they are deeply rooted in an African heritage that emerges from African locales. Hence, in this sense, the African way of doing philosophy acknowledges and takes seriously not only how place, with its contents and structures, shapes the doing and production of philosophy but also how the shared experiences that emerge from and transcend specific African places also contribute to the making of African philosophy. Janz (2009: 11) aptly summarizes the African place in relation to philosophy thus:

> Place, then, brings a great deal with it. In various ways, to address place we must also address identity, history, memory, aspiration, family and social connection. Places stand in for all these things – disparaging someone's place is often tantamount to disparaging all these others as well. But it is not only a matter of subjectivity. Place is important also because it is the site for the meeting between incommensurables – materiality and idea, part and whole, self and other. Place cannot be understood without these tensions. Therefore, if we are to understand any philosophy, particularly African philosophy, we would do well to pay attention to the site on which the fundamental tensions of life and thought are played out.

Reimagining Identity

Doing philosophy the African way as has been briefly sketched out above and as I hope to sustain in the pages that follow thus, has as its central focus the reimagining of the identity of African philosophy through an affirmation of (collective) self-authenticity. The question of the identity of African philosophy has been a perennial and protracted debate ever since the consciousness of African philosophy was deliberately or accidentally woven into academia (Masolo 1994). But what has dominated this debate and indeed the ongoing practice of African philosophy is the struggle to imagine (or, perhaps, not imagine) one's identity in the image of Western philosophy. Debating the identity of African philosophy often resembles the search for how this tradition of philosophy sits well with or departs from the Western tradition of philosophy that has dominated academia. Are the categories of thought, modes of rationality, logic of reasoning and methods of philosophizing similar to or different from those of the West? For example, the emergence, acceptance or rejection of several trends in African philosophy that aimed to theorize the identity and nature of African philosophy in the last half of the twentieth century, such as ethnophilosophy, sage philosophy and professional philosophy, were often imagined on the extent to which they synced with or departed from Western philosophy. Ethnophilosophy, in particular, emerged in the first place as an attempt to do philosophy differently from the West. The criticism and rejection of it also emerged from theorizing how it was not 'Western' enough. Sage philosophy or philosophical sagacity was in essence the search for the Platos, Aristotles and Hegels in Africa to showcase that African philosophy resembles Western philosophy. This way of philosophizing that proceeds primarily by imagining how the self resembles another, suffocates, creates disciplinary anxiety and does a significant disservice to the self, in the same way consciously striving to be like another person (or be different from the person), creates anxiety, frustration and lack of authenticity. Thus, to prevent disciplinary anxiety and inauthenticity, African philosophy must be reimagined by zooming in on its own self in ways already elaborated above, paying close attention to place and shared experiences. Does this mean we cannot compare philosophical traditions, such as the African and the Western? The question already gives away the answer, for to compare two traditions of philosophy is to affirm and acknowledge in part that two authentic traditions exist in their own right with ideas, concepts and methods worth comparing. This is of course different from the idea that there is a tradition of philosophy whose ideas, concepts and methods constitute the yardstick for determining the existence or non-existence of another tradition. This will not amount to a comparison but a pseudo-comparison defined by a legitimating or delegitimating exercise, and it is this sort of pseudo-comparison that has often characterized comparative Western and African philosophies.

Thus, in reimagining African philosophy in ways that affirm identity, self-authenticity and legitimacy of philosophical thought, and in ways that allow the self to be and allow authentic performativity of philosophy to emerge from an African place, this book will begin in the first chapter by reimagining the very idea of a philosophical tradition. As stated earlier on in this introductory chapter, the task of reimagining a philosophical tradition in the first chapter is significant, as it settles much of the dust that may arise from rethinking and interrogating the norm of defining the identity of a philosophical tradition in the image of the West. The chapter will therefore critique the dominant criteria in mainstream academia for defining a philosophical tradition, showcasing how such excludes and marginalizes African philosophy because of its alleged failure to meet these standards. It will pay close attention to such key defining features of a philosophical tradition as textuality, individual authorship, naming and labelling, and transgenerational coherence, and challenge these through debates on whiteness, the graphocentric-phonocentric debate, literacy and ownership. The chapter will lay the foundation for the other chapters by showing that a philosophical tradition is better defined by its capacity to perform and do philosophy and its ways of doing so, and this would be made abundantly clear in the chapters that follow. The chapter that follows will therefore reimagine the identity of African philosophy by focusing fundamentally on African ways of doing philosophy and the philosophy produced therein.

In the second chapter, I explore orality as one major way in which philosophy has been done in African places and how African philosophical knowledge has been produced, stored and transmitted. The chapter begins by analysing orality as a mode of being in general and of being human in particular. Orality or speech is not a less authentic mode of being than textuality or writing but one more primordial and always in ontic relations with its forms of representation, such as writing. The chapter examines the relationship between language and orality and how there is a sustained enrichment of the former by the latter. It also examines some of the major forms of repositories of orality in African traditions, such as names, proverbs, music, storytelling, hypothetical arguments, riddles and adages. The chapter then pays close attention to one of the major critiques of orality as a source of knowledge – the question of the reliability of oral sources – by exploring the epistemic mechanism of orality. It shows that textuality suffers from similar epistemic challenges as orality and that neither repositories of knowledge are sacrosanct nor without flaws. The chapter then examines some philosophical contents of orality in African traditions, paying particular attention to concepts of truth, existential philosophy, relationality and the philosophy of personhood.

The third chapter explores symbolism as another major non-textual mode of philosophizing and repository of philosophical knowledge in African traditions. It begins by analysing the dominant aesthetic interpretation of African arts and symbols that has dominated colonial and postcolonial encounters. This analysis shows that beyond this aesthetic narrative, symbolism in Africa is fundamentally deplored to present and represent thoughts and ideas about being, knowledge, personhood, relationality, morality, values, bodies, transcendence, immanence, political philosophy and other philosophical themes. The chapter showcases this by examining symbols and arts from several sub-Saharan African traditions, including the Adinkra and Ga symbols in Ghana, motifs and textile designs among the Yorubas, and the Benin Bronzes and carvings. The focus on specific symbolisms in African places exposes us to rich sources of philosophical knowledge and the philosophical principles we can deduce from them in analysing concepts, issues and debates in philosophy.

In Chapter four, I shift attention to the textuality of African philosophy, for my aim of drawing attention to the non-textual in this book is not in any way meant to deny or reject the textual, but to show how the textual is only an aspect of the whole and how the textual is dependent on the resource of the non-textual and vice versa. The chapter examines several ways that African philosophy has related with textuality, including textual legacies, texts as resistance, texts as defence, texts as mirroring and texts as doing. These analyses of the textuality of African philosophy examine the presence of texts in precolonial periods alongside oral and symbolic forms of knowledge, and the increasing use of text as a medium for forging identity and as a repository of resistance to colonization and oppression in colonial and postcolonial Africa. Here again, it is made clear that this remains only one of several mediums and repositories. The chapter examines also how in the mid-to-late twentieth century, text became a primary and unavoidable means deployed by contemporary academic African philosophers to defend the existence of African philosophy, considering the politics of academia. But then, today, the use of text, the chapter shows, has quickly become a form of scriptism with an unconscious bias that privileges text and writing over other forms of knowledge production in Africa in an unconscious but sometimes deliberate attempt to mirror European philosophy. The chapter critically engages with this textual approach to contemporary African philosophy.

Chapter five examines the question of method in African philosophy and explores Afro-communitarianism as an authentic and indigenous African way of philosophizing within the context of our transhuman age. I conceptualize trans-textuality as a dehumanized exercise in a transhuman age, and theorize the importance of preserving a humanized textual and non-textual exercise of doing philosophy. I examine how textuality and scriptism face a crisis of relevance today with the invention of AI models that de-humanize writing or remove the production of texts from the human. More so, trans-textuality syncs nicely with subjective intellectuality that dominates mainstream academic philosophy. The chapter thus shows that re-humanizing the textuality and non-textuality of knowledge requires acknowledging place and context in philosophy, intersubjective and ecocentric intellectuality, collective authorship, and the use of means of producing and preserving knowledge beyond texts. The chapter then explores the role philosophers can play in higher education to promote the diversity and inclusivity of philosophical methods as a matter of research and pedagogical ethics and practice, and explores how Afro-communitarian philosophy enables such to happen. Afro-communitarian philosophy with its features such as palaver deliberative practices, enigmatic approach, fluidity, relationality and difference, emphasizes the power of collective agency in knowledge production by examining ways in which philosophizing in contemporary Africa can take advantage of the communitarian approach to philosophizing. It examines the relevance of deference and fluid ways of knowing, and their implications for research and pedagogy. In comparison with polemics, the chapter also discusses enigmatics as a dominant attitudinal disposition in African places.

The sixth and final chapter explores ideas of the contemporaneity and futures of African philosophy against the backdrop of the identity of African philosophy curated in the previous chapters. In this chapter, I explore street philosophy as a concept of postcolonial and contemporary Africa with specific reference to the Nigerian experience that represents a sterling example of relational, collaborative, fluid and non-textual (and disruptive textual) ways of philosophizing. The postcolonial Nigerian street (understood in both the physical and virtual senses) has become a vibrant, intensely rich and productive space, site and locus for philosophizing on the Nigerian-African existential and postcolonial conditions. What is fascinating about philosophizing in the Nigerian street is the quite hybrid form it takes where resources are drawn from indigenous and modern forms of life, while retaining and exploring several methods and repositories of philosophy, including orality, textuality, symbolism, collective authorship and humour. The chapter thus shows that the street in Nigeria has become a locus of collective agency and disruptive textuality in its conversations, reflections, critique, deconstruction, construction of normativity, and formulation of concepts and ideas about being, knowing, acting, beauty and existence. It showcases this by exploring the humorous, comic and collectively produced philosophy of existence and suffering, the philosophy of migration, and the philosophy of education, I conclude this chapter by imagining and reimagining futures of African philosophy, in particular, and global philosophy in general, in ways that blend textual and non-textual possibilities and take advantage of intersubjective and ecocentric intellectuality.

So I invite you to join me in unfolding and unpacking the performance and doing of philosophy in sub-Saharan Africa, the methods for doing so, and the philosophical theories, concepts and arguments that such performance of philosophy produce. The exciting and fascinating intellectual and embodied journey that follows does not in any way exhaust what could be said or written about the identity of African philosophy but provides, I hope, some enrichment of already existing discourses and a clear statement on being authentically African and philosophical.

1

Redefining a Philosophical Tradition

In this chapter, I begin the journey of unfolding the African tradition of philosophy, which consists of African ways of doing philosophy and the philosophy produced from such ways, by settling an important issue about how a philosophical tradition is in the first place dominantly and popularly conceptualized in academia today and curating as clearly as possible how it ought to be understood. This is crucial as it is my way of taking out of the entrance to the hall of philosophy the Western mirror that all traditions are expected to gaze into before gaining admittance. The task, therefore, in this chapter, is to reimagine a philosophical tradition in order to settle much of the dust that may arise from thinking of and defining the identity of a philosophical tradition in the image of the West. The chapter will therefore critique the dominant academic conditions for defining a philosophical tradition, showcasing how such excludes and marginalizes African philosophy because of its alleged failure to meet these conditions. It will pay close attention to clarifying dominant understandings of what makes a tradition and what makes such a tradition philosophical. It will critically interrogate some of the key defining features of a philosophical tradition, such as textuality, individual authorship, naming and labelling, and transgenerational coherence, and challenge these through debates on whiteness, the graphocentric-phonocentric debate, literacy, labelling and claims to ownership. The chapter will lay the much-needed foundation for the other chapters by showing that a philosophical tradition is better defined by its capacity to perform and do philosophy much more than the method of doing so.

The Dominant Understanding of a Philosophical Tradition

What defines a philosophical tradition? This question invariably affirms at least three things: there are many traditions; there are those that can be labelled philosophical and those that cannot; and there is the possibility that there is more than one philosophical tradition. These possibilities drag us into attempting to conceptualize what can be labelled a tradition in the first place and what could be labelled philosophical, a task that we would often shy away from to avoid the tradition-modernity debate on the one hand and the metaphilosophical question on the other. But I will attempt here to say a few necessary things about both for the sake of clarity. Tradition is often used to represent the past and the sort of relationship it has with the present, the modern. Although the past is not in dispute, the details of the past and the impact it has on the present is always debatable. As Anthony O'Hear (2005: 1023) puts it:

> Tradition is that body of practice and belief which is socially transmitted from the past. It is regarded as having authority in the present simply because it comes from the past, and encapsulates the wisdom and experience of the past. For some, the very idea of tradition is anathema. It is characteristic of modernity to reject the authority of the past in favour of the present deployment of reason, unencumbered by tradition or prejudice... Traditions often turn out upon inspection to be not so much irrational as subtle and flexible deployments of reason in particular spheres.

Tradition, then, would consist of social customs, institutions, patterns of belief, and codes of behaviour that are accepted by a community and that form its culture, inherited from previous generations, transmitted to future generations and becoming a foundation for asserting or questioning identity (Bunnin and Yu 2004). Without belabouring the meaning of tradition and getting entangled with the debate on its relevance for the present and the future as conservativists and libertarians would do, we can already deduce some ideas of what a philosophical tradition would mean. A philosophical tradition will therefore consist of the institutions, patterns of operation and ideas accepted by and becoming the authority for a philosophical community as its culture for doing philosophy, and that encapsulates the wisdom and experience of doing philosophy in the past. The idea of a dominant philosophical tradition is the idea that in the global philosophical community understood here as philosophy in academia, there exists a tradition and as we shall see shortly, the Western tradition, for doing philosophy that commands and demands control of the community, and that prevails and strives to prevail over other traditions by claiming to be the one who has done philosophy rightly and properly in the past and thus has the authority and legitimacy to not only continue to do so now and in the future but to define how others can do it if they are to be residents or citizens of the community. Thus, in making sense of this tradition and its claim of mastery of the art of performing philosophy, let us pay closer attention to its understanding of what is philosophical and what constitutes a tradition of it.

Once upon a time, this dominant Western tradition of philosophy claimed to be not just the dominant tradition of philosophy but the only tradition of philosophy. As Peter K. J. Park has elaborately shown in his important historiography of philosophy, *Africa, Asia, and the History of Philosophy: Racism in the Formation of the Philosophical Canon, 1780-1830* (2013), the claim to the sole ownership of philosophy by the West was quite prominent around the seventeenth to the twentieth century, even when there were clear historical evidences that such was not always or even the case. Besides, not many of those who the philosophers in this period of philosophy vehemently defended as the sole progenitors of philosophy would have thought of themselves that way. No doubt, there are still a few today who hold the idea of the sole ownership of philosophy by the West, but a more popular view in recent times, perhaps since the mid-to-late twentieth century because of an increasing assertion of self-identity by other traditions of philosophy, is the idea of dominance as framed above. This idea of dominance is framed in a way that presents Western philosophy as doing philosophy ideally and differently from other traditions who may claim to have their own philosophical traditions in the way in which it is systematic, technical and professional, setting the standards for the academic community. In the words of William Edelglass and Jay W. Garfield (2011: 4):

> Some have insisted that non-Western intellectual traditions lack rational argument ... (Curiously, this view was never advanced by those Western philosophers actually familiar with non-Western traditions, but frequently by those ignorant of them, a fact that raises its own questions about rational argument.) Or, it was argued, that even if non-Western traditions did possess rational inquiry, this did not constitute philosophy because the inquiry took place within a religious, soteriological framework. Properly speaking, it was claimed, this was a form of religious practice and not philosophy, which is the pursuit of knowledge for its own sake. Such a narrow view, based perhaps on certain forms of recent Western philosophical practice, is blind to the varied philosophical styles and approaches that constitute the Western philosophical tradition, and would exclude from 'philosophy' much of what is generally considered philosophy from the Greeks to the Early Moderns and even some contemporary philosophers.

Thus, in the idea of a dominant philosophical tradition, a distinction between the philosophy of the West and a suspicious philosophy of the rest emerges. For example, pioneers of professional philosophy as an approach to or trend of doing African philosophy in the late-twentieth century keyed into this distinction in defining how African philosophy should mirror Western philosophy for legitimacy. For the pioneers of professional African philosophy, such as (perhaps, best to say early) Kwasi Wiredu and Paulin Houtondji, African philosophy is only just beginning to emerge in imitation of the Western (often disguised as the universalist) way of doing philosophy and it is the Western style of philosophy done by Africans (Bodunrin 1981). This sort of distinction between Western philosophy and the pseudo philosophy of the rest is captured by Masolo (1994: 59) when he writes that:

There are two senses of the word philosophy, but with a good deal of relation to each other. The first sense is usually also called the ordinary sense, and refers to some kinds of opinions and commitments to certain ideas or ways of interpreting things, to values and beliefs about the general nature of things. This sense of 'philosophy' is quite reflective and can sometimes be 'argued' even vigorously. The 'arguments' in it, however, are usually also sorts of established opinions, views, and related beliefs which are called upon for justification. This is the sense of philosophy which is usually expressed in the form 'my philosophy is . . .' In this sense, philosophy can be held by individuals and be assumed of groups – communities, societies, etc. – as part of the covert culture which is made up of the reasons behind the observable cultural practices and expressions.

He (1994: 59–60) continues:

> In the second sense, philosophy is . . . what appears as the main subject of most of the writings of Plato, Aristotle, St. Thomas Aquinas, Descartes, Hegel, Kwasi Wiredu, Hountondji, and others. In this sense, philosophy is a commitment to an investigation rather than to any specific idea(s) or opinion(s). It is a study of a variety of subjects from a specific type of approach – an open, rational analysis and synthesis – and can therefore not be expressed in the formula 'my philosophy is . . . ' Because it is not merely a body of opinions, and does not aim primarily at formulating workable principles, but rather at understanding, philosophy in this sense becomes primarily an academic practice, a study, a systematic investigation of ideas.

A similar way of drawing this distinction between the philosophy of the West (technical professional philosophy) and the philosophy of the rest (ordinary philosophy) is the distinction between philosophy as a method for technical, professional investigation and philosophy as world view (Blocker 1999). Every society, the argument goes, could be said to have its philosophy in the sense of world views, such as its philosophy of life or existence and its philosophy of the good. But in the more technical sense, it indicates a particular (dominant as it were) methodology, a specialized way of investigating and organizing ideas taught in universities that is critical, logical, analytical and systematic. In this sense not everyone has a philosophy and it is the sort of philosophy that arose at a particular point in Greek history (Blocker 1999). I have read many of this kind of distinction aimed at presenting Western philosophy as the shining example of how philosophy ought to be done, but either I am too unphilosophical and rationally sophisticated enough to understand the distinction, or my suspicion of the glaring illogicality and meaninglessness of the distinction is right. Consider for a moment these rhetorical questions. Isn't philosophy in the Western, technical and professional sense about the formulation of fundamental ideas, principles, world views and theories of being, knowing, acting and the like in the same way as it is of the critique and analysis of existing ones (Oladipo 2008)? In other words, are the so-called world views and ordinary philosophies not deeply entrenched into professional philosophy? Are the allegedly grandiose philosophies of the exalted Western philosophers not a form of the 'my philosophy is . . .' kind of postulations? When Plato, Descartes and Kant theorized the immortality of the soul and the world of forms, the cogito, ergo sum and the categorical imperative respectively, were they not postulating some sort of subjective idea or theory of being, knowing and acting, an opinion, – a 'my philosophy is . . .' (or should we continue to hold to the idea that these philosophers were merely vehicles for abstract reasoning producing infallible and objective universal truths)? What is the possibility of arriving at a philosophy of life, a philosophy of existence, an ethic of the good, without a systematic, critical and analytic reflection on lived experiences?

There is some rhetoric to these questions, of course, and if it is not already abundantly clear that this constructed distinction between the philosophy of the West and the philosophy of the rest is antithetical to and removed from the very performance of philosophy even in European history, the rest of this chapter will offer some further abundance of clarity. For it would take painstaking and deliberate dubious argumentation to prove that philosophy as a construction of principles and world views is a philosophy that is in some way different and removed completely from another kind of philosophy that is essentially about technicalities and critical investigations in the same way it will be futile to prove that scientific facts and laws are a form of science different and removed from the scientific method as another form of science. More so, if we were to agree hypothetically that genuine philosophy only exists in the technical, systematic and professional sense, we will still not be able to jump to the conclusion that for some unaccounted reasons, such only emerged and happened in Greek cultures and flourished in Europe rather than in other non-European societies. As Blocker (1999: 3) puts it, 'In this [professional] sense of "philosophy" it may turn out that some cultures have philosophy and some do not, and we cannot dogmatically assert before examining the facts that either all cultures must have philosophy or that *none* do except European cultures. We must more patiently and empirically look at each culture to see whether it does or it does not have a philosophy.'

But let us continue for now with our train of thought on a dominant philosophical tradition by not only examining the construction of an understanding of authentic philosophy as we have done above, but also the resultant idea of a philosophical tradition. The idea of a dominant philosophical tradition is in extreme cases used to argue that philosophy as an intellectual tradition is the exclusive preserve of Europe, and in less extreme cases it is used to show that although Europe dominates in displaying this tradition, there are a few others that can be shown to be like it or to mirror it in several ways. In line with the latter, Ben-Ami Scharfstein (1998; 2014) has vehemently defended the existence of only three philosophical traditions: the European, the Chinese and the Indian. In presenting this defence, Scharfstein has developed a definition of a philosophical tradition that is a good summary of what is dominant in the philosophical community and has also elaborated on why other traditions, such as the African tradition, cannot be included in the traditions of philosophy. For the rest of this section, I will expand on these points, as they provide a springboard for the critical interrogation of the basic assumptions in the idea of a dominant philosophical tradition in the rest of the chapter. Scharfstein's definition of a philosophical tradition goes thus:

> What is a philosophical tradition? A chain of persons who relate their thought to that of their predecessors and in this way form a continuous transmission from one generation to the next, from teacher to disciple to disciple's disciple. Or rather, because a whole tradition is made up of many subtraditions, it is one and the same tradition because all of its subtraditions share common sources and modes of thought and develop by reaction to one another. A tradition is by nature cumulative, and it progresses in the sense that it defines itself with increasing detail and density. I define the tradition as philosophical to the extent that its members articulate it in the form of principles – if only principles of interpretation – and of conclusions reasonably drawn from them; and I define it as philosophical to the extent that its adherents defend and attack by means of reasonable arguments – even those that deny reason – and understand and explain how they try to be reasonable. As history demonstrates again and again, no philosophy is purely rational, pure rationality being a[n] unreasonable, impossible ideal. Matters of religion, communal loyalty, reverence for teachers, and cultural habits, not to mention individual psychology, have always limited rationality, so that philosophical subtraditions or schools are rational by tendency rather than in any absolute way.
>
> 2014: 121

On the basis of this definition of a philosophical tradition, Scharfstein defends the existence of only three philosophical traditions, the philosophical traditions of Europe, China and India:

> Why say that there are only three great philosophical traditions? To claim this, one must put aside the correct but, for our purpose, insufficient definitions of philosophy as wisdom or as the group of principles, either stated or implied, by which any person or community views life. In keeping with the original meaning of the term philosophy, love of wisdom, philosophers, one supposes, have wanted to be wise, yet experience has taught that there is no good reason to think that they are necessarily so except, circularly, by their own definitions, and no good reason to think that nonphilosophers cannot be equally wise, that is, perceptive, farsighted, and sagacious, in the ways that their particular lives have taught them. Nor is there any good reason to

suppose that traditions that are not philosophical by the definition I have adopted have not had their own depth of sophistication and practical intelligence (which is implicitly also theoretical) ... Let me pause briefly to give a few examples of what I mean by this last statement. The definition of philosophy that is adopted here implies that ancient Mesopotamia and Egypt had no philosophical tradition. This implication holds true even though the Mesopotamians' religious texts show that they were trying to grasp universal and permanent principles that lie below the surface of things.

2014: 122

Scharfstein thus shares the sentiments of the above definition of philosophy that distinguishes technical professional philosophy from philosophy as the pursuit of wisdom and the search for principles by asking us to put aside the latter that stays true to the etymology of philosophy, and by failing to acknowledge that the traditions of philosophy he is vehemently defending are very much saturated with the kind of philosophical principles he is putting aside and distancing himself from. With reference particularly to African philosophy, it is Scharfstein's view that Africa has no tradition of philosophy and only recently in the second half of the twentieth century because of the pioneering work of 'professional' African philosophers is such an African tradition of philosophy beginning to be born. He attempts to legitimate this line of reasoning about African philosophical tradition by co-opting the views of key African pioneers of the professional philosophical trend of doing African philosophy, which roots anything that can be termed African philosophy in the restricted, technical and professional sense attributed to European philosophy: 'In essential agreement with the restrictive definition of philosophy I have given here, Kwasi Wiredu, *an Oxford-educated philosopher from Ghana*, considers traditional African thought, however humanistic, to be only a "folk philosophy." An African philosophy distinct from traditional world-views is still to be created, he says ... And *the French-educated philosopher Paulin Hountondji* denounces "ethnophilosophies" as European constructs unknown to the Africans to which they have been attributed and insists that the theoretical creativity of the African peoples, arrested by colonialism, is yet to be liberated.' (2014: 124; emphasis is mine.)

The key points or defining features that stand out as supreme in defining a philosophical tradition in Scharfstein's and similar accounts include individual authorship, textuality, transgenerational coherency, literacy, the politics of naming and the whiteness of philosophy. We will explain and contest the claimed supremacy of these defining features of a philosophical tradition in the sections that follow, not with the aim of dismissing them as important features of philosophical traditions, but of questioning their alleged supremacy, critiquing conventional understandings, and showcasing how they constitute only some and not all of the features that are prevalent in philosophical traditions. These contestations and analyses will result in a more inclusive and realistic understanding of a philosophical tradition that invariably and undeniably includes the African tradition of philosophy.

Contesting Individual Authorship

One of the key defining features of a philosophical tradition as dominantly understood in academia is that in this intellectual tradition, the philosophical ideas, concepts, theories, debates and arguments that are produced, are produced and authored by individuals. This is what Scharfstein captures above as a tradition that develops from 'teacher to disciple to disciple's disciple'. I refer to this key defining feature as individual authorship where philosophical knowledge and ways of philosophizing are attributed to identifiable and specific individuals in the history of the tradition of philosophy. These individuals take credit for original contributions to the development of the tradition of philosophy, such as in terms of the ideas and methods that they develop, enjoy recognition for, and ownership of, the contribution they have made, and can be held accountable for them. A philosophical tradition is thus conventionally understood to be developed by identifiable individuals over a period of time, such that there is also transgenerational coherency – another feature we will examine in more detail later. Individual authorship is therefore a fundamental condition for presenting the conventional history of philosophy, a Greek-European-Western history, and you only need to pick up a 'History of Philosophy' text in a library to encounter the individual authors and producers of philosophical knowledge that have been presented to us in this history, from the pre-Socratic philosophers, the Socratic philosophers, the medieval philosophers, the philosophers of the Enlightenment to contemporary philosophers.

Individual authorship of philosophical knowledge in this dominant Western tradition fits aptly with the broader understanding of knowledge production in this tradition of philosophy. Western epistemology has always been concerned with understanding how the individual subject with its cognitive powers acquires and justifies knowledge claims – not until recently in the twentieth century were there bold and clear interests in social epistemology (e.g. Goldman 1999). Knowledge production in the broader array of Western philosophy has always fundamentally been a subjective experience. It is the self that has self-contained properties and qualities, such as reason, thinking ability, consciousness, agency, logic and the senses to participate in the knowing process. For example, René Descartes' cogito (the subject that thinks, doubts and reflects) is one of the most defended epistemic foundations in this tradition for the possibility of any certain knowledge claim. And similarly for Immanuel Kant, knowledge would not be possible without the active structuring experience of the subject using its sensory input and mental categories. In theorizing this knowing self-contained and autonomous subject without whom knowledge is not possible, this tradition has managed to construct comprehensive sexist and racist/Eurocentric perspectives about the nature of the knowing subject where the male subject allegedly knows and thinks better than the female subject (Miller 2002) and the European (white male) subject knows better than the non-European subject (Strickland and Wang 2023).

Once established as a defining feature of the dominant philosophical tradition, individual authorship becomes a basis for the rejection of traditions often labelled as folk philosophy or cultural philosophy because of the unfelt presence of numerous individuals independently authoring philosophy in such traditions. To claim that a group of people has a philosophical tradition would be therefore to claim that one can show evidence of individual authors in that tradition coherently developing that tradition over a long period of time. Anonymous authors of philosophy or philosophical knowledge collectively produced by groups or collaboratively authored by a number of individuals would become difficult to admit as philosophy. Folk philosophy will become at best some raw material or object of discourse for the real philosopher as a knowing subject to analyse, refute or accept. This knowing subject, this individual authoring philosophy is thus presented as if standing back, detached from and removed from the folklore or culture he or she philosophizes about as if he or she is not in the first place shaped and influenced by the experiences, language and thought in place.

The privileging of individual authorship in the definition of a philosophical tradition raises at least two key challenges: the trivialization of collective epistemic agency and the holism-individualism challenge in relation to the epistemic canon of philosophy. Concerning the first, the privileging of individual authors as the sole source of philosophical knowledge treats as trivial or unimportant group knowledge, collective epistemic agency, epistemic heritages and collaborative efforts in doing philosophy. The idea of collective agency in knowledge production even within philosophical circles is the acknowledgment that in human traditions down through the ages, there has always been co-dependency, cooperation and solidarity in knowing the world around us, such that if we were to be sincere with ourselves, individual authorship would always be hanging in the balance. This collectiveness and relationality in the production of knowledge and epistemic heritages, such as language and group-held world views and beliefs that individuals draw on in producing their ideas, may in many cases be suppressed and not acknowledged because of deeply entrenched politics of cognition in spaces of human dwelling where the one or a few with the louder voice and the institutional power to proclaim (such as the power to publish in books or to air in media) what has been cognized seize ownership and authorship. To be sure, there are clear and specific manifestations of individual cognition in which the cognizer deserves credit for an excellent contribution to the cognitive process, but even such cognition would not come to be without the support from a wider community of cognizers. But the dominant understanding of cognition as purely subjective and self-contained blinds us to this salient fact of solidarity in cognition, always shifting our gaze to the subjective and individual rather than to the intersubjective and communal. As I have explained elsewhere as the concept of communo-cognition, when individuals bring together their individual cognitive capacities:

> There is a collective relational perception at play. To perceive in this web of interlocked perceivers is not merely to individually, subjectively and independently see, hear, feel, sense or think; rather, it is to intersubjectively perceive and acknowledge the multidimensional nature of perception, where what A perceives may be quite different but not better or less important from what B perceives ... Collective relational perception thus indicates that we depend on others for meaningful, comprehensive and complete perception of the world we live in. It is the acknowledgement of complementary cognition, recognizing that we never completely cognize things independently and that a robust and more comprehensive cognition emerges from the interwovenness of perceivers.
>
> Imafidon 2023: 53

So, when we think, for example, of the famous *Dialogues of Plato* (Plato 1997) and the nature in which it has been textually presented and represented in human history, one cannot help but notice the trivialization of the collective and the emphasis and elevation of the individual self. The very conventional title, *Dialogues of Plato*, is a contradiction as dialogues or conversations cannot be of an individual but of individuals, and we know for certain that there were several persons involved in the dialogues and Socrates was often a major character. So, the popular idea that Plato is the author and philosophical architect of the dialogues is perhaps an idea we do not question enough. Think for example about *The Theaetetus* (Plato 1997). When we read through the essay, we can identify several individuals involved in this dialogue about knowledge, such as Euclid, Terpsion, Socrates, Theodorus and Theaetetus. Interestingly, Plato is often not one of those involved in the dialogue as with many other dialogues. Plato simply becomes the author primarily for being the individual that produced the text. Would this not amount to academic dishonesty and fraud today? Would the epistemically responsible thing to do not be to list the actual interlocutors involved in the dialogue as authors and listing Plato only as the editor? But today and even here as I am expected to do in line with academic regulations, Plato will be cited as the author of the essay. This attitude of taking ownership of knowledge that may have been collaboratively achieved permeates philosophy in particular and academia in general, and perhaps we are all in one way or the other guilty. We rely heavily on epistemic heritages, such as language, knowledge and information acquired from learning and education; we benefit from discussions and conversations with students, friends and colleagues in classrooms, offices, hallways, conferences, seminars, pubs and other public spheres, discussions and conversations that spark and bring to life those ideas and intellectual journeys that are credited to us and us alone. In reality, what is perhaps truly ours in this intellectual journey, in an essay or book published, may be no more than some sprinkles on the collectively baked cake (originality), how we did the sprinkles (method) and how the sprinkles contributed to the cake as a whole (contribution to knowledge). We have found ways to acknowledge to a certain degree (and I dare say that it is never to a full degree) the collaboration in knowledge production through the Acknowledgement and References sections of our publications, for example, but more important it seems to me is the acknowledgement of intellectual humility, relational cognition and the collaborative nature of knowledge production.

Beyond our dependence on, and collaboration with, others for knowledge and the questions this raises in relation to the idea of individual authorship, there is an even more significant challenge to individual authorship that emerges from the understanding of group knowledge and epistemic heritages that is aptly captured in the holism-individualism debate. We know that we can speak meaningfully of group knowledge by saying, for example, that Christians know so and so, scientists know so and so, or the Akans know so and so. We can also meaningfully speak about group philosophy, such as Greek philosophy, German philosophy, Yoruba philosophy or Mexican philosophy. So, when we refer to Greek philosophy or German philosophy, do the sum of the work of the individual Greek or German philosophers in this group constitute what we understand as the group philosophy or is there more to it? Is German philosophy, for example, the sum of the philosophy of all German philosophers or is there an epistemic heritage that goes beyond this sum to include, for example, commitment to specific ideologies and ontologies that are collectively held and a certain kind of attitudinal disposition or spirit of the time? German philosophy cannot thus be understood solely as the combination of all German philosophers and their thoughts. It goes beyond this to include a commitment or reaction to the culture, ideologies and ontologies of the time. More so, the German language used in writing German philosophy as part of the epistemic heritage that an individual philosopher in the group assimilates and uses, fundamentally defines the sort of philosophy that is produced. This is why it is difficult, for example, for non-German speakers to thoroughly grasp the philosophical thoughts of Martin Heidegger when relying on translations of his work, when compared to how a German-speaking philosopher might access and understand his texts, and the difference in the many translations of his texts often centres on how best a particular translation has aptly captured the original meaning that Heidegger intended to convey with specific German words or concepts.

Therefore, there are always collaborative efforts not often properly acknowledged and group factors and agency that transcend the specific individual that is authoring philosophical thought, but yet are fundamental for making sense of the individually authored philosophy. We cannot possibly understand the philosophy of Plato outside the context of the collective spirit and traditions of the Greeks and of Greek philosophy, the political philosophy of Niccolò Machiavelli outside the Renaissance spirit and Florentine politics, and the African philosophical thought of Kwasi Wiredu or Kwame Gyekye outside the collective episteme of African (Akan) traditions. In an attempt to legitimate African philosophy by mirroring the West, some African philosophers proposed in the late-twentieth century models such as professional philosophy and sage philosophy to define and defend African philosophy as similar to the dominant understanding of Western philosophy hinged on the feature of individual authorship. Professional philosophy defended the claim that African philosophy is the philosophy authored by individual African philosophers and sage philosophy defined African philosophy as the search for specific individuals in African communities who were filled with wisdom and knowledge that included but went beyond philosophical ideas collectively held in the community (Oruka 2003). Although these trends or models of African philosophy were largely well intended at a time when African philosophers were under pressure to defend the existence of African philosophy, there was always the danger of doing disservice to the robust cognitive empire and development of African philosophy in ways that ignore and fail to acknowledge the rich philosophical heritages of African peoples and in ways that encourage individual African philosophers to use the resources of this philosophical heritage without proper credit or acknowledgment. Individual authorship is no doubt important and a major source of philosophical knowledge. It would be a self-contradiction to claim otherwise considering that I am an individual philosopher writing this book. However, it remains only one way in which philosophy is produced and authored and is always fused and intertwined with collective, collaborative and group authorship. Just as we can legitimately write and speak of the philosophy of Plato, Descartes, Confucius, Fanon, Camus, Wiredu, Tutu and Hountondji, we can also legitimately speak of Greek philosophy, Mayan philosophy, Shona philosophy, Yoruba philosophy and Polish philosophy. Much of the methods for doing philosophy and the philosophy produced therefrom discussed and analysed in the chapters of this book take seriously group philosophy in sub-Saharan African traditions. While I, as an individual author, will contribute to the narrative of philosophy that emerges from this text in terms of style, concept making, analysis, methods, arguments and drawing conclusions, it would amount to a lack of intellectual humility and epistemic injustice against African peoples if I were to take full credit for the philosophical ideas produced in this text. For example, I may have been defending in the last few paragraphs group agency as legitimate and as relevant as individual agency in the production of philosophical knowledge, but I do so by relying heavily on my African experience of such group agency at play in communities. Thus, a fusion of individual and collective authorship of philosophy is indispensable in defining a philosophical tradition and in achieving just and inclusive repositories of philosophy.

Contesting Textuality

> Philosophy, until very recently, has been defined as strictly textual. The pre-judgment is that, in order for something to be accepted as philosophical, it must be written. African philosophy in particular has suffered considerably from this prejudgment, or what others may explicitly call a Eurocentric racial gaze. The colonial and imperial projects on Africa produced narratives of what philosophy is and is not, and imposed it on the continent of Africa, from which emerged the new and dangerous view that the colonized African subjects were by definition impervious to logical thinking, to systematic thought, to organized opining, and to conceptual formations, four definitions of philosophy. Africans as human beings were thus denied the capacity to think, an essential characteristic of human beings, and through this denial, they were excluded from philosophical activity as logical thinking, systematic thought, opining, and concept formation.
>
> Kiros 2017: 181

A second key defining feature of a philosophical tradition that has often been enlisted by the West in its attempt to dominate and be the hegemon of the discipline is textuality. Textuality understood in the context of an intellectual cum philosophical tradition conveys the idea that texts or written works within that tradition form a coherent, structured and meaningful body of knowledge about that tradition. The whole corpus of texts in a philosophical tradition authored by individuals in that tradition will in some way amount to the complete heritage of the tradition. Western philosophy mobilizes all facets of textuality, such as intratextuality, intertextuality, materiality, genre, style and convention, and authorship available in its tradition to argue for its first place in owning the discipline. For example, the intertextual relationship between Heidegger's texts and those of the pre-Socratic and Socratic philosophers – as Heidegger draws heavily on Greek concepts and compares them with German concepts – would make for a fine argument of intertextuality over a long period of time. Having asserted its place in philosophy, the West can then, out of its generosity, screen other traditions to see which ones resemble the self in being faithful to textuality, and on this basis determine who is or is not qualified to be admitted into the hall of philosophy. The specific qualifying notion in this sense would be that to show that a tradition has philosophy, it must showcase its philosophical texts that it has used to preserve and transmit its philosophical knowledge from one generation to another. The absence of, or lack of consistent and coherent presence of, such texts would imply the absence of a philosophical tradition.

This understanding of the textuality of philosophy has been crucial in the denial of the existence of African philosophy before the existence of texts that could be classified as African philosophical texts in the mid-twentieth century. It is for this reason that the 1945 text of Placide Tempels, *La Philosophie Bantoue* (Bantu Philosophy) is considered by some to be the beginning point of the development of systematic African philosophy as a contemporary discipline as against pre-systematic or non-technical philosophy that may have existed before this time – a distinction already familiar to us in this chapter

(Chimakonam ND). One of the foremost pioneers of the model of African philosophy known as professional African philosophy, Paulin Hountondji, thus defines African philosophy this way:

> By 'African philosophy' I mean a set of texts, specifically, the set of texts written by Africans and described as philosophical by their authors themselves … African philosophy is a body of literature whose existence is undeniable, a bibliography which has grown constantly over the last thirty years or so.
>
> 1983, p.20

This centring of text in contemporary academic African philosophy in line with the expectations of the gatekeepers of academic philosophy, the West, is being uncritically sustained in academic circles of African philosophy today, to the extent that the contemporary textual history of African philosophy has been described as 'forward looking', while engagement with non-textual repositories of philosophical knowledge in Africa before this alleged textual age is regarded as 'backward looking' (Kwame 2017). By implication, an African philosophical tradition was non-existent until one began developing in textual forms – and still in the stage of development – in the 1940s. This embrace of textuality in African philosophy in a bid to be like the hegemon of philosophy has implications for the discipline. More so, the very idea of textuality in Western philosophy raises a few questions worth paying attention to. But it is important, I believe, to first say a few things about the politics of materiality and intertextuality inherent in the idea of textuality that we have been discussing, as it would further help us to appreciate the problematics of the textual narrative before us.

The politics of materiality and intertextuality in the textuality discourse consists of examining and understanding the power structures and dynamics of what can be considered texts on the one hand and what can determine the coherency of many texts over a long period of time on the other. It also consists of how such an understanding shapes what is included into the textual canon or excluded from it. For example, in terms of materiality or the physical form of a text, in scripting a textual history of philosophy, do the use of hieroglyphs and logograms receive the same treatment and acknowledgement as alphabets, or are alphabets much more privileged than they are? Would ancient Egyptian hieroglyphics, Yoruba hieroglyphics and Akan Adinkra symbols have the same standing as the alphabets? Are papers and inks more privileged and desired in this textual history than papyrus, walls, clay tablets, parchment, stone and metal? I do not intend here to elaborately answer these questions. I believe we have a fair knowledge of the textual history before us to determine what the glaring answers are. To be sure, the arguments for alphabets over the rest often revolve around preferences for simplicity, representation of sounds, durability, straight-forward readability and ease of production over complexity, representation of words, stories, ideas and experiences, non-durability, multi-layered readability and complex production systems. But these preferences have nothing or, perhaps, very little to do with the knowledge and wisdom inherent in all forms of textuality or scripting, for it is only ontically human to script things be it on paper, wood, tablets, walls and even bodies. More so, the idea that alphabetical texts and scripts are preferable is based on a constructed narrative, as none of the reasons often proffered are beyond questioning. For example, its simplicity is no doubt contextual and not universal. The politics of textuality is even more obvious in the claim of intertextuality. Who determines what texts are intertwined and the conditions that makes such intertwining possible? Does the quest to showcase intertextuality not deliberately or non-deliberately lead to the exclusion of certain texts? And are texts only intertwineable with other texts? We see clearly from the recent history of Western philosophy that many women were excluded and neglected in the dominant history of Western philosophy, partly to exert patriarchy and to achieve intertextuality (Kotevska 2022). What the politics of textuality brings to mind is that the very idea of textuality is portrayed and narrated in specific ways that are favourable to the dominant tradition of philosophy and could potentially exclude other traditions. But even when we agree to go by the Western narrative of textuality that aims to portray textuality as different from and opposed to non-textual forms of epistemic repositories, such as orality and symbolism, we still run into several challenges.

One major challenge of the primacy of textuality in the dominant understanding of a philosophical tradition is how it undermines non-textual repositories of knowledge, even in ways that contradict its history. A typical example is the Socratic puzzle. The enduring debate in the history of Western philosophy as to whether Socrates existed or he was simply the creation of Plato is not unconnected with the fact that there are no Socratic texts available, texts directly authored by him as undoubtable evidence of his authorship of philosophical ideas. Not many universities today would offer Socrates a lectureship position as his proof of ingenuity in doing philosophy will largely be determined as with academics today by his publications. And again, Socrates was always fond of a conversational and collaborative style of philosophy, which in many ways departs from individual authorship as examined above. The focus on texts in the search for philosophy could make us look the other way and fail to recognize philosophy even when it stares us in the face in non-textual repositories of knowledge. To be sure, the question of whether texts are more important than non-textual forms of knowledge, specifically oral forms, has resulted in the graphocentric-phonocentric debate in the history of Western philosophy. While philosophers such as Plato and Ferdinand de Saussure (1983), defend phonocentrism by upholding the superiority of speech over writing as a direct, immediate expression of thought, emphasizing the ephemeral and living nature of spoken language, the norm of the tradition of Western philosophy has become graphocentric, privileging text over speech. In Plato's *Phaedrus*, for example, writing is analysed as flawed. This is because writing destroys memory by producing forgetfulness in the minds of those who learn to use it, and writing is unresponsive. More so, writing is in-human and thing-like and does not defend itself. For Plato, writing or the written word is of little worth (Hung 2018; Ong 1967). This debate on the superiority of writing over speech and vice versa is misplaced as far as I can see it, as It fails to recognize that speaking, writing and even symbolizing have equal ontological standing in the presentation, representation, preservation and transmission of thought. We employ these varied ways of being in capturing and passing along our thoughts. Perhaps Jacques Derrida (1976) in his theory of deconstruction best attempts in the Western philosophical tradition to move away from a superiority debate to the acknowledgement of this equal and complementary ontological standing, by arguing that writing is not secondary but foundational in shaping meaning and presence. Derrida contends that all language, whether spoken or written, relies on systems of difference and deferral, undermining the traditional privileging of speech over writing. And this brings us to another challenge of privileging text, the category mistake. It is a category mistake to present text as philosophical knowledge in itself rather than as a repository of philosophical knowledge. Philosophical knowledge emerges from solitary, relational or collaborative processes that showcase the fondness, quest and search for wisdom. Texts, speech and symbols are ways of capturing that process and not necessarily the process in themselves. For we do not write before we think individually or together of what to write or before we enter into a dialogue about what to write.

Texts always exist side-by-side with non-textual forms of knowledge in human cultures. In the seeming embrace and centring of text and the de-centring, exclusion and marginalization of non-texts in contemporary academic African philosophy, the texts produced by individual African philosophers are saturated and profusely permeated with references to the non-textual oral and symbolic repositories of a more enduring African philosophical tradition consisting of African languages, concepts, folklores, proverbs, storytelling, adages, sculptures, artefacts, textile materials, symbols and the like. When we as African philosophers write in texts about the concept of the mind, the idea of personhood, the understanding of reality, the idea of community, the critique of doubt, the notion of virtue, the concept of truth, and other issues and problems in African philosophy, we draw heavily on the non-textual repositories of knowledge in African places, and we deliberately or non-deliberately acknowledge the collaboration with collectives and communities of selves in producing the knowledge we produce, questioning the very idea of individual authorship and textuality. When we make such claims in our texts about the Akan concept of truth, the Yoruba concept of virtue, the Shona concept of knowledge, and the Zulu notion of person, we are in effect affirming the power of collective agency in producing philosophical knowledge, rethinking the idea of individual authorship and affirming the relevance of oral and symbolic repositories of knowledge in African places for doing philosophy.

Thus, there is a danger of epistemic irresponsibility in the centring of texts and the marginalization of non-texts in African philosophy. Being epistemically irresponsible in this way by not acknowledging the non-textual, even while relying on it, results in exclusion, misrecognition and non-recognition of knowledge producers, dehumanizes knowledge production and causes the poverty of philosophical knowledge. The centring of texts immediately marginalizes and excludes other repositories of philosophical knowledge, or at the very least, fails to give other repositories the acknowledgement due to them. It trivializes the diversity in the ways humans produce, store and transmit knowledge, and in an age of legitimate emphasis on equality, equity, diversity and inclusion, this produces different levels of epistemic injustices. Also, the focus solely on texts and their individual authors results in the non-recognition or misrecognition of other non-individual producers of knowledge, the collective self which is central in African philosophical traditions, and this further perpetuates the coloniality of knowledge. The lack of acknowledgement of other human modes of producing, storing and transmitting knowledge beyond text dehumanizes knowledge production systems because it ignores the diverse, rich and inclusive ways in which humans have done so in human history. The culmination of these challenges is the poverty of knowledge. If we focus our attention in African philosophy solely on textuality and individual authorship, we are bound to de-historicize and de-content the field of enquiry leading to unprecedented poverty of philosophical knowledge emerging from African places. This invariably reinforces epistemic colonization as African philosophy becomes an addendum in the history of European philosophy that only came to light under the academic systems and structures of Europe and America. Texts are no doubt important sources of philosophy. After all, I am right now writing a text and using this medium to narrate African philosophy. But it remains one of several ways of presenting philosophical ideas that flows seamlessly, or at least ought to, from and with other repositories, and the question of superiority of the one over the other should not be taken seriously, particularly bearing in mind the realities of African philosophy.

Contesting the Politics of Naming and Transgenerational Coherency

Weaved into the narrative of a dominant philosophical tradition and often deployed as defences for why this tradition is fundamentally Western, are naming and transgenerational coherency. The argument from naming or labelling is that the concept of philosophy and the many other concepts it deals with as a field of enquiry, such as ontology, epistemology, ethics, metaphysics and aesthetics, are deliberately chosen Greek labels or categories enlisted to describe experiences that are uniquely Greek and European and cannot thus be said to emerge from other places. Philosophy, for example, is a Greek concept that captures the experience of the pursuit of wisdom in ways that are uniquely Greek and different from the business with wisdom in other traditions. As William Edelglass and Jay W. Garfield (2011: 4–5) put it:

> Instead of grounding their arguments in descriptive accounts of non-Western philosophy, some Western thinkers have simply argued that 'philosophy' is by definition a Greek-European project and is only mistakenly applied as a universal category to the intellectual traditions of other cultures. On this view, there may indeed be wisdom in the classic texts of other traditions, but again, these texts are not, strictly speaking, philosophical; rather, they are best approached through the methodologies of other disciplines, such as religious studies, intellectual history, anthropology or cultural studies. Such views marginalize non-Western intellectual traditions, making them objects of cultural study,

limited by their cultural particularities, and excluded from the realm of philosophy (that is, Western philosophy...), which is thought to transcend cultural location in its pursuit of universal truth. We are left, on the one hand, with an often explicit claim of universal reason, and on the other, with the implicit claim that access to this universality is restricted to particular geographic locations.

In this sense, naming or labelling becomes the welding of political power where the one who has the power not only to name an experience or enquiry but to project that name into the global space, claims ownership of not only the name or label but also of the experience or enquiry, as well as the entitlement to determine who can use the label and how it can and cannot be used. Philosophy is not simply the human love, fondness and search for wisdom; it is a uniquely Greek and European systematic way of doing so. Ontology is not simply the human discourse of being; it is a specifically Greek labelled way of doing so. Thus, when we find similar interests in the pursuit of wisdom and an understanding of being in other traditions, it might be far-fetched, in line with this politics of naming, to label them philosophy or ontology. But to name or label a human experience is not to own it. What we own when we are ontically driven to label or name an experience is our understanding of, and approach to, that experience, which we make concerted efforts to validate, legitimate and justify. The beauty and richness of a human experience is to be found in the many names, forms and interpretation it takes in different times and places. To limit a human experience to a specific label, category or name without acknowledging and engaging with similar categories and labels, stifles the experience and freezes it in time and space. More so, the politics of naming have been deployed in human history to perpetuate epistemic injustice by claiming ownership of what is not rightfully ours. Claiming, for example, that Christopher Columbus was the first person to land in a beautiful island, and his people naming the island Jamaica was to perpetuate a Eurocentric history that he discovered Jamaica resulting to a claim to ownership (in the form of colonization) of this discovered land by him and his people. To be sure, this Eurocentric narrative perpetuated epistemic and physical injustice and violence against the Taino people who owned the land long before Columbus's alleged discovery. There are similar and credible arguments in philosophical circles that the attribution of the alleged unique and systematic thought system labelled philosophy to the Greeks fails to acknowledge its roots and legacy in the Egyptian way of doing philosophy. The claim to the Greek ownership of this allegedly systematic approach based on providing the label for it would according to this line of reasoning be epistemologically unjust to its Egyptian roots (Onyewuenyi 2005; James 2001).

Concerning transgenerational coherency, Scharfstein (2014: 125–6) describes what this would mean as he fleshes out his defence of the three philosophical traditions that can be accounted for in his history of philosophy (Europe, China and India):

> To justify classifying each of the three great traditions as distinct, one therefore has to show that it has a unity that prevails over all the internal differences it exhibits. Or if the attempt to show that unity prevails seems tenuous or subjective, one has to show that each of the three has pervasive habit of thought and a history of self-reference – of person to person, of intellectual group to group, of intellectual group to authoritative person, tradition, or text, and so on. This would demonstrate unity in two separable senses, that of continuity and that of self-reference. Continuity is the relationship that makes everything subsequent in the tradition lead back to the same beginnings in time, place, or attitude – the Vedas, say, in India, the godlike culture heroes in China, and the Greek philosophers in Europe. Self-reference, in contrast, is the quality that makes any isolated statement or philosophy difficult to understand without setting it in the contextual web that determines what is internal to the tradition and what is external to it, belongs to another world of thought and, no doubt, action.

There is some sense and meaning in conceptualizing transgenerational coherency as Scharfstein does here in terms of continuity and self-reference. For traditions would naturally showcase some level of continuity and reference to ideologies, values, cultural, spiritual and social practices, perennial and protracted themes and debates, and notable figures and groups. The issue that resurfaces however is why such features can only be found in Scharfstein's three traditions and nowhere else. An obvious reason perhaps is that Scharfstein hinges such continuity and reference fundamentally on individuals in these traditions in line with his argument for individual authorship as a defining feature of a philosophical tradition – 'the Vedas, say, in India, the godlike culture heroes in China, and the Greek philosophers in Europe'. Transgenerational coherency of a tradition can therefore be proven, in Scharfstein's terms, by showcasing only how individuals in that tradition reference one another and develop each other's thought and thus would exclude consistency in collective agency and thought. There is something amiss in the focus on individuals in understanding the transgenerationality of a philosophical tradition, as it seems to be deliberately enlisted for the benefit of specific traditions. If such trangenerationality emerges from the ability of a tradition of philosophy to remain recognizable and meaningful to several generations and successive generations, foster a shared identity and connection to the past, sustain certain foundational principles, and maintain a fine balance between preservation and evolution, then it is secondary whether these are achieved through individual agency or collective agency. Much of the contents of this book attest to these qualities of the transgenerationality of African philosophy made possible through both individual and collective agencies, and considering the violence that has been done to African epistemic traditions for centuries through empires of slavery, colonization and neo-colonization, the study of African philosophy may perhaps contain the litmus test of how a philosophical tradition remains coherent for many generations despite deliberate attempts to silence and undermine it.

Contesting Whiteness and Literacy

Engrained in the dominant idea of a philosophical tradition are the qualities of whiteness and literacy carefully curated and constructed in ways that serve the colonizing and hegemonic agenda of the West. In this understanding, to do philosophy or to have the ability to philosophize is intrinsically interwoven with being white and being literate in a white way. These features of Western philosophical tradition, particularly in relation to how they are deployed in latently stating the non-existence of African philosophy, are presented and represented in subtle and radical ways in grandiose and elaborate justificatory theories of racial hierarchies, eugenics and colonization that dominate Enlightenment philosophy. When Immanuel Kant wrote, for example, about racial hierarchies and how the white race was more perfect than others with the black race with little or no cognitive functions, when David Hume reiterated similar views about the inability of thought for black people and when G.W.F. Hegel considered Africa as ahistorical, there was a deliberate narrative of the whiteness of philosophy being curated by these great minds of the Enlightenment period and such narratives have had significant impact on our received view of philosophy today.

The whiteness of philosophy meant at least two things. First, it meant that only a certain group of people could claim to have a tradition of philosophy or lay claim to the ownership of philosophy. Any other human tradition claiming to have an authentic philosophical system of its own would be considered to have produced a pseudo kind of philosophy inferior to that of the West or would have to owe its philosophical trajectory to the West. Scharfstein (2014: 126–7) says, for example, about the Jewish and Islamic traditions of philosophy that:

> No doubt, pride in one's Jewish or Muslim heritage may prompt one to minimize this dependence on European, that is, Greek and Roman thought. Each of Al-Farabi, Ibn Sina (Avicenna), and Maimonides has his own sometimes considerable degree of philosophical independence, but the thought of no one of them can be conceived without the Aristotelian and Neoplatonic principles that underlie it. The Muslims themselves reserve the term philosophy for thought based on these Aristotelian-Neoplatonic principles. The often philosophical theology that departs from the principles is called *kalam*, which may be translated dialectical theology. For its logic, *kalam* depends on Hellenistic, especially Stoic logic, and for its practices of debate and its

dissociative kind of atomism – which denies natural causality – perhaps on Indian philosophy.

It is thus not surprising that there is often a silencing of place in the dominant Western narrative of the history of philosophy. For if philosophy has only one legitimate place of origin and only one tradition, it is tautologous to markedly and repeatedly identify it when narrating the history of that tradition of philosophy. Books, book series, journals and journal articles have since the Enlightenment presented the history of the tradition of philosophy with this understanding. If you picked up ten books in a library today, each roughly and variedly titled 'A History of Philosophy', the chances that the contents of each of those books will be solely about the Western tradition of philosophy (such as narrating the ideas of key thinkers of the pre-Socratic period, the Socratic period, the medieval period and the modern period of Western philosophy) is certain, for because of the nearly subconscious understanding that philosophy is white and Western, there would be no reason for these authors and editors to indicate that each of the books is 'A History of *Western* Philosophy', an indication that would no doubt acknowledge even in principle that there exist other traditions. Only recently are there noticeable efforts to do things differently by explicitly identifying place in doing philosophy. To be sure, this understanding of the whiteness of philosophy is still very much entrenched into the pedagogy of philosophy today. Globally today, the expected learning outcomes and skills acquired in the philosophy curriculum are still very dominated and defined by the Western tradition. Only gradually but slowly is the interest in non-Western traditions of philosophy emerging in academic curricula.

Second, it meant that for any other group of people to be able to claim to have a philosophical tradition or system, or to develop one, it would have to undergo a *whitening process*. A process that actively suspends and gradually erases the heritage and identity of the group of people while embracing the identity and heritage of whiteness. With particular reference to the African experience of the whitening process, the crux of colonization and ongoing neo-colonization has been to achieve the assimilation by Africans of the white ways of doing things while rejecting, suspending and erasing African ways, and key to this process is the white idea of literacy meant to replace a constructed idea of African illiteracy. With particular reference to philosophy, this meant abandoning one's ways of learning, language and epistemic structures for the Western ways of learning and for Western languages. With particular reference to the African experience, it meant that speaking an African language and learning, co-learning and pursuing wisdom the African way would constitute illiteracy, while speaking, reading and writing a Western language, such as English, French or Spanish, and learning within the formal setting of Western education, would constitute literacy. For example, this whitening process produced a distinction in African places between formal literate languages (the languages of the West) and vernacular illiterate languages (African languages), and the vernacularization of African languages has resulted in the distancing of Africans from their own languages in the pursuit of literacy. Thus, within this framework of the whitening process and the pursuit of literacy, it would follow that without critical interrogation of these ideas, the learning and doing of philosophy will be seen as only possible and achievable by paying attention to Western individual authors of philosophy and Western philosophical texts and pedagogy. As Edelglass and Garfield (2011: 5) put it:

> Philosophers in subaltern cultures are encouraged, in order to work internationally, to attend primarily to the philosophical ideas, texts, and figures of dominant cultures, thus simultaneously alienating themselves from their own cultural context and reinforcing the view that there is not much there worthy of attention in the first place. However, the current global dominance of Western discourse in philosophical debates is due in no small part to the Western dominance of non-Western peoples over the last four centuries; political, military, economic, and technological power have as much to do with the framework of contemporary philosophical discourse as any alleged universal truths of Western philosophy that are unique in their transcendence of cultural and historical location.

There are several problems with the imposition and gradual assimilation of whiteness and literacy as conditions for, and benchmarks of, doing philosophy in the African context. One such challenge in relation to whiteness is the possibility of taking whiteness as a fact or an actual state of reality rather than for what it is, a deliberate construction and radical colouring of race for purposes of power and dominance and for sustaining a radical dichotomy of the self (as white) from the other (as non-white). In terms of doing philosophy, it would mean assimilating and promoting the philosophy that emerges from whiteness as superior to (in the specific case of Africa) the philosophy that emerges from blackness, which if at all existent is of an inferior kind. It is thus quite a reductionist and an essentialist approach to thinking about philosophy and a philosophical tradition that reduces and essentializes the rich, diverse and robust philosophical traditions of the world to the Western or anything else that resembles the Western. Another challenge in relation to literacy is the streamlining of philosophy to what has been captured in written or oral forms in specific Western languages and transmitted and learned in specific Western pedagogical ways. If language is fundamental in accessing the philosophy produced by a specific human tradition, such as how concepts have been constructed to capture ideas about being or knowledge, reducing the literacy of philosophy to specific Western languages and pedagogies results in the dismissal, erasure and ignoring of the philosophical thoughts and methods in the many African languages, such as the concepts and ideas that have been carefully stored up in the languages of many African peoples. This amounts to the delegitimizing of thought in African languages as illiterate and by implication the gradual erasure of thought.

What is a Philosophical Tradition?

What we have perhaps demonstrated so far in this chapter is what a philosophical tradition is not or at least what it cannot be reduced to. The contestations above show that a philosophical tradition is not reducible to a purely textual tradition or the philosophical ideas produced or authored only by specific individuals over a period of time. They also show clearly that a philosophical tradition is not one owned by the West alone. How then can we define a philosophical tradition? I suggest here three important features that help define a philosophical tradition in ways that are epistemically responsive and humanizing of the discipline. To be sure, these features should already be discernible from the contestations above and are by no means exhaustive. Flowing from the foregoing, therefore, a philosophical tradition is an epistemic tradition in that it produces philosophical knowledge and it is driven and validated by these three features: epistemic commitment, epistemic durability and epistemic humility.

A philosophical tradition is epistemically committed in so far as it showcases and demonstrates a sustained commitment to the pursuit of wisdom, the asking and answering of philosophical questions and puzzles, the development of specific methods for doing so, and to the production and revision of philosophical ideas, concepts and theories. Who does the asking and answering, develops the methods and produces the philosophical knowledge – be it an individual or a community of selves – becomes secondary to the actual performance of these philosophical activities. This of course allows for the inclusion of diverse epistemic agents, methods and knowledge forms into the global heritage of philosophy. We will see in the chapters that follow how African traditions of philosophy have been committed to the doing of philosophy in ways that allow individual and group knowers, textual and non-textual forms of knowledge, as well as solitary and deliberative processes of knowing, to flourish and grow. A philosophical tradition is epistemically durable in so far as it is capable of sustaining, preserving and transmitting over a period of time its philosophical knowledge and methods, resisting as much as possible external and internal attempts to break, deteriorate or minimize its relevance. The specific repository(ies) developed for achieving this durability – be it textual, non-textual or a blend of both – becomes secondary to the actual actualization of durability. This of course acknowledges and allows for flexibility in how the durability of a tradition is accomplished, bearing in mind that different methods for doing so may dominate different phases of human history. The chapters that follow explore how African traditions of philosophy have achieved an epistemically durable tradition and the contemporaneity and futures of its philosophical knowledges, methods and practices. A philosophical tradition showcases epistemic humility by deliberately or inadvertently acknowledging the fallibility of its philosophical knowledge and system, the possibility of other perspectives and the possibility of revisions to previously held perspectives as the dialogue unfolds. Epistemic humility does not threaten authenticity, reliability and robustness of a tradition but rather affirms it, for one realization that is commonly shared in the many traditions of philosophy in their fondness for and pursuit of knowledge is the fallibility of philosophical knowledge, which makes it subject not only to questioning, debate and analysis but also the possibility of fresh ideas and new perspectives. The discourse specifically of collaborative strategies in philosophizing and the enigmatic nature of philosophizing in African places compared to a more dominant polemical method in academia in Chapter Five, strongly capture epistemic humility in African traditions of philosophy.

Thus, what unfolds in the chapters that follow is a comprehensive exploration of the epistemic commitment, durability and humility of African philosophical traditions that will be made evident by focusing on the enduring fondness for wisdom, the styles and methods of performing philosophy, the textual and non-textual repositories of philosophy, and ideas of fluidity, relationality, difference, enigmatics and fallibility that are inherent in the tradition.

2

The Orality of African Philosophy

If the shift away in the previous chapter from a restrictive and essentially Eurocentric understanding of philosophy and a philosophical tradition is an important inclusive and epistemic step to take toward a robust and rich encounter with the philosophical traditions of the world, then it opens up the way, particularly in an African context, to rich non-textual repositories of philosophy, which this chapter and the next primarily focus on. Non-textuality in this context consists of the deliberate and systematic activities of knowledge producers in African traditions to produce and store up knowledge, in this particular case, philosophical knowledge, in forms other than written or printed forms, such as texts, at least as understood in the conventional sense. Non-textual knowledge forms will therefore include oral, visual, symbolic, unconventionally scripted, embodied and kinetic knowledge forms. These will specifically include folklore, storytelling, names, adages, proverbs, paintings, sculptures, motifs, dancing and performance arts, fabrics and textiles. These non-textual forms of knowledge are often accessed aurally, visually and kinetically. Philosophical concepts, ideas and theories preserved in non-textual forms immediately evoke the urge for philosophical and hermeneutical engagements, debates and analysis. Non-textual philosophy is not detached from or separable from textual philosophy, as the former feeds into the latter and vice versa. In the rest of this book, the richness of non-textual African philosophy, its deliberate, systematic and methodical prowess, and its inseparability from textual African philosophy, will become obvious.

Let us begin our journey into the non-textuality of African philosophy by examining orality in this tradition of philosophy. I am interested in examining in this chapter why African philosophy can be described partly as an oral tradition, analysing some of the major repositories of orality in African traditions, and examining how such repositories are produced and sustained. This chapter will also focus on analysing the dynamism and transgenerationality of oral forms of philosophical knowledge and the extent to which we can consider oral traditions reliable epistemic sources, particularly when compared with the more dominant textual traditions. The chapter will then engage with the specific performance of oral philosophy in African traditions or the philosophical exercise of producing specific forms of oral philosophy, namely the philosophy of existence, truth and relationality. In exploring oral African philosophy, we will be thrown into a space of vibrant non-textual epistemic systems where knowledge and understanding are collectively negotiated and used to saturate community life in mundane, performative, discursive, humorous and artistic ways. What becomes obvious in this chapter and further on in this book is that orality is a human way of performing philosophy and producing and transmitting knowledge.

Oral Repositories of Philosophy

> An oral tradition is a transmission of thought over generations by the spoken word and techniques of communication other than writing. Under this definition, such items as poems, lyrics, proverbs, and maxims, of course, qualify as elements of our oral traditions. So too do drum texts and art motifs. But languages do have embedded in their syntax and semantics various notions about reality and human experience. Through these, our habits of speech influence our habits of writing. And so we cannot regard written traditions as altogether independent of orality.
>
> Kwasi Wiredu (2009: 8)

African communities are permeated with aural learning and pedagogies as much of what can be learnt or taught is produced, transmitted and preserved in oral forms. I grew up in an African community where listening attentively, remembering and recollecting, memorizing, communicating properly and respectively, and actively participating in conversations in public spheres that punctuated everyday life were valued and cherished skills that I was encouraged to develop from a very young age if I was to successfully learn about, gain knowledge of, and contribute to producing knowledge of the world I live in. I have encountered many teachers, knowledge producers and knowledge transferers, including parents, uncles, aunties, community elders and school teachers who do not only teach the formal curriculum but communal values, the stranger on the road who corrects, instructs or disciplines me as my parent would do, those singing songs, making music and saying greetings, and those systematically playing with words in forms of adages, proverbs, slogans, parables, maxims and riddles to capture some experience or reality. For example, a greeting said to an elderly person on my way to primary school would often not result simply in getting a response to that greeting but also some brief and quick instructions about life, corrections where necessary and commendation for good behaviour, which includes the very act of greeting. While one pedagogical actor may or may not be aware of the other, you could feel a strong sense of collaboration of these actors to produce a coherent body of knowledge, and this learning would take place all through the day from the time I rose from bed to the time I went back to sleep. Considering how deeply rooted oral repositories of knowledge and aural learning are in sub-Saharan African communities, the search for philosophical knowledge and the performance of philosophy in such communities must take orality seriously. My intention, therefore, in this section is to examine three questions in this regard: What makes a tradition of philosophy an oral tradition (just in case this is not already obvious) and why can we describe African philosophy at least in part as oral philosophy? What are some key oral repositories of philosophical knowledge in African traditions? How are the repositories of oral philosophy produced and sustained?

A tradition of philosophy is an oral tradition if it is constituted at least in part by oral forms of producing, preserving, sustaining and transmitting philosophical knowledge, concepts, ideas, arguments and theories. An oral philosophical tradition will therefore consist of the oral ways of doing, practising and performing philosophy as well as oral forms of preserving and transmitting theories that emerge from such practices. No doubt, all philosophical traditions practise and produce philosophy in ways other than writing or textual forms. Even today, oral debates and deliberations on philosophical issues in conferences, seminars and workshops have a place in mainstream academic philosophy and such are often preserved and transmitted in audio and visual forms, such as through podcasts and social media. However, the challenge that oral philosophy faces in mainstream academia revolves around emphasis on a deeply rooted epistemic hierarchy that privileges the primacy of texts in producing systematic, technical and academic philosophy over speech, as if the production of text is not invariably dependent on oral practices in philosophy. Orality, however, takes a central place in the philosophical enterprise of African peoples. Sophie Oluwole, a prominent contemporary Nigerian philosopher, vehemently defends the orality of African philosophy in her classic, *Philosophy and Oral Tradition* (1998). She challenges the idea that philosophy must be written by exploring the significance of oral tradition in shaping philosophical thought, showing how African oral traditions contain deep philosophical insights. Oluwole pays close attention to African indigenous knowledge systems, such as proverbs, folktales and maxims, and how they serve as legitimate sources of philosophy. Her objective in this seminal work was apt: to decolonize mainstream academic philosophy and to show that African philosophy is not inferior to Western philosophy but is simply expressed in different forms. Since Oluwole's work, there have been other deliberate attempts to showcase the orality of African philosophy (Wiredu 2009; Ikuenobe 2018; Graness 2021). I am intentional in describing Oluwole's and similar literature as deliberate in defending the legitimacy of oral philosophy as there are many who rely on African oral traditions in doing African philosophy without deliberately acknowledging and defending it – a point we have made earlier in this work and that we will elaborate on much later in this chapter. Philosophy in the African context is thus largely performed and preserved orally in varied oral forms and philosophy is learnt largely aurally. Oral philosophy in this sense produces a lived philosophy, one that is always present in daily life rather than detached, removed or secluded to a particular place or in a particular form, such as an academic library. It is therefore more readily accessible to many and also bridges the gap between abstract theorization and lived practices.

What are some key oral repositories of philosophy in African traditions? Oral forms of doing philosophy and storing up philosophical concepts, debates and theories that are prominent in African places include language, names, enigmatic sayings, storytelling and music. Language is perhaps the best place to begin as not only its components, such as words, concepts and phrases used orally, are bearers of thought but also other repositories, including textual and non-textual ones, emerge essentially from the use of language. African languages, it seems to me and in my experience, are carefully curated repositories of thought that have been painstakingly developed over a long period of time and that continue to be developed to harbour, at least only partly, the philosophical systems, thoughts and practices of African peoples. At the surface, an African language, like every other language, is used for communication. In fact, many have argued that African languages are simplistic and not particularly robust and sophisticated like Western ones. But below the surface for anyone who is keenly interested on unravelling its richness, an African language is a complex system of philosophical thought. I have grown up knowing in my language (Igueben) – a variation of the Edo language of the ancient Benin (Bini) Kingdom of Nigeria – that the word for 'evening' is '*akota*'. So, at the surface level as I have done many times in life, I would simply translate *akota* as evening. Only recently have I paid closer attention to the word '*akota*' and realized it is a compound word formed from two other simple words '*ako*' and '*ota*', which translates as 'coming together' and 'discourse' or 'talk' respectively. Thus, below the surface, *akota* represents a collaborative discursive deliberative practice, a rich meaning that is lost at the surface level of translation. It makes sense that *akota* is simply translated as evening, since such collaborative deliberations are reserved in the communities for evening times when community members would have returned from their respective daily businesses and activities, and become available for discussions, but such simplistic translation does harm to the rich thought embedded in the seemingly simple work, *akota*.

Kwasi Wiredu (2002) has advocated for conceptual decolonization if we are to harness the rich philosophical resources of African oral languages. In his words, conceptual decolonization is:

> The elimination from our thought of modes of conceptualisation that came to us through colonization and remain in our thinking owing to inertia rather than to our own reflective choices ... If by virtue of a colonial history, you are trained right from the beginning in a foreign Language and initiated thereby into the professing of philosophy, then certain basic ways of thought that seem natural to native speakers might become natural to you too. Consequently, you might not even realize that those ways of thinking may not be at all that natural or, if your own language is radically different, even coherent from the standpoint of your own language. This means that you might not even be aware of the likely neo-colonial aspects of your conceptual framework. This is one of the greatest impediment to conceptual decolonisation in African philosophy.
>
> 2002: 56

Wiredu's description of conceptual decolonization and the key impediment to it, a deeply rooted colonial linguistic mentality, may explain why I would immediately think of *akota* as meaning 'evening' rather than the originally intended meaning 'coming together for discourse'. There is no easy way out of this linguistic predicament if one is to succeed in harnessing the rich philosophical concepts about being, beauty, knowledge, truth, existence, personhood and personal identity, perception and the like from African languages that does not put a heavy linguistic burden on the knowledge seeker. One suggestion that has been made by Alena Rettová (2002) is for African philosophers to write in African languages, which no doubt would immerse African philosophers into the orality of African languages. Rettová highlights several ways contemporary African philosophers have related and could relate with African languages. These include a complete refusal to engage with African languages and pursuing philosophy from a purely Eurocentric standpoint, the isolation and explication of certain concepts from an African language, grafting them into the European conceptual systems, the recourse to folk wisdom as contained in proverbs and other sayings to support the philosophical claims of the philosopher, the derivation of a philosophical system from an African language, and the consistent use of an African language to present and write African philosophy. Rettová argues that these different ways of relating with African languages overlap in contemporary times except for the last one: the deliberate use of African languages to write African philosophy. In her words:

> It is obvious that the philosophical potential of African languages is by far not exhausted ... The lack of writing in African languages is the main obstacle to writing African philosophy in African languages and to a more effective elaboration of the philosophical thoughts contained in folk wisdom. Creating a written tradition in African languages is, I believe, one possible solution to fortifying the position of African languages in philosophy and, by means of this, to an enhancement of the knowledge of African philosophical concepts in philosophy.
>
> 2002: 150

Apart from the obvious emphasis on a written, textual tradition of philosophy by Rettová here, one that I aim to de-emphasize in this book, the idea of writing in African languages does not on its own resolve the problem of loss of meaning that happens in translating African languages to other languages, as we see above with the concept of *akota*. If African philosophical thought is to be accessible by a diverse and global audience and be relevant for global issues and debates, the most important goal, it seems to me, should be the linguistic care for African languages in any context of their use, such as writing or speaking philosophy with and through them and selecting specific philosophical concepts in them for examination and analysis. The linguistic care or the care for language that I have in mind here is the careful attention paid to detail, components and building parts of words, concepts and phrases in a language. It is going below the surface in a somewhat surgical process that is therapeutic and healing for African languages. It is not simply decolonizing, since in some cases the challenge is not coloniality but disinterestedness and lack of attention to detail; it is genuinely caring with the aim of healing distortions to meaning, achieving precision and arriving as close as possible to the original intentions of the components of language, something akin to my linguistic care for *akota* above. As the overarching repository of oral philosophy, African languages require linguistic care for authentic philosophical thought to emerge.

One specific component of African languages that requires linguistic care for the philosophy within it to emerge is a personal name. Personal names emerging from the naming traditions and practices in African places were systematically and discursively arrived at. Although specificities such as the number of days that would pass after a child's birth before being named, who attends the naming ceremony, the specific procedures for arriving at the name(s) for the child, and who names the child may vary from one community to another, naming traditions and practices are generally well-structured, follow some specific methods, are done collectively by members of a kin, have clearly defined objectives, progress logically, and are replicable structures and practices. A fundamental defining objective of a naming tradition is that the deliberation results in the production or choosing from the existing oral corpus of a philosophical concept, statement or theory that is either linguistically parsimonious and easily understood or pregnant with meaning needed to be deciphered. Within the practice of such naming tradition, I was named Unuagbon by my father. In Nigeria, a common pattern of naming that has emerged from the colonial experience is that a child receives an English first name and a middle name that emerges from the indigenous naming practice in the specific tradition, accompanied by the surname. The English name may emerge from Christening rites or may be the parents' choice. The middle name on the other hand emerges from and sustains naming traditions in different communities, which is an interesting point worth exploring in thinking about indigenous resistance to the coloniality of (linguistic) power. Unuagbon at best translate, taking linguistic care, is 'the world's mouth'. On its own, it makes no immediate sense and this is because it expresses a deeper philosophical position, one that I can best describe here as existential populism. Unuagloon is a concept that presents the argument that striving to please or appeal to popular (the world's) views and perspectives (mouth or sayings) is an existentially futile exercise, as such perspectives are often in a state of flux and by nature critical of the varying possibilities or stances that you may take. Unuagbon is therefore the existential commitment to pursue a life course based on reason, evidence and conviction, rather than by playing to the gallery. Following the same naming practice, my immediate elder sister is named Aigunyibhin. This would best be translated as 'no one has a mastery of existence', which presents an existential philosophy that is quite self-evident and would not require, at least in this space, further elaboration. The Igbo people of Eastern Nigeria take pride in their naming tradition and in line with this tradition, my wife, an Igbo woman, is named Ndidi-Amaka, a common name among the Igbo people. Ndidi-Amaka translates as 'patience (ndidi) is good, virtuous or beautiful' (amaka). To be sure, the Igbo people are ready to defend, elaborate on, and debate this philosophical and ethical statement summed up in a name. I have deliberately chosen to showcase the philosophical contents of names by drawing on my own name and those of loved ones to make a point about how ubiquitous the practice is in African places. No doubt, these names and many others are borne by many community members in different periods and times to guarantee the preservation and transmission of these ideas and concepts. Naming and names are therefore significant repositories of philosophical knowledge, and the birth of a child becomes an opportunity to philosophize and for the child to be a bearer of thought. Names in this sense are not mere labels or tags but vehicles of thought.

Besides names, I group other important repositories of oral philosophy, such as proverbs, maxims, adages, thought experiments and riddles in African traditions under the broad heading of enigmatic sayings, particularly because of how they are often in need of interpretation and understanding, and how they are by their very nature pregnant with meaning. African communities are saturated with such enigmatic speeches and conversations. I will return to the discourse of enigmatics as a deliberative disposition much later in Chapter five. Enigmatic sayings permeate celebrations, mourning and other ceremonies, deliberations, public sphere discourses, healthcare encounters and familial gatherings. They are often deployed to express, preserve and transmit diverse philosophical commitments and puzzles, such as ethical commitments and puzzles, intersubjective and communitarian ideologies, epistemic paradoxes and existential dilemma. The Congolese philosopher, Nkombe Oleko, wrote extensively about the philosophical thoughts conveyed in African languages, particularly in the metonymies and metaphors built into proverbs. Writing specifically about Tetela proverbs, Oleko examined intersubjectivity or relationality that emerges as an overarching theme from many Tetela proverbs (Komo 2017). African peoples can relate to how enigmatic sayings are central to learning and understanding. One's enlightenment and epistemic prowess is often dependent on one's familiarity with and ability to relate to, understand and interpret such enigmatic sayings. The only reason such puzzles, debates and propositions are often not considered philosophical is not because of the lack of philosophical contents or deliberations about them in communities, but mainly because they are orally preserved and collectively owned, and not written and authored by an identifiable individual.

Stories, epics, music and other oral artistic performances contain more lengthy philosophical narratives. Stories, for example, would consist of a hypothetical statement, say, about an ethical principle or an epistemic condition, a detailed fictional or experimental discussion of the hypothesis and a conclusion that confirms or disproves the hypothesis. Storytelling is an effective pedagogical tool for learning, interpreting, preserving and transmitting knowledge, concepts, ideas and puzzles, as it weaves together other oral forms of knowledge, such as proverbs and riddles. As Emmanuel Obiechina (1993: 124) puts it, 'the story itself is a primary form of the oral tradition, primary as a mode of conveying culture experience and values, and a means of transmitting knowledge, wisdom, feelings, and attitudes in oral societies'. The Congolese theologian and philosopher, Bénézet Bujo, in his classic, *Foundations of an African Ethic* (2001), also relies heavily on orality, particularly stories in developing an African moral theory. He uses stories to show how ethics in African traditions prioritizes communal relationships, interconnectedness and interdependence. Stories tell us how within an African context moral decisions are dialogical and situational, encouraging reconciliation, healing and harmony, the care for others, and community and awareness of social realities.

Oral repositories in the diverse forms of spoken languages are thus important sources of philosophical knowledge in African traditions that anyone serious about gaining knowledge of indigenous African philosophy must pay close attention to and provide linguistic care for. These community-centred epistemic mechanisms for preserving and transmitting knowledge forms have been employed by Africans for centuries as effective pedagogical tools for teaching and learning philosophical concepts, ideas, methods and arguments. But how effective are oral traditions of philosophy, particularly when compared to textual traditions? This brings us to the question of the epistemic reliability of orality, as it is often invoked to dismiss oral traditions in favour of textual ones.

Orality, Transgenerationality and Epistemic Reliability

The legitimacy and relevance of orality as a form of knowledge production and preservation is often challenged on the basis that orality lacks epistemic reliability and is not effectively transgenerational the way textuality is. Texts, in this understanding, are considered as more epistemically reliable sources of knowledge because of the specific processes of coming into and remaining in being. The processes that guarantee the epistemic reliability of texts include the following. First, a text captures thought, orality and language in space and time and freezes these in a fixed state that can be passed on to others in the same and future generations. This seemingly fixed and stable repository of knowledge is epistemically reliable because its epistemic contents are stable and have not been altered, at least not significantly, and the author's intended meaning reaches the audience. We can immediately sense the superficiality of these lines of reasoning when we think of the perennial problem of the translation and transmission of texts from one language and generation to another, and the accompanying loss of meaning, the protracted debate, for example, in the Western hermeneutical tradition, on the (im)possibility of decoding and deciphering an author's intention, and the evolution of words and meanings that challenges the very idea of capturing and preserving in nearly a fixed state meanings in texts. But the main objective of these lines of reasoning about texts, it seems to me, is primarily not to argue for the ideality of texts but to show that texts are much more stable epistemic repositories than oral forms of knowledge. Second, a text is an epistemically responsible way of producing and preserving knowledge because authors of texts take responsibility and can be held responsible for the knowledge produced in their texts, and this may be difficult to achieve in oral forms of knowledge, particularly those attributed to group agency. Again, we can immediately question such claims to epistemic responsibility that present authors as responsible knowers by problematizing the very idea of authorship – as we did in the previous chapter – and the extent to which authors readily acknowledge and give credit to co-producers of knowledge, individual or collective, and by acknowledging that the history of textuality is punctuated with authorial uncertainties and controversies. But the point being made in this second line of reasoning, I believe, is essentially that textuality does better than orality in terms of epistemic responsibility. Third, in addition to being epistemically stable and responsible sources of knowledge, the materiality and tangibility of texts it is argued makes it much more easily preservable and transmittable than oral forms of knowledge. Oral forms of knowledge as 'sound exists only when it is going out of existence. It is not simply perishable but essentially evanescent, and it is sensed as evanescent. When I pronounce the word "permanence", by the time I get to the "-[n]ence" the "perma-" is gone, and has to be gone' (Ong 2012: 32). The stability, responsiveness and materiality of texts at surface level could be and have been deployed to present convincing arguments for the epistemic reliability of texts over oral knowledge in pursuit of philosophical knowledge in African philosophy. When philosophers such as Sophie Oluwole argued for the relevance of oral traditions in accessing African philosophical thought (Oluwole 1999), the criticisms against this argument mostly revolved around these lines of reasoning, rejecting the epistemic reliability of orality (Fayemi 2014). Also, a bulk of the criticism of the ethnophilosophical approach to doing philosophy in African contexts was hinged on its dependence on language in its oral rather than written forms in African traditions. In what follows, I argue that orality is epistemically reliable and that whatever challenges orality encounters in terms of its epistemic reliability are not unique or peculiar to it, but are present as well in other repositories of philosophical knowledge, including texts. In doing so, I draw on Ikuenobe's ideas of the epistemic dependence, epistemic trust and epistemic communalism of orality (Ikuenobe 2018) and Ong's ideas of orality as epistemic power and mnemonics (Ong 2018). I also highlight the ontological embodiment of orality and the power of creativity and dynamism in its fluid nature.

The epistemic engineering and mechanism of orality in African traditions, the methods of production and preservation, and the way its different forms, genres and contents are organized and shaped, do not happen by chance. There is a deliberacy and efficiency in the epistemic mechanism of orality that makes it epistemically reliable, trustworthy and dependable. Two parts of this epistemic engineering, it seems to me, that guarantee a smooth epistemic process, are the ubiquitous and inclusive pedagogical system of orality and the reliance on group agency or collective epistemic responsibility. It is commonplace to find in contemporary African philosophical (textual) literature the position that elders in African communities are the primary bearer of wisdom and custodians and transmitters of the oral traditions of the people. As Ikuenobe (2018: 29) says:

> An elder's duty requires him or her (as a 'grown-up') to display a wealth of knowledge, years of practical life experience, and good judgment by exhibiting responsible action and robust moral sensitivity. Usually, such responsible communal elders act as mentors and role models; their actions are seen as codes, narratives, abstract knowledge, and principles, and the exemplifications of the 'ideals' or exemplars of culture, values, traditions, and the acceptable modes of behaviour. By their consistent good actions, elders educate the young about the tradition and model their behaviours. Children go to elders to learn about traditions, beliefs, values, and justificatory foundations. Children learn to imitate the behaviours of elders whom they see as role models that exemplify the traditions and accepted practices of the past.

This is certainly true. I grew up in an African community and as a young person, the moral and epistemic impact of the elderly on the young is significant. But the elders are never alone in discharging this duty to teach, preserve and transmit oral knowledge forms. The pedagogical system of the epistemic mechanism of orality in African communities is designed in such a way that it is ubiquitous, such that everywhere you turn and in everything you see, hear and do, you are entangled in a learning web, in so far as you are paying close attention and taking linguistic care. Names, greetings, ceremonies, rites and rituals, stories, songs, riddles, adages, maxims and proverbs saturate communal life and collaboratively create a learning environment that prioritizes oral forms of teaching and learning. Elders are perhaps key in this learning environment because they are more knowledgeable of these oral forms of knowledge and are keenly interested in teaching them to others, but the pedagogical system and the learning environment goes beyond the elders.

This of course brings me to my second point, group agency. Oral forms of knowledge in African traditions are collectively owned and collectively cared for. The group takes full credit and responsibility for disseminating, editing, revising and organizing them, as well as for curating and birthing new ones as lived experiences unfold. The group as an epistemic agent provides a solid foundation for the reliability and transgenerationality of oral knowledges. African philosophers such as Barry Hallen (2006) have questioned the reliability of oral philosophical knowledge on this very basis. The argument is that since oral philosophy is not individually authored through a subjective rational process but rather achieved collectively, then it is not good enough, which undermines the reality that a group of persons can indeed reason together. Recent philosophical studies, even in the Western tradition of social ontology, social epistemology, communal cognition and collective intentionality show clearly that the argument against group epistemic agency is flawed (Ikuenobe 2018; Imafidon 2023). In reality, the fact that the group can reason together, create and recreate together, validate together, question together, and curate multiple repositories that interdependently and continually accumulate and absorb oral knowledges as they evolve, constitute why orality is reliable, dependable and transgenerational. Ikuenobe (2018: 36–9) captures this point of the efficiency of group agency aptly with the ideas of epistemic communalism and epistemic dependence:

> The idea of rationality in epistemic communalism and epistemic dependence involves the sharing of cognitive and epistemic responsibilities. The idea of knowledge in African traditions (as epistemic communities) requires reliance on and sharing with others who have different knowledge backgrounds and perspectives. This suggests a view of knowledge as holistic and requiring multiple perspectives and disciplines or expertise . . . The epistemic principle of communalism is [also] underscored by the contextual and pragmatic nature of justification . . . For instance, if as a herbalist, one has practical knowledge such as the effective treatment for an illness, and one refuses to share it, then one might be shirking one's communal moral and epistemic responsibilities or doing something morally and epistemically reprehensible. This illustrates the heuristic value of the principles of epistemic communalism, a cognitive division of labour, and epistemic dependence

Invariably, therefore, epistemic trust is an integral part of the epistemic mechanism of orality, since group epistemic agency does not only imply collectively doing the business of knowledge and inter-depending on one another for several epistemic activities but also trusting and relying on others as credible and reliable sources, producers, preservers and transmitters of knowledge.

The group agency embedded in orality also implies that the epistemic mechanism of orality is empowering, embodying and eco-friendly by its very nature of being for individual members of the community of selves. Sounding, voicing, venting, chuckling, vocalizing and other forms of oralization are by their very nature not only human and embodied but also non-human, empowering, healing and therapeutic. Knowing that my voice counts in producing, preserving, challenging and revising philosophical knowledge in my community empowers me to participate in the epistemic process, and develop cognitive abilities, such as listening and remembering. Ong (2012: 32) captures the power of orality thus:

> Words . . . have great power. Sound cannot be sounding without the use of power. A hunter can see a buffalo, smell, taste, and touch a buffalo when the buffalo is completely inert, even dead, but if he hears a buffalo, he had better watch out: something is going on. In this sense, all sound, and especially oral utterance, which comes from inside living organisms, is 'dynamic'.

With particular reference to mnemonics or the development of the ability to remember, Ong (2012: 34–5) adds that:

> In a primary oral culture, to solve effectively the problem of retaining and retrieving carefully articulated thought, you have to do your thinking in mnemonic patterns, shaped for ready oral recurrence. Your thought must come into being in heavily rhythmic, balanced patterns, in repetitions or antitheses, in alliterations and assonances, in epithetic and other formulary expressions, in standard thematic settings, . . . in proverbs which are constantly heard by everyone so that they come to mind readily and which themselves are patterned for retention and ready recall, or in other mnemonic form . . . The more sophisticated

orally patterned thought is, the more it is likely to be marked by set expressions skilfully used. This is true of oral cultures generally from those of Homeric Greece to those of the present day across the globe ... such as Chinua Achebe's novel *No Longer at Ease* (1961), which draws directly on Ibo oral tradition in West Africa.

More so, oral forms of knowledge resist the disembodiment that textuality produces, where the debate on the extent to which the author and his or her intention should be removed and detached from the text is prominent. Oral forms of knowledge are always embodied and lived and cannot be removed from those who intersubjectively engage with them.

Orality is thus a legitimate, rich and reliable source of philosophical thought in sub-Saharan African traditions. It is the key route to African philosophical thought before the contemporary textual phase. It is philosophy as lived, practised and embodied in indigenous communities, and anyone genuinely interested in unravelling African indigenous wisdom and thought must take oral forms of knowledge seriously. What I intend to do in the remaining sections of this chapter is to exemplify the richness of African philosophy by examining and analysing the concepts of truth, existence and relationality as they are presented in the oral traditions of selected African places.

Language, Orality and Truth

Truth is a perennially debated theme in philosophical circles. The textual history of the Western canon of philosophy furnishes us in mainstream academic philosophy with philosophical thoughts about truth as proposed by different philosophers in the tradition, thoughts that are fundamentally epistemic, propositional and analytical. In Western philosophy, truth is often theorized in relation to conditions of knowledge, such as justification and belief, analysing how we come to know what is true. It is also examined in relation to the truth-value of statements or propositions – assertions about reality that can be evaluated as true or false. In engaging in these analyses, several theories have emerged in the history of Western philosophy. The correspondence theory of truth, for example, holds that truth is when a proposition accurately reflects reality, the coherence theory argues that truth is determined by the logical consistency of a system of beliefs, the pragmatic theory claims that truth is what works or proves useful in practice, the deflationary theory suggests that truth is a linguistic convenience rather than a substantive property, and the constructivist theory argues that truth is socially constructed and shaped by power and discourse. Each theory offers a different perspective on what it means for something to be 'true', reflecting the diversity within a philosophical tradition that we can learn from. The tendency in the literature of contemporary African philosophy has often been to identify oral words and concepts in African languages that can be transcribed straightforwardly as truth to mirror the Western tradition, and to also identify which of the Western theories of truth best syncs with an indigenous African concept of truth. It is a typical example of doing philosophy in the image of the West and blinds us to the original thought preserved in such concepts that are transcribed simply as truth in contemporary African philosophy. What I intend to do, therefore, in this section is to take linguistic care of such concepts to allow the originally preserved meanings in them about truth to emerge.

I grew up in an African community in the Bini Kingdom in Southern Nigeria to learn that the words often transcribed and translated as truth are *uhu-ebhon* (typically in Edo and the Igueben languages of the Bini Kingdom) and *emuata* (typically in the Esan language of the Bini Kingdom). Thus, the statements '*Utu uhu-ebhon*' and '*Ete - muata*' would be readily translated as 'You do not speak the truth' and 'He/she does not speak the truth' respectively. However, on closely examining these words and taking linguistic care to translate them, I encountered much deeper and richer meanings consisting of fundamental ideas of what is implied by truth, which would be lost in the straightforward swapping of these words for truth. *Uhu-ebhon* is a compound word, which when broken down to its atomic components, *Uhu* and *Ebhon*, would translate as crux, substance or effervescence and debate or discourse respectively. *Uhu-ebhon* will therefore best translate as the crux, substance or effervescence of a discourse or debate. Similarly, *emuata* would best translate as the substance or essence (*emu*) of a talk, conversation or dialogue (*ata*). Therefore, as preserved in the spoken languages of my people, what is true is what stands out and bubbles forth with clarity and aptness in a discourse, dialogue, debate or argument. The truth is apt and without vagueness and ambiguities, and suspicions of vagueness, undecidedness and ambivalence would imply that what is written or spoken could be false or at the very least, not yet proven to be true. It makes sense then that within the same linguistic schemes, one of the words that would be standardly translated as falsehood is o-oghe. The closest meaning that emerges from a surgical and therapeutic translation of o-oghe is shock, confusion, wonderment and looking dazed. If truth is aptness and clarity, it makes sense that falsehood constitutes confusion and bewilderment. A fact then will be a true unambiguous state of affairs such as 'There is a cup on the table', or 'The sunflower is yellow'. But aptness and clarity as a condition for truth goes beyond expressing factuality to include accessing the truthfulness of other claims, such as one's opinion, an accusation levied against someone, one's defence of a value or custom and the conclusion drawn from arguments between interlocutors. Truth as the apt effervescence of a discourse also implies that the one who lays claim to a truth bears the moral and epistemic burden of proving one's claim. It also implies that a truth claim could be fallible and rejected if new evidence makes it unclear. This conceptualization of truth is aptly captured in an Asante proverb: *Wode nkontompo ka asem a, wobere*. This translates as: When you speak falsehood in stating a case, you become weary. It pictures how exhausting and tiring it is when one tries to explain an ambiguous and false claim, unlike the truth, which avoids such excessive exertion of the self to demonstrate its clarity (Tieku 2022).

I am married to an Igbo woman from the Eastern part of Nigeria and I have quite a number of friends from this tradition; we had a long and careful conversation about the word usually translated as truth among the Igbos, *eziokwu* – taking great linguistic care. It turns out that *eziokwu* does not literally and immediately translate to truth but that it is best translated as good (ezi) talk or discourse (okwu). This immediately presents truth as what goes beyond a subjective state, as it must be shared or 'talked about', and the interlocutor has both moral and epistemic responsibilities. It also raises the question of what would be considered 'good' within a particular context of discourse, which within many African communitarian contexts would include what is reliable and accurate, and what upbuilds, allows individuals to flourish, and promotes connections and togetherness among members of a community. The person who presents a truth claim ought, therefore, to be presenting something accurate, upbuilding and allowing individuals to flourish both at the subjective and intersubjective levels of being. Truth as good talk also implies that truth is not necessarily an ingredient for knowledge and telling the truth is not always tied up with knowing the truth. I could hold and defend as knowledge a claim that is not necessarily true in the sense of good talk and I could know the truth and still not tell it because it is not good talk. This puts the onus on the interlocutor making a truth claim to not only demonstrate that it is epistemologically desirable but also ethically appealing. A maxim of the Ga people of Ghana succinctly captures the moral dimension of truth with the saying: *Amkwale ni jwaa man le awieee*. This means the truth that will destroy or break up a town should be kept silent and not spoken (Kotei 2023).

The conceptualizations of truth in African languages and oral and symbolic repositories no doubt adds interesting and enriching dimensions to the analysis of truth in philosophy. One major impediment to harnessing these ideas from African languages is the quest for Eurocentric validation and legitimacy. This style of philosophizing often begins by identifying a concept in the West, such as in this case, truth, and proceeding to present an indigenous concept that looks like it or mirrors it. This approach hinders any linguistic care for the indigenous concept and the difficulty to appreciate its unique contribution to knowledge. For example, while Onwuatuegwu (2022) begins his paper on the Igbo concept of truth by offering a quite linguistically caring translation of it, I sense almost immediately a shift away from exploring the richness of that translation to trying to show how it fits with the correspondence theory of truth as presented in the Western canon. In his words (2022: 2):

> The Igbo equivalent of the English word for truth is *eziokwu*. Thus, *eziokwu* is actually a combination of two words: *Ezi* which translates to mean---'correct, genuine, right or good;' and Okwu which translates to either---'word or speech.' Following this understanding, one can rightly say that the word *eziokwu* can literally signify---'good talk, correct sentence, right word, or even the appropriate statement.' In other words, eziokwu means the correct response to a question or, that which is used to represent utterances that are true ... truth [is] an empirical fact, something that can be investigated and verified empirically rather than something that is intuitional. Since what is the case is asserted of a proposition which agrees with what happened in reality, it is safe to posit that it represents for the Igbo, the Western equivalent of truth as correspondence.

Thus to do philosophy specifically from language and more broadly from orality and symbolism in African places, one must sincerely and earnestly be interested in what authentically emerges from an African place and avoid a Eurocentric gaze that preconceives how that which should emerge ought to resemble similar concepts in the West.

Names and the Philosophy of Human Existence

Philosophizing about human existence, such as raising fundamental questions about the ontology of existing, the ethics of co-dwelling, the question of identity and freedom, and the facticity and onticness of life, as well as formulating theories regarding these can be discerned from various philosophical traditions. What the Western tradition of existentialism brought to the fore, in part, is how these fundamental questions and discourses of human existence become much more urgent in the face of human suffering and crises. The experiences of the late-nineteenth and early-twentieth centuries, including the World Wars, were more than sufficient for the Western philosophical tradition to produce some deep and critical thoughts on human existence captured in textual and non-textual repositories – although the focus is often on the textual. At the very heart of the philosophical discourse of human existence are debates around the human struggle for meaning, freedom and responsibility, as well as an understanding of what these mean in the first place in different contexts. Such discourse naturally leads to exploring lived experiences and qualities that may threaten or guarantee meaning, freedom and responsibility, such as death, suffering, violence, relationships, virtues, will, destiny and place.

An interesting epistemic site for accessing ideas about human existence in sub-Saharan African traditions is personal names. To be sure, African communities are permeated with non-textual existential philosophies, but I am particularly fascinated about names for several reasons. Personal names are effective vehicles of thought that capture, preserve and transmit in succinct and simple ways complex ideas about existence and other matters of philosophical interest in African places. Names are often used to preserve philosophical concepts and dictums in ways that are easy to remember and demanding of interpretation. Some names are used to capture and preserve general ideas, puzzles, perspectives and principles of life and existence; others are used to effectively convey specific qualities, attitudes and dispositions needed for human existence and survival. The brevity and primary purpose of a name as labelling a person implies that there is the danger that many could take this important epistemic repository for granted and fail to see beyond its function as merely a tag or label. The African postcolonial condition does not make this challenge easier as the colonial mentality of trivializing native names and valuing Western names is still felt today in African places and many would focus on the more manifest function of their names as labels and would not take the linguistic care to unravel the rich philosophical contents of such names. Let us explore the philosophical contents of a few names in selected sub-Saharan African traditions.

In my community, the word that is translated as 'world', 'life' or 'people' is '*Agbon*' and the word often translated as 'living', 'existing' or 'dwelling' is *unyibhin*. There are several names that would either begin with or end with 'agbon', with the rest of the name providing some principle, perspective or thought about it. My native name, for example, is Unuagbon. This would literally translate as 'mouth' (Unu) of the world or of people (Agbon). 'The mouth of the world' is meant to convey the existential truth that the world, in the sense of people or humanity, is always opinionated no matter what a person does and how they choose to live their lives. Existing only to play to the gallery or acting in ways that would attract praise from the mouth of the world threatens meaningful existence. The native name of my immediate elder sister is Aiguinyibhin, which literally translates as 'there is no mastery of living' or 'no one masters existence'. It conveys the idea that existence is an unfolding process and no one can lay claim to a perfect understanding of how to exist. Another common name in my community that I find interesting in terms of the existential truth it conveys is Agbonkhale, which translates as 'the world/people will reckon with you'. It makes the point that existence is not a bed of roses and that freedom is not without accountability; being with others implies being prepared to struggle and to be held responsible and accountable for one's action. We are not isolated from others and our lives and the decisions we make will be influenced at least to some extent by the world we live in.

We find similar names among the Igbo people of Eastern Nigeria, names that furnish us with crucial ideas about human existence. Life or existence is often captured among the Igbos with the word '*ndu*'. There are many names in the Igbo tradition that begin and end with ndu, such as Ndubuisi, Nduka and Ndukwe, presenting a manifold of resource on existential philosophy. Ndubuisi, for example, translates literally as 'Life is first' or 'Life comes first', similar to the existentialist dictum in the Western canon, 'existence precedes essence'. The name captures the primacy of life in the scheme of things, we must exist first to be able to engage in any human activity and to have a definitive purpose. The primacy of life is even more re-emphasized in the name 'Nduka', which translates as 'life is supreme'. As well as in the name 'Ndukwe', which translates as 'If life agrees', Ndukwe conveys the idea that the goals and plans we make as we exist can only be realized if we have life; life and existence take precedence over purpose, essence and objectives of life. And while there is an abundance of evidence in oral, textual and symbolic repositories of sub-Saharan African peoples that the overarching ontological, epistemological, ethical and existential principle is communality or relationality – a point to be expanded on shortly – names show that this principle does not suffocate or water down the value for individuality. For example, anyone with familiarity with Yoruba names would find many names with 'Temi' and 'Yemi' as prefixes or suffixes. 'Temi' translates as 'belonging to me' or 'what is mine', while 'Yemi' translates as 'what suits or befits me'. Many such names, as Olayemi (wealth and success befit me), Adeyemi (royalty befits me), Yemisi (honour and respect me), Ogunyemi (the deity, Ogun, suits me – an expression of an individual's preference for a form of spirituality), Temidayo (my story or life course is or will become one of joy), Teminikan (it is mine and mine alone) and Temidire (my struggles have transformed into victory) are meant to convey ones existential experience and lived realities.

In exploring existential philosophy in African places, I have deliberately narrowed my focus to a very specific form of oral repository, names. To be sure, such existential philosophy can be found in other oral, textual and symbolic repositories but the particular focus on names re-emphasizes how such philosophies saturate everyday life to the extent that they are accessible and epistemically open to anyone paying close attention and giving linguistic care to African languages.

Oralizing Relationality

To oralize is conventionally used to mean to speak out what has been written or to turn the textual into the spoken. Of course, this understanding fits well with a densely textual narrative of the human experience, which we have critically attended to earlier on in this book, one that presents a graphocentric narrative of the human historical and lived experiences as if writing is the primordial way of being human that gets to be transformed into secondary forms, such as speech and symbols. Revising and shifting away from this understanding in line with the fundamental claim in this work of the equal value of non-textual narratives, to oralize, it seems more plausible to me, is simply to speak, to speak out what has been thought of and conceptualized individually or collectively. What is oralized need not exist first in written or textual form for oralization to happen. Understood in this sense, oralizing relationality or African communal philosophy consists of ways in which African peoples produce and store up ideas, concepts and arguments for the validity and legitimacy of relationality in different spoken forms of knowledge, such as maxims, dictums, adages, proverbs, music, names, parables and puzzles, and stories and folklores.

Communal or relational philosophy is perhaps the most discussed and debated non-textual philosophy of sub-Saharan African peoples in contemporary African philosophical texts, mainly because of the way the philosophy is lived and felt in African communities. The idea of relationality or communalism in African philosophy is, to put it succinctly, the claim, at the existential ontological level, that beings are not self-contained and self-sufficient but are connected to and interwoven with other beings, both human and non-human, for existence and survival (Imafidon 2014); at the epistemological level, that knowledge is collectively rather than solitarily produced, validated and justified (Imafidon 2023); and at the ethical level, that the permissibility and impermissibility of human action is dependent on the extent to which an action promotes and sustains the community of beings (Metz 2007). Contemporary African philosophers producing a textual history of African philosophy have drawn heavily on oral repositories of knowledge in African communities to conceptualize, debate and critique the philosophy of relationality to the extent that the discourse of this overarching philosophical framework of sub-Saharan African peoples is ubiquitous in contemporary literature on African philosophy.

Perhaps the most popular oralization of relational philosophy that has become an integral part of the contemporary African philosophical literature is the Zulu maxim: '*umuntu ngumuntu ngabantu*', which means 'a person is a person through other persons', often simply captured in the shortened form, Ubuntu or Ubuntu philosophy. This maxim affirms the co-dependency of beings and how attaining personhood and meaningful existence happens in the context of relationships. It has also resulted in one of the most protracted and perennial debates in contemporary African philosophy on the extent to which the individual in the community of beings enjoys or is deprived of autonomy and freedom, resulting in the radical versus moderate communitarianism debate (e.g., Ikuenobe 2006; Menkiti 1984; Oyeshile 2006). Not surprisingly, in defending either of these perspectives, African philosophers have continued to enlist oral and symbolic knowledge forms in African traditions to argue for the necessity of the ontological priority of the community and of relationality over individuality and unchecked autonomy, but also to argue for the importance of individuality, freedom and autonomy within the communitarian framework. The Shona word 'Ukama' has also become popular in theorizing the interrelatedness of beings, particularly in terms of human and non-human relationships (Murove 2006). As Ndofirepi and Shanyanana-Amaambo (2015) explain, ukama translates roughly as relative or relation. It conveys the idea of milking an animal, and the notion of milking in the Shona culture implies closeness and affection. Milking also suggests a connection between the source, the means of livelihood and the beneficiaries. In essence, ukama is a brotherhood in which members of the group share with one another and find peace through love of all in the extended family, or clan, and reminds people of the value of sharing not only in times of scarcity, but also at all other times, because of the relational values that exist in community. I grew up in a community where dialogues and conversations were often punctuated with interlocutors beginning or ending contributions with the word '*Akomen*' or '*Akugbe*'. *Akomen* translates as 'we are better if we do it together' or 'we get better together', while *akugbe* translates as 'togetherness is our reality' or 'we are joined together'. These and similar concepts affirm the relational factuality of existence and are constantly oralized in the community for pedagogical and mnemonic reasons.

The ubiquitous oralization of relationality in African communities is thus meant to teach and remind community members as well as sustain in the very fabric and engineering of society two salient ontological facts: first, my being is intrinsically connected to the being of others, human and non-human. I do not come into existence and remain in existence solely because of certain self-contained qualities or capacities, such as anatomical properties or rationality. I also exist because others contribute to my existence just as I contribute to theirs. We see, for example, a robust genetic ontology of being human in many African traditions in which a human being is seen as coming-to-be from the rebirth of a previously physically existing being, such as an ancestor who vitalizes this new being with both physical and character resemblance. This is why the Yorubas name their children Babatunde (my father has returned) and Yetunde (my mother has returned), an affirmation that a father or mother who was physically dead has returned in physique and character in a newborn child. Also, the way Africans relate with other members of the ecosystem, such as trees, water bodies and farm produce shows an awareness of relationality and co-dependency. It is not uncommon to see people, such as care and health givers or medicine men and women in African societies, speaking with or addressing a plant, tree or water body as they would a human being during the use of these resources or a healing process. For example, a clear affirmation of the being and life force of plants is seen in the treatment of kola nuts in many parts of West Africa. Ceremonies such as marriages, child naming ceremonies, funerals, ceremonies marking the beginning of new seasons and other festivities would not begin without the breaking of the kola nut. The breaking of the kola nut is accompanied by prayers and blessings. While the kola nut is being broken, one of the key declarations would be 'the person who brings kola brings life', and then the kola nuts are broken by the eldest in the gathering and shared with all. The proverbial declaration that the one that brings kola brings life affirms the life-giving force of the kola nut in terms of its health benefits and also signifies the simplicity but profound impact of hospitality and communion in the sustenance of wellbeing (Imafidon 2025). Second, I have duties and responsibilities toward other beings in the community, human and non-human. To be sure, this is implied from the first. If my being, my personhood and the meaningfulness of my existence is intrinsically tied up with the existence of others, then it is counterproductive to care only for my rights and wellbeing and not for the rights, wellbeing and survival of others. Relational ethics is therefore useful in rethinking our social responsibilities, our relationship with the environment, the limits of freedom, autonomy and individuality, and rights, duties and responsibilities to humans and non-humans now and in future generations.

We have examined in this chapter the relevance of orality and oralization for the doing of philosophy in African traditions. Our discourse of language and other forms of orality, such as maxims, names, proverbs and adages as philosophical repositories in sub-Saharan African traditions, opens up the historicity and epistemic canon of African philosophy beyond the narrow focus on a recent, more textual history and canon to a rich, diverse and sophisticated episteme with a long and enduring tradition. The usual charges against orality and oral forms of knowledge, such as orality not being epistemically dependable and reliable, often emerge from a place of textual bias that fail to acknowledge the epistemic dependability and reliability because of qualities inherent to it, such as mnemonic, collective and transgenerational features. Oral repositories like textual repositories are not without flaws, of course, but these flaws are not sufficient for completely jettisoning them in the pursuit of knowledge. We have examined how oral repositories in African traditions furnish us with philosophical ideas about existence, relationality and truth, and can be explored for other philosophical ideas. The focus on oral repositories of philosophy is not just relevant for the doing of African philosophy but for philosophizing in a global context. There is a lot that philosophers all over the world can learn from and critically engage with in music, storytelling, film, oral histories, proverbs, maxims, adages and other oral forms of knowledge in different philosophical traditions. To be sure, such engagements with and acknowledgements of oral philosophy already exist but often in the peripheral spaces of philosophy. The goal of the exercise, such as has been attempted in this chapter, is to centre oral philosophy in philosophical activities in all its spheres, including pedagogical, scholarly and educational ones. To be sure, textual and oral forms of philosophical knowledge are not the only ways humans produce, preserve and transmit knowledge. A fundamental repository in African contexts is symbols, to which we now turn.

3

Symbolism and African Philosophy

Exploring the non-textual in African philosophy will be incomplete if we do not turn our attention to symbolic and artistic epistemic repositories. Shifting our non-textual gaze to symbolism in African traditions in this chapter is crucial because, just like orality, it often suffers from a constructed narrative in Western thought that displaces it from the realm of philosophical knowledge and thought. As we gleaned from previous chapters, oral forms of knowledge in African traditions are within this Eurocentric narrative strictly relegated to folk wisdom, religion and culture, and thus, not fitting enough to be termed as philosophy in the allegedly technical and systematic sense. Similarly, symbolic and artistic forms in African traditions are often reduced to objects of aesthetic fascination, fitting for captivating and absorbing stares in museums, art galleries and homes of the wealthy, and much less as repositories of philosophical and spiritual thought (Soyinka 2020). Symbolic and artistic expressions and forms of knowledge saturate sub-Saharan Africa. From the rich Adinkra symbols, the symbolic representations of the Odu Ifa, the Nsibidi writing system and Zulu symbols, to masks, sculptures, word carvings, textile and body arts and motifs, symbolic and artistic representations welcome you in an African place. Of course, the dilemma of whether we ought to treat many of these symbolic expressions as symbols in themselves or as forms of textual writings simply not fitting into the conventional canon of textuality, a point we discussed in Chapter one in our contestation of textuality, remains. No doubt, the materiality of textuality is often different in African traditions. Rather than paper, fabric and textiles, stools, bodies, buildings and other forms of materiality were deployed to imprint these symbols. For example, to date, Adinkra and Nsibidi symbols are commonly found on textile materials and, by implication, clothes that people wear in communities. But the question remains: Did the Akan people of Ghana and the Igbo people of Nigeria, as instantiations, originally think of the Adinkra symbols and the Nsibidi symbols respectively as symbols or as forms of scripting? I will suspend this question for now – perhaps, one to take up more robustly elsewhere – because the answer we provide to it, it seems to me, will not alter the epistemic significance of African symbols or non-canonical forms of writing, however we view it, that we pursue in this chapter in relation to philosophy.

In what follows, I begin by problematizing the aesthetic interpretation of African symbolic and artistic forms, a problematizing that I hope shifts our gaze from an aesthetically loaded hermeneutics of African arts and symbols to an epistemically balanced hermeneutics. Flowing from this, I then proceed to analyse symbolism in African traditions as a deliberate and conscious process of curating philosophical knowledge. The rest of the chapter examines specific ways in which such symbolic curation of philosophical knowledge happens, by examining specific ontological and ethical themes embedded in African arts and symbols, such as transcendence, immanence, destiny and relationality. These analyses open up more broadly the repositories of philosophy.

Problematizing the Aesthetic Hermeneutical Encounter

One of the effects of the West–Africa encounter, specifically the colonial encounter, which indicates the obvious power control of the former over the latter, was the encounter with African artefacts, including symbolic and artistic objects in different African cultures. This encounter with African arts and symbols resulted in fascination with their aesthetic value, acknowledging and accessing their worth and significance based on beauty, form and appeal, and by implication, the impulse to own, driven by a combination of curiosity, admiration and a desire to assert dominance. European colonizers were captivated by the intricate craftsmanship, vibrant colours, and manifest meanings embedded in African art and cultural artefacts. This fascination often led to the systematic and forceful looting of these items, as colonizers sought to bring them back to Europe to display in museums, galleries and other institutions. The aesthetic value of African art is highly prized, and these artefacts are often showcased as exotic treasures, quite similar to the Orientalist experience in Asia and the Middle East (Said 1979), meant to showcase the colonizers' perceived superiority and their control over foreign lands. The often forceful taking and owning of African arts and symbols results in the displacement of cultural heritage (Adjei and LeGall 2024; Wainwright 2024), stripping African communities of their historical and spiritual artefacts, which are important epistemic repositories, and leads to a skewed representation of African arts in the global narrative that focuses essentially on the aesthetic value while neglecting its deeper cultural, historical and philosophical meanings. Today, with an increasing call by African and African-Diasporic peoples for cultural restitution and the return of looted artefacts, Western institutions, such as the British Museum, notorious for proudly housing such items, still argue that they continue to hold on to them because it is safer with them as the self-proclaimed preserver of global cultural heritages. There is thus a continuous and persistent resistance by Western institutions to return stolen artefacts to Africa primarily because of the market worth and aesthetic value of such objects. For example, as a person of Bini heritage, I observe, often with jaw-dropping effect, some of the weird conversations and defence from European, specifically British institutions, on why the thousands of stolen bronzes from the Bini Kingdom in Nigeria, looted during the 1897 Benin massacre, cannot be returned to the owners. The anti-restitution logic that prioritizes an aesthetic hermeneutical encounter of African arts and symbols, such as their market value, beauty, appeal and pleasure for the Western audience, is problematic for several reasons.

First, the hermeneutic encounter of the West with African arts and symbols prioritizes and privileges the gaze of the beholder/interpreter (the aesthetically fascinated Westerner) over that of the creator of what is interpreted. In a sense, rather than a genuine encounter taking place – of course, this will be difficult considering the violence of the encounter, there is the silencing and suspension of the creator's perspective, and only the interpreter's perspective dominates. Hans-Georg Gadamer explains in his magnum opus, *Truth and Method* (2004) how a hermeneutic encounter, in this case, between an interpreter and an artwork or symbol situated in a tradition, ought to be a dialogical encounter where meaning emerges from a fusion of perspectives, or in Gadamer's term, a fusion of horizons in which understanding occurs when the horizon of the interpreter (their historical, cultural and personal context) merges with the horizon in which the artwork or symbol was created. The fusion of horizons is characterized by a historical consciousness and the acknowledgement and awareness of pre-judgements and fore-understandings. The historical consciousness and pre-judgements are important because the historical consciousness constitutes the acknowledgement of the historical context of both the artistic forms and the interpreter, while the pre-judgements constitute the awareness of preconceptions and prior understandings that could impact the interpretive process. To be sure, in the broader hermeneutical tradition, the emphasis is on aiming to genuinely understand the intentions and motives of an author or creator as one encounters a text or an artwork rather than imposing meanings on it. But can we legitimately describe the aesthetic hermeneutics of African arts and symbols by the West as one emerging from a genuine hermeneutical encounter, where a fusion of horizons or the deciphering of the creator's intentions has at the very least been attempted? What is often available is the dominance of the Western narrative of such arts and symbols, such as the exoticist and paganistic interpretations of African masks and sculptures. Perhaps, from the onset, this was not a genuine hermeneutic encounter in any form, aesthetic or otherwise, and should not be described as such, as it was characteristically a violent and oppressive encounter that was never geared toward understanding, nor was it an instance of misunderstanding but a deliberately constructed non-understanding of the other. Or the Western colonial encounter of African arts and symbols was a form of, in Yong Huang's (2006) conceptualization, a hermeneutics for self-fulfilment or self-creation as distinct from a hermeneutics for genuine human solidarity. In hermeneutics for self-fulfilment, the goal is to find and be interested only in what resembles, mirrors or edifies the self in the understanding of the other; there is barely a genuine interest in allowing the other to reveal itself. As Huang (2026: 189) puts it, 'When interpreting a text, a tradition, a culture – in short, an "other"– the interpreter's main concern . . ., the primary or ultimate purpose of our interpretation of the "other" is not to understand the "other," but to understand ourselves through our understanding of the "other". On the other hand, hermeneutics for human solidarity consists of entering into the exercise of interpretation not merely with the goal of self-understanding or self-edification but primarily with the goal of understanding the other, its unique ideas and ideals, habits and customs, culture, religions and philosophies. The colonial encounter with the artistic and symbolic contents of African traditions was heavily defined and shaped by pre-judgements, mostly aesthetic ones, for the edification and fulfilment of the Western mind.

Second and following from the first is the coloniality of power and knowledge (Quijano 2000) that essentializes and reduces African artistic and symbolic expressions to aesthetic objects and, by implication, trivializes the ontological, epistemological, ethical, existential and spiritual contents. The Eurocentric and capitalist narratives of African arts and symbols often miss the authentic indigenous interpretations of these non-textual forms of knowledge production. The violent owning, classification, structuring and presentation of African arts and symbols as capital and objects of pleasure rather than cultural ways of being and knowing has left an enduring disruption of the perception of African arts and symbols. More so, the Eurocentric power to decide and structure ways of knowledge production and repositories of knowledge, one that prioritizes textuality and individual authorship, invariably excludes, or at least pushes to the periphery, African arts and symbols as sources of (philosophical) knowledge. This would explain why, because of the coloniality of the process and consciousness of learning, African arts and symbols do not often enter into the colonial and capitalist epistemic structure until it is attended to in texts by individual artists and authors trained in the capitalist cognitive system to validate and legitimate them as valuable aesthetic objects. Since African non-textual forms of knowledge, including arts and symbols, gain epistemic relevance by going through a textualization and an individuated intellectualization process, then, perhaps, what I am doing right now, writing about the philosophical contents of African arts and symbols, serves this colonial legitimization process. This would be the case if, in writing about African artistic and symbolic forms, the motive was to fit them within the Western aesthetic narrative. Thus, writing or speaking about ways of being and knowing in African places is in itself neither colonial nor decolonial, as the coloniality or decoloniality is embedded in the motive and intention for doing so. In so far as my motive here as an African with vested interest in the liberation of African episteme is not to further essentialize African arts and symbols as fundamentally aesthetic but to attempt a liberative hermeneutics that opens up the narrative to authentic indigenous understanding of African arts and symbols, the exercise here is best situated within the pursuit of the decoloniality of knowledge and power.

Third, the reductionist aesthetic perspective on African arts and symbols misses the deliberate hermeneutical intentions of the curators and authors. African arts and symbols, while showcasing creativity and aesthetic intentions, are deliberately curated to be pregnant with meanings which, when accessed, contain rich insights into the philosophical thoughts of African peoples. That symbols are pregnant with meanings beyond the manifest aesthetic appeal has been defended by hermeneutic philosophers of both Western and African traditions, such as Paul Ricoeur (1974), Theophilus Okere (1983) and Louis Dominique Biakolo Komo (2017). Okere (1983), for example, asserts that African philosophy is fundamentally the exercise of interpreting symbols. As he (1983: 115) puts it, 'African cultures have their own symbols pregnant with meanings. A reflection on these symbols, with a view of making the implicit meanings explicit, will constitute African philosophy.' African philosophy defined in this sense, quite in line with the Socratic idea of philosophical midwifery, would be fundamentally the hermeneutics of African arts and symbols, an interpretive exercise geared toward unravelling and birthing philosophically relevant meanings latent in them. To be sure, other African hermeneutic philosophers have opened up this interpretive exercise beyond arts and symbols to include orality, such as proverbs and languages (Oleko 1979) and lived colonial and postcolonial experiences (Serequeberhan 1994). A major point made by African hermeneutic philosophers and indeed the global traditions of philosophical hermeneutics, is that philosophy is essentially interpretive and the focus of such interpretation varies from texts, art, symbols, language, to lived experiences. The reductionist aesthetic encounter with African arts and symbols fails to appreciate the deeper and richer contents of African arts and symbols as relevant for a philosophically inclined interpretive exercise, and thus would occlude them from the global canon of philosophy. In what follows, I hope to shift the gaze from an aesthetic to a philosophical hermeneutic one to showcase their relevance in the doing of African philosophy.

Creating, Performing and Curating Philosophy

I have witnessed quite recently an upsurge of interest in academia in the Global North in creative and co-creative outputs. Creative and co-creative outputs are increasingly being recognized as relevant as much as traditional, scholarly and textual outputs in actualizing scholarly and pedagogical goals and as important epistemic repositories. Although this is a welcome development, particularly considering how academic spaces can hold on tenaciously to traditional scholarly methods and outputs, I am often uneasy about how in some circles, certain individuals and groups quickly take credit for pioneering and masterminding the interest in creating and co-creating knowledge in academia. When we amplify creation and co-creation in academic spaces today as important means of knowledge production and preservation, we are not pioneering or inventing new ways of being human or doing enquiries, we are in fact learning from the traditions of the world, old ways of being and knowing and exploring their relevance for our academic life today. It takes epistemic humility and a check on the radical individualization of knowledge to acknowledge this salient fact that today's academia is not pioneering creative and co-creative learning and scholarship, but learning and re-learning how to do so from rich global heritages. Indigenous sub-Saharan African places produce and preserve knowledge, including philosophical knowledge, in creative ways. Creating knowledge could be done individually or collaboratively, and is deliberately curated in ways that are performative and visual. They include sculpting, carving, printing, textile making, bronze casting, artefact making, cultural symbol designing, ceremonial dancing, music making and a combination of these. Thus, the search for authentic indigenous African philosophy, such as philosophical thoughts about reality, truth, mind, beauty, knowledge, the good, and personal identity would require paying close attention and examining closely and critically the carefully (co-)created, curated and performed knowledge systems of African peoples. The symbolism of African philosophy, therefore, is the acknowledgement of the use of symbols and other artistic expressions in the doing of philosophy in African places, a creative performance of philosophy that complements textuality and orality. For example, the textile industry in sub-Saharan Africa has been used for many years to script into cloth and fabric the collectively held values and philosophies of African peoples. Ivor Agyeman-Duah (2024: 143) writes that, 'The designs ... had been based on history, socio-cultural matters and philosophy – of proverbs and gold weights and Adinkra symbols with their stamps.' It was also interesting to read on one of the wall panels in the National Museum of Ghana the following about Ghanaian textiles:

> Textiles, beyond aesthetic values, reflect the cultures from which they come and are valuable vehicles for the personal, political, societal, and religious cultures of a people. In Ghana, textiles are a significant marker

of our cultural identity and embody customary values and spiritual connotations ... Ashanti kente are brightly coloured geometrically patterned with the majority having the famous Adinkra symbols embroidered on them. The Ewe kete also has symbolic inlaid motifs, more subtle and less colourful than the Ashanti kente. Ewe kete is more unified in composition and applies the tweed effect technique.

Also the National Museum, Lagos, explains the following in one of its wall panels about ancient Benin (Bini of Southern Nigeria) arts:

> Benin art, originating from the ancient Benin Kingdom in present day Edo state Nigeria, is a captivating and intricate artisic tradition that has fascinated art lovers and historians for centuries. This royal art form is renowned for its stunning beauty, symbolic significance, and historical importance, offering a glimpse into the kingdom's rich cultural heritage. The Benin Kingdom, situated in the southern region of Nigeria, was a powerful and influential empire that flourished from the 13th to the 19th century, Its strategic location allowed for trade and cultural exchange with European nations, African kingdoms and other parts of the world. Benin art has played a vital role in the kingdom's history, serving as a symbol of royal power and authority, a means of storytelling and historical record-keeping, a reflection of the Kingdom's spiritual and cultural values, and a showcase of artistic expertise and craftsmanship. The art forms distinctive characteristics, including intricate designs and patterns, geometric shapes, naturalistic depictions of humans and animals, symbolism, and advanced craftsmanship ... demonstrating the kingdom's artistic genius. The use of geometric shapes, such spirals, circles, triangles, and squares, carry specific meanings, representing concepts like growth, unity, balance, and stability ..., strength, and beauty.

Philosophizing through arts and symbols has been pedagogically effective in African places for several reasons. It guarantees epistemic accessibility and transgenerationality; it bridges the gap between philosophy as theory and philosophy-in-practice; and it showcases the transdisciplinarity of knowledge and the value of epistemic collaboration or co-creation. Artistic and symbolic forms in African communities are embedded into every facet of life, such as clothing, jewellery, body arts, architectural designs, music, dance performance and everyday home utensils, such that symbols and the knowledge conveyed through them permeate the society, and are easily accessible, sustainable and transgenerational, leaving a strongly felt presence of knowledge. The Adinkra symbols, for example, are found in clothing, buildings, sculptures, furnishings and pieces of jewellery, making these philosophical symbols accessible to everyone (Kissi, Fening, and Asante 2019). To be sure, access is not equivalent to understanding; the accessibility of African arts and symbols and their reproduction in different spheres of everyday life may guarantee their felt presence and sustenance from generation to generation but may not always translate to understanding and deciphering of the deep philosophical meanings they embody. To adequately understand African arts and symbols, we must proceed with the assumption that they are pregnant with meanings and refuse to be satisfied with the manifest impressions that come across when we encounter them, aiming always to probe further into the deeper philosophical and spiritual meanings and implications. Artistic and symbolic forms of philosophy are also carefully created and curated in ways that sync with rather than detach abstract ideas from lived experiences. Symbolic philosophy presents and sustains in society philosophical ideas not merely as abstract thought removed from community, theories and ideals that community members need to formally learn in dedicated spaces, but as philosophical thought weaved into the fabric of society and serving as foundations for understanding practices and experiences in the community. For example, it is not rare to come across symbolic representations of ontological ideas of personhood, personal identity and destiny in African traditions, say in the many sculptures of body forms, in the very spaces where such ideas are practised, such as from healing spaces, royal palaces to festivals, ceremonies and individual homes. There is, therefore, no constructed gap between theorizing philosophy and practising philosophy. The non-textual nature of African philosophy, including its oral and symbolic forms, accounts for why African philosophy can be described as lived philosophy, since it is woven into every sphere of being in community in oral and symbolic ways rather than kept away in textual forms in spaces that require specialized skills to gain access.

Concerning transdisciplinarity and epistemic co-creation, symbolic and performative philosophy are by their very nature collaboratively produced, re-produced, performed and preserved in African communities, bringing together community members with similar and different interests and expertise, and persons spanning several generations actively pulling their agency together for knowledge production and re-production. One example that has often fascinated me in my heritage (the Bini–Esan traditions), particularly in the way it weaves together ideas about personal identity, patriarchy, power, agency and the interwovenness of past, present and future generations, is the symbolic representation of ancestorhood, the *Ukhure* staff. *Ukhure* is a symbolic representation of a family's paternal ancestor. This 3–4 feet long staff, often made of wood, designed with cowries, and consisting of a carved head or hand at the top and several markings on the body, is created or commissioned by the first son of the immediate past ancestor and used as the focal point for familial meetings, deliberations, prayers and sacrifices. The *Ukhure* remains in the care and trust of the first son of the family, giving him agency, power and responsibility over family matters. He uses it, for example, to perform rituals aimed at cleansing and blessing the household, a practice rooted in Bini and Esan ontology, consisting of the deeply rooted belief in the flow of energy from the ancestors to the physically living, and the need to maintain a connection with ancestors to ensure familial wellbeing and harmony. The ancestral shrine may contain several *Ukhure* at a given time, dating as far back as three generations. Thus, a carefully curated and preserved ancestral shrine would only be collaboratively achieved after several generations, since the different *Ukhure* on it would have been created by different persons over a given period of time, but yet seamlessly capturing the interwovenness of the past and present and the potentiality of the future through cosmic forces. The co-creation of philosophical knowledge is also clearly seen in the way symbols with rich philosophical meanings permeate different facets of life. They are, among other things, printed on clothes, drawn on bodies, crested on walls, told in stories, sung in songs and worn as pieces of jewellery. Community members become stakeholders with epistemic and ethical responsibility to actively use their expertise and interests to preserve the philosophical wisdom in their tradition.

Thus, there is a sense of deliberacy in the creating, curating and performing of African arts and symbols, an intentionality that fundamentally includes the making, performing and storing of philosophy. Creating and performing philosophy in the manner present in African traditions makes indigenous African philosophy accessible, transgenerational, lived and collaborative, allowing for many opportunities for co-creation of knowledge. In the rest of this chapter, I examine specific instances of philosophy symbolized, focusing on symbols as sources of ontological, existential, feminist and moral philosophies in African traditions.

Symbolizing Ontological Commitments

African traditions use arts and symbols to effectively present, represent and communicate the entities and ways of being that are implicitly and explicitly recognized in the community of beings, a community of interacting forces (Imafidon 2014). Symbols are crafted and designed, figurines are carved or sculpted, and other artefacts such as stools, staffs and textiles are made to symbolize the nature and reality of human and non-human entities, such as ancestors, deities and animals, as well as the ontological interconnectedness of such beings. Arts and symbols are also enlisted in showcasing specific ways of being and understanding reality, such as afterlife realities for humans, as, say, ancestors, extrasensory perception, destiny, freewill and determinism, and transcendence and immanence. For example, the ancestral *Ukhure* staff discussed earlier, what it represents and how it is used, symbolizes the idea that although physically dead, the person represented by the staff remains in the family and is actively collaborated with in family affairs. To be sure, *Ukhure* is only one of many ancestral arts across sub-Saharan Africa meant to showcase not only artistry but, more importantly, how ancestors as non-human persons are an integral part of the community shaping value, structure and power, and forming a solid foundation for aspects of causal explanations of events and realities. Similar to the *Ukhure* are the Dogon ancestral elongated and simplified wooden figures that are placed in family shrines as the embodiment of the spirits of deceased family members. Also, the stool takes a central place in many Ghanaian traditions, such as the Asantes and Ewes. It represents the soul of a person. The sacredness of the Asante stools, the symbolic markings on them, and their use and functions connect family members and communities with the energy of the owner who, although physically dead, lives on in the community as represented by the stool. As N. K. Dzobo (1992: 91) explains it,

> The stool as a symbol of the individual's soul has become a highly valued personal property. Thus, if the owner is not sitting on it, theoretically nobody else is allowed to sit on it and so it is generally laid on its side. The stool is conceived as a female principle and its seat part is shaped like a crescent and represents the warm embrace of a mother welcoming her beloved child home from a journey or from the day's labours. The crescent part of the stool is called atuu, which is a word used to embrace a person arriving from a journey.

The vigorously performative *Egungun* masks festivals among the Yorubas and the energetic acrobatic *Ikpabonelimin* (clap for the spirits) performance among the Esan people of Southern Nigeria, one I have witnessed in awe several times in my life time, are also performative and embodied philosophical processes meant to keep the knowledge of the existence, power and active agency of ancestors in the mind of community members, as relationship with the ancestors and other cosmic forces significantly impacts every aspect of the life of a person, including health and wellbeing. As Bénézet Bujo (1998: 182–3) puts it:

> The community of the diseased is also not forgotten since a disease might be caused by the disturbed relationship of the patient with the

world of those who have passed away ... Health, therefore, implies safe integration into the bi-dimensional community as the place where life grows ... If interpersonal relationships are not well maintained, sickness can affect the members.

A careful examination of specific Adinkra symbols reveals quite a number of ontological commitments, including the belief in a Supreme Being, the creative powers of such a being, the source and sustenance of the human energy and soul, and the inevitability of death (Mensah, Obeel and Babah 2020; Kissi, Fening and Asante 2019). I have deliberately not included the actual symbols here as they are easily accessible online. *Gye Nyame* is perhaps the most popular of the many Adinkra symbols and often translates as 'Except the Supreme Being' or 'if not for the Supreme Being'. I am obviously deliberately avoiding the use of 'God' in these translations as it is, in my understanding, a Christianized labelling of the Supreme Being in African contexts, which may not aptly capture the names given to such a being in specific African contexts. As far as I can tell, the name for such a being in many African communities immediately connotes creativity. They would often translate as the creative being. This stands out as well in *Gye Nyame*. *Gye Nyame*, a symbol prominently featured in the Ghanaian banknote of 200 Cedis, denotes that nothing would exist if not for the creative being. It is also how community members explain their ability to surmount very difficult challenges – the Supreme, Creative Being came to their aid. The creativity and power of this Supreme Being is further captured in another Adinkra symbol, *abode santann*, a symbol that visibly combines planetary bodies and communal artefacts, such as the sun's rays, the moon and the stool in forming an eye-like symbol. *Abode santann* symbolizes the totality and interwovenness of all that is made possible by the epistemically conscious, universally present and watchful *Gye Nyame*. It is this creativity and consciousness of *Gye Nyame*, partly consisting of being the source of human soul and life, that explains the validity of the Adinkra symbol, *Nyame Nwu Na Mawu*, often translated as 'The Supreme Being never dies; therefore I never die.' Of course, the originators of the ever-evolving Adinkra symbols are aware of the inevitability of physical death. The Adinkra symbol in the form of a ladder, *owuo atwedee* (ladder of death), clearly asserts this as it symbolizes the inevitability of death. Thus, *Nyame Nwu Na Mawu* denotes that one does not cease to exist because of physical death, since one's energy or force that comes from the Supreme Being is indestructible and can take up new forms of existence, such as being an ancestor.

Another ontological commitment that permeates African societies is the strong conviction in the reliance on supernatural forces and beings in the explanation of phenomena and events through extrasensory perception. In different aspects of life, such as in understanding diseases and healing, seeking protection and in decision making, community members frequently communicate with non-physical entities and forces through persons known to have a heightened awareness of their surroundings beyond what the senses perceive, often symbolized as the inner eye that sees beyond the physical. An indigenous healer among the Igbo people of Eastern Nigeria, called a *dibia*, would usually have his or her eyes and forehead marked with the native chalk, partly as a symbol of heightened and deeper vision and understanding of issues brought before him or her. One artistic performance that is fascinating in its use as access to and as a symbol of extrasensory perception, is embodied performance aimed at embodying the knowing process and stimulating the senses. Such embodied performances are not simply about creating a mood; they are often integral to altering states of consciousness, opening channels to the spiritual realm and embodying the presence of insights gained through extrasensory perception. Embodied performance would include auditory and visual stimulations, such as vibrant dancing, drumming, singing and chanting, often done collectively in spaces particularly fitting for such performances.

Ideas and beliefs about being, the entities that exist and the relationship, encounter and engagement with non-physical entities and forces in African traditions, are thus not merely abstract and intellectual but symbolic, performed and embodied. A vast territory of philosophical repository is left unexplored if the search for African understanding of being ignores artistic and symbolic forms of knowledge.

Symbolizing Individuality in Relationality

One of the most heated debates in the more recent history of African philosophy, the contemporary, more textual period, is the individual-community debate often weaved around questions of freedom, individuality, relationality, ontological priority, autonomy and collective survival. Both sides of the debate draw on ontological and normative principles in African traditions to imagine, re-imagine and analyse the relationship between the individual and the community in African contexts and to understand who a person is and what a community is. This debate is often referred to as the radical versus moderate communitarianism debate or, sometimes named after their key proponents as the Menkiti-Gyekye debate, since the Nigerian-Igbo philosopher, Ifeanyi A. Menkiti is often regarded as the key pioneer of radical communitarianism in his seminal work '*Person and Community in African Traditional Thought*' (1984) and the Ghanaian-Akan philosopher, Kwame Gyekye is often regarded as the key pioneer of moderate communitarianism in his seminal work, *African Cultural Values: An Essay on Philosophy and Humanism* (1996). Radical communitarianism not only affirms the ontological primacy of the community but argues for the subordination of individual interests and autonomy to the collective will. This perspective emphasizes the importance of communal cohesion and stability in the individual-community relationship, often at the expense of individual liberties, leading to critiques that it risks stifling individual rights and choices, and fostering authoritarian tendencies. Proponents of this view emphasize the interconnectedness of individuals to such a degree that individual identity becomes virtually indistinguishable from the communal identity, potentially suffocating individual will and freedom. This stance, although rooted in the perceived need for social harmony, raises concerns about the suppression of individual agency and the potential for the community to become a vehicle for oppressive conformity. In contrast, moderate communitarianism seeks a nuanced balance between individual rights and communal responsibilities, acknowledging the inherent value of both individual autonomy and social interdependence. This perspective recognizes the individual's embeddedness within the community, emphasizing the relational nature of personhood, but it simultaneously affirms the individual's right to pursue personal goals and exercise freedom within a framework of shared values. It contends that genuine individual flourishing is contingent upon a supportive communal environment, where individual freedoms are exercised in ways that contribute to, rather than undermine, the collective wellbeing. Moderate communitarianism advocates for a reciprocal relationship, where individuals contribute to the community while simultaneously benefitting from its support, thereby fostering a harmonious co-existence that safeguards both individual liberty and communal stability. This view argues that individuals in African communities still enjoy freedom but must do so in ways that protect the community, which he or she needs for survival and flourishing. This debate between radical and moderate communitarians, to which many have lent their voice (e.g. Oyeshile 2006; Ikuenobe 2006; Imafidon 2012; Etieyibo and Ikuenobe 2020; Maqoma 2020; Ansah and Mensah 2018), seems to me to be an intellectual exercise that can be avoided if one pays closer attention to orality and symbolism in African traditions. As we discussed in the previous chapter, African oral philosophy does not suffocate individuality, autonomy and freedom but emphasizes that these must be enlisted to preserve and sustain the ecosystem for survival and flourishing, the community. Similarly, there is abundant evidence from artistic, performative and symbolic expressions in African traditions that showcase the value for autonomy, freedom and individuality within the communal context.

There are numerous symbols to explore in understanding the African philosophy of individuality and communality, but I will pay attention here to a selected few in the Asante tradition (Adinkra symbols), Ga tradition (Ga Samai symbols) and Yoruba tradition (Adire symbols). The Adinkra collection of symbols is replete with many symbols dedicated to the expression of the interpretation of individuality, diversity in personality and freedom. The Adinkra twisted symbol,

Nkyinkyim, represents existential facticity and difficulties but also resilience and progress in the face of life's difficulties. It is used in connection with the initiatives, dynamism and versatility that an individual strives to showcase while navigating life's complexities with adaptability and thus acknowledges and justifies the necessity for diverse individual approaches. *Ananse Ntontan*, which resembles a spider web, signifies wisdom, creativity and the intricate nature of life, acknowledges the unique cognitive and inventive capacities inherent in each individual, and highlights the value of diverse perspectives in the construction of knowledge and social fabric. The *Aya* symbol in the form of a fern leaf, represents endurance and resourcefulness, reinforces the recognition of individual resilience in the face of adversity, and implicitly validates varied strategies for survival and flourishing. The *Bi Nka Bi* symbol expresses the pursuit of peace and harmony through tolerance and non-interference. Allowing people to flourish as individuals, tolerating individual differences so far as it does not threaten the community, is fundamental for attaining a peaceful society. Also, the symbol *Fawohodie* is primarily used within the Adinkra framework to represent independence, freedom and emancipation. Thus, while *Bi Nka Bi* promotes a social framework where individual differences are respected, it advocates for a pluralistic society where diverse personalities and viewpoints coexist without oppressive dominance. *Fawohodie* explicitly champions the right to self-determination, emphasizing the importance of individual agency and autonomy. These symbols, taken together, demonstrate that the Akan conceptualization of community is not antithetical to the recognition and celebration of individual diversity and freedom, but rather seeks to integrate these values into a harmonious social order. They provide cultural context to the moderate communitarian argument that individual freedom and community support are not mutually exclusive.

The Ga Samai wisdom symbols are also punctuated with symbols expressing ideas about the self, freedom, agency and individual authentic existence. Two Ga symbols that express individuality and self-preservation come to mind. *OkƆlƆ* is a Ga symbol showing three figurines with different heights holding walking sticks of different lengths. It represents the Ga proverb, which says, 'it is your height that determines the length of your walking stick'. It emphasizes the need for an individual to know his or her capabilities and limitations and act accordingly within the limits of his or her means (Kotei 2023). It represents an individual's worth and value, and the need to be realistic about one's plans and expectations. *Hençkwɛ̃mç*, often translated as self-preservation, represents the Ga adage: 'Self-preservation and personal safety are a person's responsibility, which one cannot relegate to others. Just like you cannot take medications on behalf of a sick person as the sick has to take the prescribed medication themselves, individuals have full responsibility for self-determination and preservation, including accessing and benefiting from the social structures available for their wellbeing' (Kotei 2024). This symbol underscores the moral autonomy of the individual, emphasizing the responsibility inherent in exercising freedom and the consequential nature of authentic self-expression. It highlights the Ga understanding that true freedom is inextricably linked to ethical discernment and the acceptance of personal accountability, thus enriching the broader African philosophical discourse on the balance between individual agency and communal responsibility. In Adire textile design in the Yoruba tradition, specific symbols serve not only as aesthetic functions but also convey profound philosophical and cultural meanings. One such symbol is *Orita Meta*, or the 'three-way crossroads', which represents a moment of decision and the complexity of choice, an embodiment of individuality and the exercise of personal freedom. Within Yoruba ontology, the crossroads symbolizes a sacred space where physical and non-physical beings and forces converge and intersect, resulting in tensions, disruptions and interweaving that could put the individual's autonomy and the responsibility that accompanies free will to the test. This motif, often found in Indigo-dyed Adire cloth, reflects the Yoruba belief that each individual must navigate their own life path, bearing the consequences of their decisions. Other motifs, such as *Eyin Ifa* (the eye of divination) and *Irin Ajo* (the journey motif), also echo themes of self-determination and destiny, reinforcing the notion that freedom is intertwined with duty and moral accountability. Together, these symbols articulate a nuanced worldview where artistic expression intersects with ethical and existential reflection, making Adire textiles not only visual statements but also carriers of philosophical thought about individuality.

The point, then, in the emphasis on the ontological primacy of the community, is not to suffocate the individual but to always keep in the individual's fore the need to preserve, sustain and care for the community in which he or she is able to be, to exist, in the first place. Hence, alongside these many symbols of individuality in African traditions are symbols expressing solidarity, togetherness, pursuing unity, building community and cooperation for the wellbeing of community members. Staying with the traditions we have been examining, perhaps the most popular in this regard in the Adinkra symbols is the *Funtunfunefu Denkyemfunefu* (unity-in-diversity or pursuing unity amidst differences) symbol, the conjoined crocodile. Other Adinkra symbols expressing the need to build community and for cooperation include the *Boa Me Na Me Mmoa Wo* (help me and let me help you) symbol, and the *Bese Saka* (bunch or bag of kolanut) symbol. The *Funtunfunefu Denkyemfunefu* symbol, depicting two conjoined crocodiles with a shared stomach, illustrates the paradox of conflict amidst shared destinies. It symbolizes the necessity of unity and cooperation despite differences, underscoring that communal survival depends on collaboration rather than rivalry. Similarly, the *Boa Me Na Me Mmoa Wo* symbol directly communicates the principle of mutual aid and reciprocity as an ethical foundation for social cohesion and collective progress. This symbol emphasizes the importance of interdependence as a moral and practical imperative in community life. *Bese Saka* symbolizes wealth, abundance, and the social capital that emerges from cooperative labour and economic collaboration. Traditionally, the kola nut is not only a valuable commodity but also a symbol of hospitality and alliance, reinforcing communal ties. Together, these symbols articulate a deeply ingrained ethos of unity, mutual support and shared prosperity, reflecting the centrality of community in Akan philosophy and social organization. The Ga Samai symbol, *Aguyaa*, which depicts two net weaving needles crossed together, symbolizes how an individual's worth, respect and dignity is determined by the ability not only to pull people together and build a strong community (akin to weaving a fishing net), but to hold the group together maintaining peace and progress (Kotei 2023). And the popular *Agbole* (circles in boxes) symbol in Adire clothing emphasizes family, community, dwelling together, household, strong bonds and relationships.

African philosophical traditions, therefore, as represented in African symbols, emphasize relationality and community not as mechanisms to suppress individuality or autonomy but as frameworks that ground personal freedom in mutual responsibility. This communal orientation fosters a conception of the self that is inherently interdependent, where individual rights are acknowledged alongside other-regarding duties (Molefe 2018). These duties highlight the moral imperative to consider the wellbeing of others in one's exercise of freedom, situating autonomy within a network of social obligations. Rather than negating selfhood, this ethical orientation enhances it by promoting a sense of responsibility, reciprocity and solidarity, thereby achieving a balance between individual agency and communal harmony that is central to African philosophical and moral thought.

Symbolizing Knowing and Learning

From our discourse so far, we can glean that African symbols, akin to orality, constitute in themselves a robust epistemic system that becomes an epistemic route to the philosophical, cultural, religious and broader intellectual and embodied thought of the people. It is expected, therefore, that such a system of symbols would consist also of meta-epistemological frameworks for pursuing, validating and analysing knowledge, wisdom and learning. I pay close attention in this section to the epistemological thought embedded in Adinkra symbols and a popular symbol that stands out in the Adinkra collection of symbols as an epistemic framework for encountering knowledge forms, symbolic or otherwise is *Nyansapo*, the wisdom knot. Kwadwo A. Okrah (2003: 6) explains the wisdom knot symbol thus:

> Nyansapo means 'wisdom knot' and suggests that, when the wise ties a knot it takes an intelligent mind to untie it. The saying implies that there are underlying meanings behind all symbols and figures of speech and activities of the Akan people. It takes a person with insight and profound intelligence to understand the true meanings of their actions ... [For example] a foreigner observing ... indigenous people will take everything by the face value and conclude as such ... [This] one may assume for example, that they were making noise when they were actually singing; that they were pagans when they were actually religious; that they were lazy when they were actually in recreation.

The wisdom knot thus emphasizes the complexity and sophisticated nature of knowledge forms, and the need for the knowledge and wisdom seeker to be ready and willing to carefully untangle and decipher meanings and intentions in the same way one would take the pain, patience and care to untangle a complexly tied knot. When we encounter a proverb, a story, an adage, a text or a symbol, we are encountering a wisdom knot, and require, among other things, intelligence, perseverance, patience and will to untie it and make sense of it. The wisdom knot symbol as an epistemic framework thus brings together intellectual and moral responsibilities in pursuit of knowledge as figuratively untying a tightly knotted cord of information, knowledge and wisdom requires, genuine interest and curiosity, readiness, determination and deliberacy, patience, perseverance and a sense of obligation, and intellectual humility to acknowledge when one requires assistance to successfully untie the knot. On this last point, the need for intellectual humility and, by implication, a collaborative epistemological outlook, the collection of Adinkra symbols is very rich.

Intellectual humility is often described as the recognition and acceptance of the limits of one's knowledge and epistemic gaze, along with an openness to new ideas, evidence, approaches and perspectives.

It involves acknowledging that one's beliefs, assumptions and knowledge claims might be wrong, particularly in the face of new perspectives and evidence, and thus being willing to revise them when warranted. This virtue encourages active listening, critical self-reflection and respectful engagement with differing viewpoints. Intellectual humility does not mean lacking confidence but rather balancing confidence with curiosity and a readiness to learn. At its core, it supports constructive dialogue, deeper understanding and responsible enquiry. More importantly, intellectual humility necessitates a collaborative epistemological outlook in which a knower, realizing the limits of his or her knowledge and epistemic outlook, willingly collaborates and works with other knowers and is open to actively learning from other knowers. It leads to the prioritization of communal or collective cognition, an inclusive approach to knowledge production and validation where different perspectives are taken seriously (Imafidon 2023).

The Adinkra symbols, *Kyemfere* (potsherd) and *Dwennimmen* (ram's horn) are particularly meant to represent intellectual humility and humble learning. The potsherd symbol represents the adage 'the potsherd says it is old; what then does the potter who made it say?' Old age is usually associated with wisdom and vast experience, so claiming to be old in this context is claiming to know, to be wise and experienced. But the potsherd is quickly reminded of two things: the potter is older and, by implication, more experienced and knowledgeable; the potter made the potsherd. In the context of the pursuit of knowledge, then, there would always be others more epistemically competent than us, and we owe a chunk of our competency to the efforts of others. The ram's horn symbol, on the other hand, which is prominently displayed in the University of Ghana logo, expresses a balanced view of epistemic humility and strength. *Dwennimmen* teaches that true wisdom involves the ability to pair inner strength and confidence with humility and openness. Just as the ram, a strong and assertive animal, lowers its horns in a gesture of humility, the learner must be willing to set aside ego, acknowledge the limits of their knowledge, and remain receptive to correction and new understanding. The symbol thus reinforces the idea that intellectual growth is fostered not through arrogance, but through a humble, disciplined yet courageous pursuit of truth.

With this emphasis on intellectual humility, Adinkra symbols also consist, therefore, of representations of collaborative and retrospective learning. The *Kokuromotie* (thumb) symbol and the popular *Sankofa* (go-back-and-get-it) symbol are apt representations of collaborative and retrospective learning, respectively. The thumb symbol is often expressed with the saying, one cannot bypass the thumb in tying a knot. This reiterates how everyone involved in knowledge production and validation brings something to the table. Just as the thumb enables the hand to function effectively in coordination with the other fingers, individual understanding is enriched through collaboration with others. This symbol underscores the value of interdependence, mutual respect and shared intellectual effort in the pursuit of knowledge. It affirms that learning is not a solitary act but a communal process, where diverse perspectives contribute to deeper insight and innovation. The Sankofa (go-back-and-get-it) symbol, on the other hand, often depicted as a bird turning its head backward to retrieve a valuable egg, conveys the profound principle of retrospective learning, the necessity of drawing wisdom from the past to inform present and future actions (Slater 2019; Kwarteng 2016; Asante and Archibald 2023). In educational contexts, Sankofa emphasizes the philosophy that meaningful knowledge production is rooted in historical, spiritual and transgenerational consciousness and critical reflection. It advocates for the recovery and re-engagement with cultural heritage, ancestral knowledge, and past experiences as essential resources for learning and growth. By encouraging learners to revisit and reevaluate traditions, heritages and prior understanding, Sankofa promotes a dynamic and fluid model of knowledge and learning, one that values tradition while enabling transformation through reflection and reinterpretation.

To be sure, the emphasis on intellectual humility, collaborative learning and retrospective learning in no way trivializes the need to develop epistemic competence at the individual and subjective level. In fact, collaborating, reflecting and displaying humility in the pursuit of knowledge when done with others requires a deliberate and intentional willpower to proceed. Hence, there is substantial emphasis on developing individual epistemic competence in Adinkra symbols, such as critical reflection and the pursuit of quality and excellence expressed in the *Hwehwemudua* (measuring rod) symbol, craftiness and intelligence represented in the *Dame dame* (Checkered) symbol and the *Ananse Ntentan* (Spider web) symbol, and the self-determination to know more and know better as embedded in the *Nea Onnim* (not-knowing) symbol. Emphasizing precision, excellence and quality, *Hwehwemudua* or the measuring rod symbol signifies the importance of critical enquiry and precision in, and clarity of, thought, urging the learner to apply intellectual standards and careful evaluation in assessing information and truth claims. *Dame-Dame* or the checkered symbol, represents the necessity of intellectual agility, foresight, craftiness, display of strategic intelligence and adaptability in problem-solving and in navigating complex knowledge systems. *Ananse Ntentan* or the spider's web symbol, linked to the wisdom and creativity of the spider *Ananse*, promotes cognitive flexibility, innovation and interconnected thinking, emphasizing that knowledge is multifaceted and woven through diverse sources. *Nea Onnim* or not-knowing symbol represents the thoughts in the Akan adage 'If he who does not know learns, he knows'. It serves as a humbling reminder that acknowledging one's ignorance is the first step toward genuine understanding and it promotes lifelong education and learning, and the continuous quest for knowledge. It thus calls for epistemic humility and an active commitment to learning. Collectively, these symbols encourage a balanced epistemic posture that values rigour, creativity, strategy and openness, which are fundamental layers of intellectual competence and responsible knowledge-seeking.

African symbols, particularly the Adinkra symbols that we engaged with in this section, offer rich epistemological insights into knowledge production, validation, and the processes of learning and education. These symbols encapsulate indigenous philosophies that emphasize the interconnectedness of intellect, morality, and individual and communal responsibility. Symbols such as *Nyansapo* (wisdom knot) and *Sankofa* (go-back-and-get-it) illustrate the complexity of knowledge and the relevance of reflection and cultural, historical and transgenerational consciousness. Others like *Dwennimmen* (ram's horns) and *Kyemfere* (potsherd) promote the necessity of a balance between intellectual, epistemic strength and humility, while *Kokuromotie* (thumb) underscores collaborative learning. *Hwehwemudua, Dame-Dame, Ananse Ntentan* and *Nea Onnim* collectively highlight individual epistemic virtues, such as critical thinking, adaptability, creativity and the courage to acknowledge ignorance. Together, these symbols present a holistic, values-based approach to knowledge that integrates cognitive skills, collaborative pedagogy, teamwork, ethical grounding and cultural continuity.

In this chapter, we have zoomed in on African visual and performative arts and symbols as significant repositories of philosophical thought in African places. Although these are aesthetically appealing, an appeal that defines the usual fascination with and gaze on them, they serve more fundamental purposes as knowledge bearers and transferers. There is a deliberacy in African traditions to craft, curate and perform knowledge. The detailing and effects, as we have seen, are very intentional and purposeful. I am particularly fascinated with the intertwinement of these symbols and how they are crafted with different facets of the human and non-human: trees, animals and their parts, planetary bodies, insects, fruits, plants, humans and human parts, etc. It showcases not only the interconnectedness of all beings but also the relationality of thought. We see in these artistic and symbolic expressions again the reminder that thinking and philosophizing is not always a self-contained project but a collaborative one, a point we will return to more fully in Chapter five. Our reflections are ontically connected to and impacted by the beings and forces, human and non-human, around us. Of course, the key challenge as we have examined remains the possibility of misinterpretation as well as of multiple interpretation where a symbol could have multiple meanings rather than a fixed, rigid meaning, and these multiple meanings will be legitimately valid and defensible in different contexts and situations. For example, the Adinkra conjoined crocodile symbol can be described as conveying the quest for unity in diversity, a sense of humanism, the importance of cooperation, and the need to avoid unhealthy competitive and individualistic practices that threaten the collective. These interpretations are multiple and can be useful in different specific contexts, such as in theorizing democratic practices, promoting a healthy sense of individuality or in theorizing cooperative business ethics. But, they are not radically opposed to one another and can all be validly defended as emerging from the same symbol. This is not peculiar to African symbols but is in the very nature of arts and symbols. I find it interesting, for example, how widely used emoji symbols online have, in the past decade, created legal and ethical issues because of misinterpretation and multiple interpretations of a single emoji. As Eric Goldman (2018: 1227) aptly puts it, 'Emojis are an increasingly important way we express ourselves. Though emojis may be cute and fun, their usage can lead to misunderstandings with significant legal stakes such as whether someone should be obligated by contract, liable for sexual harassment, or sent to jail.' But again, as we have discussed, the challenge of misinterpretation and multiple interpretation (if and when the latter can be deemed a challenge) is not peculiar to symbols and arts but one encountered in the different repositories of knowledge, including textual and oral ones. It is therefore not a sufficient reason to deter us from paying close attention to African arts and symbols and their relevance in the doing of African philosophy. More so, we get closer to the authentic interpretation(s) of African artistic and symbolic knowledge forms not when we enter into the hermeneutic gaze in search for what mirrors oneself but when we are genuinely interested in dialoguing with and understanding the other, taking place, context and embodiment seriously. Then, the ontologies and metaphysical commitments, moral philosophies and ethical principles, epistemological frameworks and other philosophical ideas embedded in arts and symbols will emerge.

4

The Textuality of African Philosophy

As we continue the exercise of reimagining the identity and performativity of African philosophy that we have been engaged with from the first pages of this book, it will no doubt be a disservice to such a reimagination if the focus was solely on the often underexplored and neglected methods and repositories for the performance of philosophy in African places, such as oral, artistic and symbolic ones. A robust reimagination and reconceptualization must also focus on and reimagine textuality in African philosophy as this chapter and the next one do. Perhaps, this should put your mind at ease if you felt for a moment, after reading the past two chapters, that my goal here is fundamentally aimed at downplaying or trivializing the relevance of texts in doing African philosophy, for that will be no doubt a performative contradiction as I am right now textualizing my thoughts on African philosophy. The key point, I believe, that is discernible then from our discourse so far, is the interwovenness of textuality with non-textuality, such that texts that can legitimately be described as being about African philosophy are densely permeated with references to the non-textual as legitimate sites of subjective and intersubjective thought. This is already obvious in this text before you, for example, as there have been plenty of references to proverbs, adages, maxims, artistic performance, symbols and the like in presenting African philosophical thoughts on themes such as relationality and individuality, freedom and existentiality, ontological commitments and the meaning of truth. Doing African philosophy, particularly in textual forms, is thus not a purely subjective and intellectual matter with a linear progression from self-contained intellectual and cognitive states of the self to scripting, but one that is embodied and positioned, emitting a spirit of collaboration and inclusion of all that it means to be African.

To reimagine textuality in the context of African philosophy then, it seems to me, is to re-examine and question the taken-for-granted assumption and dominant imagination of African philosophy as essentially textual and to rethink what exactly it means for it to be textual and the place of texts in the performativity of philosophy in Africa in the past and present as well as the future possibilities. To be sure, such reimagination would consist of rethinking the dynamics of power and the fluidity of knowledge production. Why is the reimagining of textuality important for doing African philosophy? Well, as we discussed in Chapter one in the contestation of textuality, textuality has been a defining feature of African philosophy, its history and current and future status. It has played a key role in shaping what we commonly receive as the legacy of African philosophy, in defining expectations from the gatekeepers of academic philosophy, and in shaping the contemporary identity of the discipline. In what follows, I examine textuality within the context of legacies, resistance, defence and mirroring. I show how dominant narratives of the history and legacies of African philosophy are heavily textual and examine the implications that the search for an exclusively textual legacy has for African philosophy. I then examine the textuality of contemporary African philosophy by analysing the different ways texts were enlisted as forms of resistance to colonization and marginalization, in defending the existence of African philosophy and in showing that African philosophy resembles Western philosophy. I conclude by exploring what the future of texts looks like in African philosophy.

Legacies

The characterisation of Africa's precolonial indigenous cultures as significantly ahistorical in character has been dismissed as patently false ... This false ahistorical stereotype had profound consequences for Africa's status vis-à-vis philosophy as an international enterprise. 'Early' human societies anywhere in the world were not thought to have developed the capacity for the intellectual refection definitive of this supposedly sophisticated discipline. Therefore Africa's indigenous cultures were, in both principle and fact, disqualified from occupying a place in the philosophical arena . . . The response on the part of many African philosophers, scholars, and intellectuals to this falsely ahistorical, as well as deeply offensive, typing of the cognitive significance of their civilisations has been sustained and vigorous.

Hallen 2002: 3

The points made here by Barry Hallen, a renowned African philosopher with expertise specifically in Yoruba philosophy, are clear and succinct. African scholars and philosophers, particularly in the past seven to eight decades, have been very keen on unearthing, curating and presenting legacies of African philosophy in human history, specifically in textual forms to counter centuries of epistemic injustice and false ahistoricization as well as to make concrete a history that contemporary African philosophers and students of African philosophy can lean on as a pillar of identity, even if only partly so. Drawing heavily on the histories of ancient Egypt and the broader Northern Africa to the Abyssinians and broader sub-Saharan, curating a textual history of African philosophy, which include unearthing texts and individual authors, was significant to showcase to the gatekeepers of mainstream academic philosophy that the demand for texts as evidence can be met even though it may not be as detailed and comprehensive as the gatekeepers may have or may desire.

Let me briefly attend to and perhaps wish away two issues before exploring more fully this textual history of the legacy of African philosophy, issues that tend to quickly emerge in conversations of this sort and become distracting to the more concrete matter at hand. Our discussion of doing philosophy the African way in the Introduction to this book may already be a sufficient response to these issues, but it is perhaps useful to recap them here. First, what qualifies an authored text (and also the author) in ancient history or the legacy being considered to be African and about African philosophy? The textual corpus before us in the curating of this legacy shows that the curators are clear on what fits in. The texts originated from and were about the African experience and conceptualizations of things, and in cases where they originated elsewhere, they were still about the African experience. So, being an African author but writing on topics completely removed from or remotely related to the African experience and narrative may mean, at least for many like myself, exclusion from this legacy or, at the very least, a controversial inclusion. The Ghanaian philosopher, Kwasi Wiredu, attends to this issue in relation to Augustine of Hippo thus:

> These thinkers were Africans and were responsible for a considerable body of thought. But did that formation of thought constitute an African philosophy? ... these philosophers, though African, thought and wrote within the context of a Western tradition ... Augustine's consciousness was not untouched by his African roots, and it is speculated that some of his views were conditioned by that circumstance. In the final analysis, it is the degree of dedication to the advancement of an African tradition of thought that must make the difference ... By comparison with either Augustine or Amo, the place of Zera Yacob and Walda Heywat in African philosophy is totally unmistakable. It has been known for a long time that Ethiopia has a remarkable tradition of written philosophy.
>
> Wiredu 2004: 23–4

Many of those who have devoted much energy to unearthing the textual legacy of African philosophy have focused more on the 'unmistakable' legacies, and it makes sense to do so, as it provides a sufficient corpus to work with, one that continues to grow. Second, isn't the claim to such a legacy an Afrocentric sentimentality such that the legacy itself or parts of it are overrated and perhaps not factual? The short answer is 'No'. One cannot possibly respond in the affirmative without raising the ugly heads of racism, Eurocentrism and epistemic injustice (Hallen 2002; Obenga 1992). The texts from Egypt, Ethiopia and other African places drawn upon in this legacy are factual and scientifically validated. Their absence in the mainstream academic corpus is not because of their non-existence but because of other marginalizing factors. As Molefi Kete Asante says about the Egyptian legacy, for example:

The antiquity of African philosophy is unique and stands alone in its foundational dimension because its antiquity is far beyond that of other philosophies. While civilizations such as the Sumerian and Minoan produced pottery, vases, and frescoes during the period of the earliest dynasties, only Egypt produced a body of work consistent enough in ethical, spiritual, and moral aspects to be called philosophy. It would be much later, nearly two thousand years, before the Greeks influenced by Egyptians would develop their own philosophy.

Asante 2000: 10

The textual legacy of African philosophy consists of a rich corpus from different African places, periods and times. The history section of one of the most important African philosophy texts in the twenty-first century, *A Companion to African Philosophy* (2004) edited by the Ghanaian philosopher Kwasi Wiredu, provides quite a detailed sketch of this legacy. In this section, Théophile Obenga (2004) explores the Egyptian philosophical legacy, focusing on such ancient Egyptian texts as the *Inscription of Antef*, which he argues provides the earliest definition of a philosopher, and the philosophical texts and tradition developed by important figures in ancient Egypt, such as Imhotep, Kagemni and Ptahhotep. Obenga also examines specific themes in Egyptian philosophy as contained in texts and hieroglyphics, such as Egyptian Logic, conception of the universe as endless totality, the problem of evil and the idea of immortality. Examining one of the most important texts in ancient Egypt, *The Litany of the God Ra*, he shows the centrality of the principle of Maat in Egyptian ontology and ethics, tracing similar concepts for the same principle across several African places. Molefi Kete Asante is perhaps the one who has provided a comprehensive exposition of the textual legacy of Egyptian philosophy in his work, *The Egyptian Philosophers: Ancient African Voices for These Times* (2000). He examines in some detail the ontological, ethical and axiological thoughts of key thinkers, such as Kagemni, Imhotep, Ptahhotep, Amenhotep, Amenemhat and Akhenaten. A read of this book shows that Asante's aim is to showcase a rich philosophical legacy in ancient Egypt and reclaim ancient Egyptian thought as the foundation for African philosophy. For example, Kagemni's textual legacy reveals a commitment to deontological and communitarian ethics and an ecological philosophy. In Asante's (2000: 75) words:

> An explanation of this text reveals that Kagemni's renown rested not so much on his statecraft which evidently was well thought of but more on his intelligent approach to service and generosity. He proffered a way of looking at the world which involved the true understanding and appreciation of other people and all creatures. He may have been the first ecologically interested philosopher because he spoke on behalf of the principles which demonstrate generosity to the land as well as to the people. To use the Bennu bird, often called the phoenix, and the tekenu or obelisk as figures in his moral teaching also shows a person who is attuned to the myths, intellectual properties, and metaphors of his own time.

Continuing with the history section of Wiredu's *A Companion to African Philosophy* (2004), D. A. Masolo examines African philosophers in the Greco-Roman era, focusing on such Christian philosophers with some African origin as Origen and St. Augustine. Of course, this is one contribution that raises the question of whether and to what extent Masolo is right to classify them as African philosophers. Souleymane Bachir Diagne (2004) draws attention to an often-ignored but robust tradition of philosophy in precolonial Africa, the Arabic tradition. From Morocco in North Africa to Mali or Timbuktu in West Africa, there existed important textual sources of philosophy that are often excluded from the corpus. A shining example that Diagne discusses is the Malian scholar of the sixteenth-century Ahmad Baba al-Timbukti, who developed important ideas on jurisprudence, justice and identity in the context of the trans-Saharan slave trade. No other than Claude Sumner (2004), being the most qualified to do so considering his pioneering efforts to make accessible Ethiopian philosophy, writes a chapter on the two most prominent philosophers of the sixteenth and seventeenth centuries in the Ethiopian tradition, Zera Yacob and Walda Heywat, the first being the master and the second being the disciple. He discusses their major works and ideas, and succinctly explains the context in which their philosophical thoughts emerged and developed, and the relevance of their philosophy. The chapter is no doubt a finely concise introduction to the more comprehensive work of Sumner (1994). Ethiopian philosophy, both in oral and written forms (Gutema and Verharen 2013), is no doubt one of the most important legacies of African philosophy as a longstanding and enduring tradition. As Teodros Kiros (2017: 182) aptly puts it:

> Classical Ethiopian philosophy is a source of great pride for the continent of Africa because it satisfies the conditions that Africans were fated to prove that in order for something to be philosophical, it must be written. Ethiopia points to its great historical presence on the world stage as a possessor of both written texts and orally transmitted wisdoms of the highest standards. The existence of an original Ethiopian philosophical text, written by Zara Yacob in the seventeenth century, sent tremors of epistemological and moral shock to the Western world. This discovery was a mighty blow to the Eurocentric gaze, which too confidently conceived thinking as an exclusively Western gift. There were those who had the audacity to deny that this was an African/Ethiopian philosophical product. Claude Sumner has answered the doubters by contending that modern philosophy began in Ethiopia contemporaneous to Descartes.

To be sure, there are now plenty of relevant texts written on the ancient, classical, medieval and early modern legacies of African philosophy drawing on factual scientific evidence and realities from places such as Egypt, Mali, Ethiopia, Morocco, Ghana and Nigeria to resist and challenge the Eurocentric narrative. We will return more fully to the question of resistance shortly, but first, let us dwell a bit more on the immediate impact and implications of a textual legacy. The proclamation, affirmation, awareness and availability of these histories of philosophy in Africa and their enduring, ongoing and lasting impact on the field of enquiry today, results in the availability of reliable textual historical records of philosophical investigations in Africa that refute the ahistorical presentation of African philosophy as a field of enquiry that was birthed only recently in the second half of the twentieth century with sufficient credit of that birth to European philosophy. As Hallen (2002) explains, this false ahistorical stereotype no doubt had profound consequences for the status of African philosophy, since its basic assumption is that Africans in history did not develop the capacity for the intellectual reflection definitive of this supposedly sophisticated discipline called philosophy, and this meant that Africa's indigenous cultures were, in both principle and fact, disqualified from occupying a place in the philosophical arena. Thus, the historicization of African philosophy through the documentation of its legacies thoroughly rejects this assumption. Also, the unearthed legacy signals that there is perhaps more history hidden and buried deliberately or non-deliberately to be uncovered. It is therefore a call on African philosophers to be keen on re-searching and unearthing the history of African philosophy and not to be satisfied with and work solely within a historiography of African philosophy that restricts it to developments in the twentieth century. But there is also a danger in focusing essentially on the textual, one we have reiterated several times in this work, a trivialization and non-development of the rich and comprehensive non-textual. There is no doubt that in curating this legacy, there has been some focus on the oral and symbolic non-textual, such as the Ma'at principle in Egypt and the Safuu principle in the Oromo tradition in Ethiopia. However, because the curating was primarily meant to be a response to the Eurocentric denial of philosophy in Africa on the basis of textuality, the legacy has been more intensely a textual one. Perhaps, what has been presented in the pages of this book is an attempt to present a fine balance between the textual and the non-textual as equally relevant sources of the legacies of African philosophy.

Resistance

Textuality and its forms of performativity – writing, reading and translating – have been used effectively for many years as tools both of oppression and resistance. Texts, how they are written, produced, read and translated, have been fundamental in constructing and creating power structures, norms and oppressive systems (Matusov and St. Julien 2004). Much of what we would consider as integral facets of the global system today, including religion, philosophy, economy and art, are often defined and sustained not necessarily by an ontic global history but by a selective textual one dependent on what was opportune by the power structures in specific times to be documented, transcribed, translated, written, and available to read and conversely, to be undocumented and thus, un-translated, un-written, and unavailable to read. When we think, for example, about how painstaking, time and labour-intensive, and costly it was to produce papyrus or parchment materials and scribe on them or, in more recent history, to print copies of text, we can readily discern that access to textuality would be limited and determined by power structures and gatekeeping. More so, the fragility of, and controlled accessibility to, historical texts meant that gatekeepers could determine what is handed down, what survives or what is destroyed, and generally what becomes available and accessible to us today. Beyond the controlled mechanisms of textuality, the contents can be deliberately or non-deliberately enlisted to promote and reinforce for generations harmful and oppressive ideologies, stereotypes, and systemic prejudices meant to marginalize and exclude specific groups of people (Devereaux 1990). The history of European philosophy as we have seen in the Introduction and the first chapter of this book is replete with the sort of texts that labels through elaborate writing often funded by power structures, specific sexes or races as not rational enough to perform and produce philosophy, thereby sustaining harmful patriarchy and racism, and in our specific context of discourse, the denial of African philosophy.

Conversely, forms of textuality are equally relevant and effective in performing resistance. The way a text is written and preserved, the telos for writing, the mechanisms of production, the care for translation, and even how and where it is read – or whether it is read in the first place – can create atmospheres of resistance. From critical reading groups to refusal-to-read activism and selective production choices, textuality can be an effective form of resistance. Text as resistance, therefore, consists of enlisting forms of textuality to challenge and disrupt, marginalizing and excluding power structures and oppressive systems. It involves writing, reading, translating, producing texts, rewriting, re-translating, rereading, refusing to read and refusing to produce in specific ways, sometimes at a high cost, such as exiling, denial of freedom, non-recognition and even death. For example, resistance literature has been a major and effective tool for feminist activism and in disrupting oppressive patriarchy (Ahonen, et. al. 2020; Smith 2011; Flynn 1996; Clark 1991; Lyotard 1984). As Pasi Ahonen and her colleagues collaboratively write about writing resistance together in academia (2020: 447) 'Writing is a form of collective resistance for Gender, Work and Organisation ... we desperately need a space to breathe, to move beyond the boundaries imposed on us by the disembodied metrics that are put into place to evaluate our intellectual abilities as academics. They favour quantity devoid of meaning in our academic production as opposed to impactful, meaningful knowledge.' An example of refusing to write in ways as standardized and expected that has always fascinated me is the rebellious writing of a foremost contemporary ancestor of African philosophy, the Ugandan poet, Okot p'Bitek, for which he was denied his doctoral degree at the University of Oxford in 1970. p'Bitek's writing was rebellious and a clear case of writing resistance, as although he wrote, he refused to write about African spirituality, philosophy and cultures in ways expected by the dominant Eurocentric gaze. Of course, the politics of writing and textuality in academia are widespread. The French philosopher, Jean-François Lyotard, wrote extensively about this in *The Postmodern Condition* (1984). He says, for example, that 'Research funds are allocated by States, corporations, and nationalized companies in accordance with this logic of power growth. Research sectors that are unable to argue that they contribute even indirectly to the optimisation of the system's performance are abandoned by the flow of capital and doomed to senescence. The criterion of performance is explicitly invoked by the authorities to justify their refusal to subsidise certain research centres.' (1984: 47). There is thus an unending tension between the system, power structures and the producers of texts as to who produces what and why it is produced or should not be produced.

African philosophers in contemporary times have used text as a weapon of resistance against marginalization, oppression and the denial of African philosophy. There are at least two interrelated ways, I believe, that we can frame text as resistance in contemporary African philosophy: resistance to the ahistoricization and the coloniality of African thought, and resistance to the multi-layered dimension of violence and oppression of Africans for the purpose of reclaiming dignity and identity and projecting authentic narratives. Concerning the first, there were several texts written particularly during the phase of Enlightenment philosophy to ahistoricize Africa and, by implication, deny the possibility of knowledge of any kind emerging from within Africa. Thus, it was the coloniality of African thought in which Africans are first denied the capacity of thinking, cognition and knowledge production and then, purportedly taught how to think and understand the world by the same folks who deny their capacity to think. For example, Hegel wrote a philosophy of history and postulated a crafty historical metaphysics that excluded Africa from anything historical (1956). So, when Africans took up the task to re-historicize Africa through writing, as we saw, for example, in the previous section, they were clearly resisting the ahistorical narrative and affirming the art, philosophy, spirituality and other knowledge forms of African peoples. The textual accounts of the legacies examined above, then, are in themselves a resistance to exclusion from philosophy. More so, the critical reading and rereading of, and textual commentary on, several Enlightenment texts previously held in high esteem to expose the racism and coloniality of African thought buried within them become and continue to be a significant part of this resistance. For example, my guided reading of Immanuel Kant's works during my undergraduate studies was with Eurocentric lenses focusing on core ideas such as the categorical imperative and pure aesthetic judgement. My eyes were trained by the system and its structures to see only and not beyond these allegedly lofty and universalist ideas. My encounter in graduate study days with Emmanuel Eze's *Race and the Enlightenment: A Reader* (1997) was my first liberation from such gazing. Eze produced a critical reader, an anthology that disrupted and resisted the narrative of innocence and high-standard scholarly excellence and ethics of Enlightenment thinkers, such as Kant, Hume, Hegel and Jefferson, exposing previously hard-to-access aspects of their work, which clearly showed how the works of these thinkers were racist and marginalizing to African peoples. No one encounters Eze's text without thinking differently and digging deeper. It achieves what a resistant text ought to achieve and there are many of its kind now in African philosophy.

Concerning the second, African philosophers (and I dare say both by training and disposition) have used texts to resist and critically challenge the many facets of the oppression of African peoples, such as colonization, slavery, economic oppression, racism, imperialism and neocolonialism. So, beyond resisting the coloniality of thought and philosophy through the exclusion of African thought from history, African scholars and philosophers seized and used textuality as a space for African liberation from marginalization and oppression. African philosophers and allies such as Frantz Fanon, Amílcar Cabral, Julius Nyerere, Aimé Césaire, Ngũgĩ wa Thiong'o and Chinweizu Ibekwe used their writings not only as political tools but also as philosophical interventions that articulated the conditions of oppression while asserting African agency, identity, epistemologies and philosophies. You should be quite familiar with these names and many more, as well as the insufficient summary I provide here. In *The Wretched of the Earth (1961)*, for example, Fanon critically analyses the psychological effects of colonization and advocates for a philosophy of violence, a revolutionary praxis through which the colonized can reclaim their subjectivity, agency and identity. He challenges both colonial and neo-colonial systems, arguing that decolonization must be total, affecting political structures, consciousness and cultural expressions. Similarly, Aimé Césaire's *Discourse on Colonialism* (1950) indicts European colonialism for its barbarity and hypocrisy, turning Enlightenment humanism on its head by exposing the dehumanizing logics underpinning colonial expansion. Amílcar Cabral's political writings, particularly in *Unity and Struggle* (1979), emphasize the role of culture as a tool of resistance and the necessity of cultural liberation in anti-colonial struggles. He famously argued that culture is simultaneously the fruit of a people's history and a determinant of history, thus highlighting the philosophical dimensions of cultural reclamation. Julius Nyerere, through essays such as *Ujamaa: Essays on Socialism* (1968), articulated a vision of African socialism grounded in traditional communal values, aiming to construct a post-colonial society rooted in indigenous African philosophies and political ethics. These intellectuals, along with others such as Ngũgĩ wa Thiong'o, particularly in *Decolonising the Mind* (1986), and Chinweizu, particularly in *The West and the Rest of Us* (1975), challenged the epistemic violence of colonial discourse and laid the foundations for an emancipatory African philosophy. Through their texts, they asserted the philosophical legitimacy of African worldviews and thought systems and actively contested the discursive mechanisms that sustained African marginalization.

Textuality as resistance brings to mind at least two considerations. On the one hand, I ponder about the burden of performing resistance through text, which drains a great deal of one's time and energy that could be devoted to doing African philosophy. But of course, the resistance is part of the doing of African philosophy, since although what is being resisted is not self-created, it is necessary. African philosophers and allies bear the necessary burden of vindicating African philosophy from false representations against it, and protecting and defending it from the harm that has emerged from such false representations. This self-vindication remains an ongoing process, and part of the textuality futures imagined of African philosophy is perhaps self-exoneration in which African philosophers have sufficiently resisted to the extent that they are released from the obligation to keep doing so. On the other hand, within the context of the resistant texts of

African philosophy, it is hard not to think about the sometimes blurred lines between friends and foes of African philosophy. In the recent history of the discipline in academia, there are some who would readily act like they identify with African philosophy and its challenges. They would readily show their fascination with and acceptance of the relevance of specific philosophical principles in African philosophy, such as the Ubuntu-communitarian theory of personhood, relational ontology or consensual democracy. But, they would trivialize and downplay by their action or inaction, particularly in how they write, read, comment and translate within African philosophy, the burden of resistance and self-vindication. Such subtle antagonism to textually curated resistance in African philosophy takes different forms: the resistance done already is enough – let's move on; the critique of Enlightenment philosophers is over-reactive because it does not take note of the fact that they wrote within the context of their time; the corpus of African philosophy produced in the past few decades is sufficient – there is no need to think too much about the past if there's even one to think about; African philosophy is a fascinating philosophy of culture in the periphery of conventional academic European philosophy and this is a sufficient place to hold; resistance in order to rekindle the authenticity of African thought is a waste of time as Africa has pressing developmental challenges to deal with and there is much to learn from the West in doing so; and so on. Of course, the undermining of textual resistance in African philosophy is not always subtle but sometimes radical. When we think, for example, about the kind of arguments Olúfẹ́mi Táíwò makes against noble projects of decolonization, reclaiming agency and identity for African peoples in such works as *Africa Must be Modern* (2014) and *Against Decolonisation: Taking African Agency Seriously* (2022), the rejection of such resistance and even of indigenous African philosophies and the embrace of the West as the only route to modernity is obvious. This complicates the burden of resistance for anyone who is ethically committed to resisting the documented and deeply entrenched false narratives about African peoples and philosophies.

Defence

I am well aware of the unavoidable overlaps between resistance and defence, since to defend involves in some way some form of resistance or refusal to accept, in this case a narrative. Thus, some intersection can and will be discerned between what we have been discussing in the previous section and what we will examine in this section. However, to defend is not just about resisting or refusing a narrative, in this case of the non-existence of African philosophy. It fundamentally involves presenting, fighting for and protecting a different narrative from that being resisted, one that assents and elaborates the existence of African philosophy. In this section, I examine briefly how texts have been mobilized not necessarily in resisting but in defending and fighting for the existence of African philosophy, particularly since the middle of the twentieth century. The mobilization of texts in defending the existence of African philosophy emerged primarily from the mixed reaction from the mid-twentieth century onward to a particular text that through the study of the Bemba and Baluba peoples of the Bantu tradition, had at least in the surface, the sole purpose of rejecting the denial of African philosophy and affirming the existence of African philosophy. The text I speak of here is no doubt the book by Placide Tempels titled *Bantu Philosophy* (1952). The title of the book and the claimed objectives in the Preface and Introduction show clearly that the goal at least was to affirm the existence of African philosophy. How this objective was carried out and developed throughout the work, and whether he accurately captured the features of African philosophy, is another matter that legitimately became the focus of many other texts.

The Preface to Tempel's *Bantu Philosophy* (1952) written by E. Possoz states clearly that European researchers and ethnographers in Africa have always denied philosophy and abstract thought to African peoples, exalting themselves and denigrating Africans. The book had the sole aim of correcting this falsehood and affirming the philosophical systems of African peoples through Bantu philosophy. Scholars have rightly noticed several issues with how this was then developed in the book. Okot p'Bitek, for example, elaborates on how the book itself remains primarily in the praise of European philosophy even while affirming the existence of African philosophy:

> Fr. Tempels writes: We do not claim, of course, that the Bantu are capable of formulating a philosophical treatise, complete with an adequate vocabulary. It is our job to proceed to such systematic development. It is we who will be able to tell them, in precise terms, what their innermost concept of being is. They will recognise themselves in our words and will acquiesce saying, 'you understand us: you know us completely: you "know" in the way we know...' Elsewhere, we read: that Bantu wisdom consists in the Bantu's discernment of the nature of being, of forces: true wisdom lies in ontological knowledge...
>
> 1976: 13

p'Bitek continues:

> If all this is true, then is it not strange that not even a single Bantu elder should be able to give a rough description of Bantu Philosophy...? A crucial question arises as to the attitude and role of the student of African thought-systems. It is, to say the least, unhelpful pride to start off by holding that a people do not know what they believe, or cannot express it; and that it is the student who, after discovering it, will tell them what this belief is.
>
> 1976: 13

More so, the details drawn by Tempels as to the very contents of African philosophy could amount to hasty generalization, since Tempels had studied the thoughts and philosophical systems of a small group of Bantu-speaking people only and expects us to label his findings as 'African' philosophy without first analysing the connections and disconnections with the many other traditions – Zulu, Yoruba, Igbo, Shona, Ganda, Akan, to mention a few. The renowned Congolese philosopher, Valentin-Yves Mudimbe has also written extensively on how Tempel's *Bantu Philosophy* and similar works after it, such as Alexis Kagame's follow-up book, *La Philosophie Bantu-Rwandaise de l'Etre* (1966) were meant to serve the ideological practice of Christianity in

Africa, showing how Christianity offers similar ontologies to those indigenous to Africans and by so doing encourage Africans to be more receptive to Christianity. This line of reasoning makes sense considering that Tempels, Kagame and others who hailed his textual presentation of African philosophy were trained to serve the Christian missionary agenda.

> Placide F. Tempels, a Belgian missionary in Central Africa from 1933 to 1962, offered his Bantu Philosophy to colonialists of good faith as a possible aid to the building of a Christian Bantu Civilisation. Tempels had lived more than ten years among the Luba Katanga people, sharing their language and cultural background... when he decided to publish his experience... Rather than a philosophical treatise, his Bantu Philosophy could be understood as, simultaneously, an indication of religious insight, the expression of a cultural doubt about the supposed backwardness of Africans, and a political manifesto for a new policy for promoting civilisation and Christianity. But this complexity is not what is commonly discussed when specialists speak of Tempels' philosophy.
>
> Mudimbe 1983: 133

And of course, *Bantu Philosophy* is a text heavily loaded with denigrating colonial categories for African peoples: primitive, semi-primitive, tribal people, savage, pagan and so on. The usual dismissal of any legitimate concerns about such words and concepts, one that I often find too trivial to take seriously, is that Tempels wrote in his time and could not have written better.

Notwithstanding these serious matters with Tempel's text, it did usher in a phase of serious textual defence of the existence of African philosophy, and a heated and protracted debate on documenting the defining features of the discipline. As the Nigerian philosopher, Peter Bodunrin, explained it in 1981, 'Philosophy in Africa has for more than a decade now been dominated by the discussion of one compound question, namely, is there an African philosophy, and if there is, what is it? The first part of the question has generally been unhesitatingly answered in the affirmative. Dispute has been primarily over the second part of the question as various specimens of African philosophy [have been] presented …' (1981: 161). This dispute or heated debate over specimens, or what the Nigerian philosopher, Godwin Sogolo, at the time called 'options' in African philosophy (1990), was primarily about defining what features made African philosophical thought authentically and uniquely African. Some options were presented in ways that mirror European philosophy by either arguing that African philosophy looks like or could look like Western philosophy, an approach we will examine more fully shortly; others were presented in ways that African philosophy seemed secluded and isolated from global patterns of philosophizing, and yet others were committed to presenting African philosophy as philosophizing about the African experience with a commitment to African ways of doing so. There is much to learn from these specimens, options, paradigms, trends or models of African philosophy that emerged from the debate on the meta-philosophical question of what defines African philosophy, both prospects and flaws. But what emerged from this defence strategy that went on for decades is that African philosophy was at this time an essentially meta-philosophical exercise. To be sure, there is always some meta-philosophical exercise going on in any philosophical tradition at any given point in time; the question of defining and redefining what exactly we are doing here and now never goes away, and we have been doing so in many ways even in this text. But devoting many decades of an era to producing works specifically on the meta-philosophical question of African philosophy is a substantial undertaking that perhaps distracted many from the task of doing philosophy beyond defining it. The question should never have been: does African philosophy exist? Of course, another way of rephrasing this question that should never have been is: are humans of African traditions capable of thinking philosophically? Any answer besides an affirmative one would no doubt be open to charges of racism, marginalization and epistemic injustice. Likewise, the question of what defines African philosophy – a question that hovers about all philosophical traditions – should have been a question in the background, the answer to which always lies in the residues of the doing and practice of philosophy.

Mirroring

Mirroring signals several related events. It could indicate the act of confirming if the one looks like the other, and if not, it would then include the process of achieving the desired resemblance. Mirroring is also a useful exercise for observing not just the self-other similitude (and even dissimilitude) but the surroundings and environment in which the similitude or dissimilitude is being assessed. The environment is key to the aesthetic judgement in a mirroring exercise, since the clarity and success in mirroring of a subject is very much dependent on the surroundings in which the mirroring happens. There are many ways in which the textual narratives of African philosophy in recent times, as presented in at least some of the specimens and paradigms we have been discussing, the critique and practice of such specimens as well as in the very way of doing philosophy, were and continue to be attempts to mirror European and Western philosophy. In this section, I examine briefly how professional philosophy, sage philosophy and ethnophilosophy as paradigms and trends in the defining of African philosophy were shaped in the shadows of European philosophy by a similitude-dissimilitude exercise. I also examine how the performativity of philosophy in Africa is still often haunted by a resemblance urge invested not only in mirroring the meta-philosophical assumptions of Western philosophy but in showcasing resemblance in the broader geography of thought, such as similarities of themes and concerns.

Professional philosophy as a trend in contemporary textual African philosophy is perhaps the most ideal example of this mirroring of Western philosophy, particularly in the sense of making sure whatever is called African philosophy is something that resembles Western philosophy in methods and thematic concerns. The specimen of professional philosophy as the sense of performing African philosophy often tended to present African philosophy as (Western) philosophy done by individual Africans trained in Western philosophy, or thematically about Africa by both individual African and non-African philosophers. This doing of philosophy is African because individual philosophers subject African experiences or what is often labelled as traditional thought to the systematic rigour of Western philosophy. In this sense, Africa, its body of thoughts and beliefs, and experiences become a subject of discourse for Western philosophy, an enquiry within the peripheral Western philosophy of culture. It is for this reason that advocates for African philosophy as professional philosophy are very critical of what has often been labelled the ethnophilosophical specimen, which prioritizes and is keen on demonstrating the presence and relevance of authentic and indigenous African epistemic forms and methods in the discourse of philosophical themes and problems (Oruka 1998). There is thus a strong emphasis, as would be expected in this mirroring exercise, on textuality and individual authorship over and against the non-textual and group/collaborative episteme in African traditions. A major proponent of the professional philosophy trend, Peter Bodunrin (1981: 177–8), says thus that:

> Surely, writing is not a prerequisite for philosophy but I doubt whether philosophy can progress adequately without writing. Had others not written down the sayings of Socrates, the pre-Socratics and Buddha, we would today not regard them as philosophers, for their thoughts would have been lost in the mythological world of proverbs and pithy sayings ... The remaining point is this: what does an expression like 'British Philosophy' mean? It does not mean the philosophy of the average English-man, nor a philosophy generally known among the British people ... the philosopher should be allowed the intellectual liberties allowed his colleagues in other disciplines. He may be asked to apply his training to the study of his culture and this would be an understandable request, but it would have to be understood that his reaction will be guided by his own philosophical interests ... Philosophy as a discipline does, and must have, autonomy.

But as G. Salemohamed (1983) explains, when Bodunrin writes this way about (autonomous) philosophy, what he has in mind is simply the British-American philosophical tradition. Although he is quite happy that this should co-exist in African universities with continental philosophy, he does not investigate from the latter point of view what might be the merits of including in the philosophy curricula of African universities everything that he at present rejects, primarily ethnophilosophy.

Ethnophilosophy, on the other hand, is the ideal example of dissimilitude, not wanting to resemble or mirror the philosophy of the West, as a specimen of African philosophy. Of course, this too is a problematic approach, for resembling or not resembling the other is only secondary to the key issue of denial and suffocation of authenticity and peculiar ways of being philosophical and doing philosophy. Understandably, such denial and suffocation can at least be justified on the basis of not mirroring a standard but only partly so – the reasons are often far more complicated. Besides, comparative philosophy in particular and more broadly speaking, comparative enquiries, thrive on exploring resemblances and non-resemblances. The time and labour spent to prove non-resemblance can be draining, and paradoxically, one still needs to look closely at the mirror in which the other reflects in order to accurately identify points of dissimilitude. Hence, ethnophilosophy has been haunted by the Western mirror of philosophy, since every attempt to present, say, an African concept of time, mind, personhood, death or truth, almost involuntarily yields the urge and yearning to comprehensively present the Western perspective first in order to show how it is significantly different from that of the self. It is a typical case of living in the shadow, margin and fear of the other, and African philosophy must transcend this urge to prove itself to the West for it to thrive.

Sage philosophy and nationalistic ideological philosophy as models of African philosophy that became popular in the textual discourse of the nature of the discipline also did not escape the mirroring challenge. In essence, the programme of sage philosophy was to prove that just like the West, African philosophy could fulfil the condition of having individual philosophers, sages in African communities. In staring at the Western philosophical mirror and identifying individual authors, such as Plato, Aristotle, Kant, Rawls and Rorty, what would reflect back would be identifiable individual sage philosophers in African traditions. Similarly, the nationalistic ideological model of African philosophy was very much committed to questions of decolonization, liberation and freedom of African peoples. It often aimed to approach African political and existential philosophy in ways that resist and liberate Africans from the political colonialist ideologies of the West. But key proponents such as Léopold Senghor and Kwame Nkrumah often played into the very same ontologies and ideologies that the model was meant to move away from. There was often an emphasis on mirroring European socialist/Marxist philosophies. As the Ethiopian philosopher, Tsenay Serequeberhan (1994: 33) explains about Nkrumah, for example, 'the language Nkrumah utilized fails to grapple with the historicity of the African situation. By unreservedly employing the abstract and worn out language of Marxism-Leninism, the language of "scientific socialism" and "means of production" and by framing the problematic of African freedom in these terms, Nkrumah occludes the foundational and grounding character of the question of freedom in Africa.'

Beyond the challenges faced by the proposed models and specimens of African philosophy in texts as they grappled with mirroring or not mirroring Western philosophy, the ecology of identity and the geography of thought on African philosophy is profusely surrounded and saturated by the Western legacy of philosophy for the usual obvious reasons, such as colonization and neo-colonial systems, such that no matter where the African philosopher looks in this mirror, the self is surrounded by multiple layers of the other, including categories and language. It takes more than the usual level of consciousness and determination for an African philosopher to see an authentic image of oneself in the densely compromised mirror. When an African philosopher, for example, writes about evil and suffering primarily in relation to the category of sin in medieval and Judeo-Christian philosophy, destiny within the category of fatalism, freedom within the category of European human rights and individuality, you sense the constant struggle not to simply resemble the other but to do philosophy differently. But the struggle to do philosophy differently, in ways that are authentically African, is no doubt worth it as it helps the discipline to flourish, thrive and genuinely contribute to a global discourse of philosophy rather than simply re-echoing the Western voice in the discourse.

Doing

In discussing texts in African philosophy as performance and repositories of legacies, resistance, defence and mirroring of Western philosophy, I have no doubt already presented, at least in part, how African philosophy has been done in existing texts and may continue to be done. So, in this section, I am particularly interested in briefly exploring the doing of African philosophy in textual forms that goes beyond, is not necessarily and foundationally about, and is not so much distracted by presenting and defending a legacy of the discipline, resisting the negation of African philosophical tradition, defending the existence and identity of African philosophy or showcasing the resemblance of the discipline to that of the West, but is primarily concerned with doing African philosophy in itself rather than in the shadow of the West, whatever reactionary forms that often takes – resisting, defending or mirroring. To be sure, a fundamental aspect of doing African philosophy in itself includes the definition and interpretation of self. Such definition and interpretation of self may sometimes understandably include the need to resist, defend and showcase or refer to legacies, but it does go beyond such needs to include a more definitive and interpretive exercise to present and elaborate on different facets of what one actually does and how it is done, similar to what we have been doing so far in this book and what many other African philosophers have done. A recent text in mind here that had the clear goal of doing African philosophy in this sense of definition and interpretation of the discipline is Pascah Mungwini's *African Philosophy: Emancipation and Practice* (2022). Understandably, he begins with the reactionary approach (the emancipation discourse of defence and resistance) but then moves on to a more definitive and interpretive account of African philosophy (the practice discourse), exploring such themes as interculturality and orality as characterizing contemporary African philosophy. Other African philosophers focus on defining a delimited and specific area of African philosophy, such as Uchenna Okeja (2022; 2024) has done with African political philosophy, Thaddeus Metz (2021) and Munyaradzi Murove (2009) with African ethics, James Ogude (2018) and Motsamai Molefe (2019) with philosophy of personhood, and as I have been doing with the philosophy of disability (Imafidon 2019, 2021, 2025). Thus, as a definitive and interpretive exercise in the doing of African philosophy, the goal is to lucidly and unambiguously present in texts what doing African philosophy in general involves or what doing specific aspects of the discipline involves.

Another way African philosophy has been done through texts is as a collaborative practice, which includes forms of non-textuality and interculturality. As a collaborative practice, African philosophy fundamentally consists of enlisting the non-textual in achieving the textual. This involves drawing on the rich oral and symbolic epistemic repositories in African traditions to textually conceptualize methodological and thematic concerns in African philosophy. This is why it is nearly impossible to write about concepts of truth, knowledge, justice, being, beauty, personhood, democracy, freedom, community, mind, destiny, identity, disability and so on without referring to an African adage, proverb, dictum, symbol, sculpture and the like. More so, the core methodological framework for African philosophy today is Afro-communitarianism, which is derived from oral repositories of sub-Saharan African peoples, such as Ubuntu among the Zulus and Ukama among the Shonas. Similarly, African philosophy as collaborative practice is intensely invested in interculturality, an interculturality that transcends the urge to merely mirror another tradition (as comparative philosophy can be reduced to a mirroring of Western philosophy (Wiredu 1984; Udoidem 1987)) to an active involvement and preoccupation with a genuine interest in comparing with and learning from another culture. One can see such interculturality attempted in, for example, Bert Hamminga's *Knowledge Cultures: Comparative Western and African*

Epistemology (2005), Grivas Kayange's *The Question of Being Western and African Analytic Metaphysics* (2021), and Kwasi Wiredu's *The Concept of Mind with Particular Reference to the Language and Thought of the Akans* (1987). We shall dedicate significant space to analysing and exploring the meaning and relevance of collaborative practices in academia from the lens of African philosophy in the next chapter. But in the current context, what is obvious is the strong presence of the exploration of collaborative practices in African philosophical texts.

Doing African philosophy as presented in textual forms also consists fundamentally of writing philosophically about the African experience in ways that are interpretive and problem-solving. There is a commitment in this textuality of African philosophy to exploring how indigenous philosophical concepts, methods and principles, as well as those interculturally derived, can be useful in interpreting the nature and problematics of the multi-layered dimensions of the African experience, as well as laying the foundation for exploring solutions to them. In other words, doing African philosophy textually involves writing about the philosophies behind and interpretive of African experiences, such as identity, corruption, gender, trauma, xenophobia, disability, health, femininity, political crises, violence, relationships, religion, technology, developmental challenges, education and justice. In doing philosophy this way, there are at least three questions in mind: What is the philosophical foundation of this experience in its current state? What philosophical concept, theory or principle can be enlisted in improving the experience? If the experience is problematic because of an underlying and deeply-rooted indigenous philosophy, what steps can be taken to re-theorize and revise the philosophy? In focusing on these questions, there is often a heavy reliance on the non-textual in making sense of it and recommending improvements, but in some cases, some African philosophers explore how philosophical theories and concepts from the West can help improve the African experience. In the latter approach, care must be taken not to fall into the danger of putting a round peg in a square hole, as we saw Senghor and Nkrumah do in the mirroring exercise above (intended or unintended). For there is a thin line between interculturally drawing from the global heritage of philosophy and drawing from the Western philosophical tradition in ways that undermine one's own tradition, since the global is very much dominated by the Western.

In this chapter, we have examined the forms that textuality takes in shaping and doing African philosophy. Although there is a legacy of texts on African philosophical thought, we ought to continue to explore such legacy, considering how much such a legacy has often been ignored, unknown and suppressed in the global history of philosophy. There has clearly been an increased reliance on texts in doing African philosophy in recent times. The core purpose has often varied and may include one or a combination of several reasons, such as curating and scripting resistance, defence, resemblance of another, interpretive of methods, themes and lived experiences, and forging and exploring collaborative practices. When done right, the ongoing curating of the textual repositories of African philosophy is always done in collaboration with non-textual repositories such as orality and symbolism. Doing African philosophy textually in ways that are removed from non-textual repositories threatens the very essence and substance of African philosophy. The different forms of the textuality of African philosophy have not evolved as different and distinct phases of its history, with one detached from the other. Rather, these forms of textuality are often interwoven and intersecting as African philosophy evolves. When the Egyptian and Ethiopian philosophers scripted their thoughts, they were primarily using text in the form it existed at the time, and as it is with the crafting of history, the presentation of such texts as a legacy only happens after. Similarly, the textuality of African philosophy today as defence, resistance and doing will in the future serve not only their original purpose but also as legacies that future generations can refer to. And speaking of African philosophy futures in the specific context of textuality, what does the future of texts look like within African philosophy and what does the future of African philosophy look like as textual repository continues to be curated? On the one hand, text in its different forms will remain relevant in the doing of African philosophy, in accessing a global audience with philosophical ideas indigenous to African peoples, and useful for understanding and dealing with problems emerging from the human and non-human conditions. But, of course, this must always be done in collaboration with the non-textual. On the other hand, African philosophy must like other disciplines grapple with the unfolding crises of relevance for texts in what I refer to in the next chapter as our trans-textual age. This would include philosophizing about textuality by drawing on important African philosophical concepts and principles that can be enlisted in the search for sustaining a tradition of both textual and non-textual repositories. The chapter that follows engages with some of these concerns.

5

Trans-textuality and Collaborative Strategies

My aim in this chapter is to focus on the question of method in African philosophy futures in particular and, by implication, the future of doing philosophy as a global human enterprise. This, I believe, is important, in the transhuman times we live in, which threaten the most popular approach to doing philosophy in mainstream academia: the individual authorship of philosophical texts. In thinking about the performativity of African philosophy in the past three chapters, we have examined several aspects of the non-textual and textual processes, repositories and approaches that are intrinsic to thinking, philosophizing and practising philosophy in African traditions. What can be gleaned from the discourse so far about the methods for doing African philosophy or the processes that African philosophers have employed in exploring ideas, arguments and the fundamental assumptions behind human experience include (i) A non-textual approach to philosophizing, such as collectively or collaboratively oralizing and artistically symbolizing philosophy as a deeply embedded method of philosophy in African traditions; (ii) however, the individual authorship of texts has also been an important part of the African philosophical legacy sometimes in forms that may be different from what would be the norm today, but there has been an upsurge of the textuality of African philosophy in recent years for varying reasons, some of which we examined in the last chapter; and (iii) the non-textual and textual approaches continue to coexist and collaborate in the doing of African philosophy today. Speaking specifically of collaborations, the collaborative practices in African philosophy, what we can deduce from the discourse so far, is not simply between the non-textual and the textual as we see, for example in relying on proverbs, adages and parables in writing about truth, but in the very methods, practice and modes of doing philosophy in African places, such as the enigmatic deliberation scenarios we will examine shortly. There are, therefore, promising possibilities, I believe, to sustain the collaborative spirit that African philosophy emits in the discipline's futures as well as in broader philosophical and academic practices. And this emphasis on working together as humans collectively pursuing knowledge is even more fundamental now that we are confronted with transhuman possibilities with real impact for textual and academic futures.

In this chapter, I begin, therefore, by analysing the crisis (and perhaps, prospects) of relevance for textuality in a transhuman age by exploring the concept of trans-textuality. This analysis is important considering that academic philosophy today relies heavily on textuality both as a defining feature and as a primary repository. Of course, in line with this heavy reliance on texts is the reliance on individual philosophers who produce these texts as the primary producers of knowledge. Thus, while we may have communities of philosophers as knowledge producers in the community, there is no active pursuit of collaborative philosophy. Thus, I then proceed to examine what we can learn from the ontological commitment to collaboration and relationality, the fluidity of thought, and the acknowledgement of ontic and epistemic difference in African philosophy in doing philosophy today and in the future. In this regard, I focus specifically on such aspects as relational cognition, collaborative ethic, the agency and capacity of individuals to contribute to the collective, and the enigmatic processes of discourse and deliberation in African places. On the basis of these methodological gems from African philosophy, I then proceed further to imagine non-textual possibilities in our global and transhuman realities, and explore ways of rehumanizing research and building collaborative pedagogies. The conversation we are about to enter into in this chapter, then, is crucial not simply for understanding the doing and practising of African philosophy but also for exploring more broadly possibilities of encountering and critiquing the coloniality of academic spaces and the transhumanity and dehumanity of academia today.

Trans-textuality and the Crisis of Relevance

To have a good understanding of the trans-textual realities and possibilities that I have in mind here and also why a post-textual phase of human history is unimaginable, it is important to reiterate succinctly a few points discussed already in this book. In our critical analysis of individual authorship and textuality as defining features of a philosophical tradition in Chapter one, the point was elaborated and clarified that textuality in philosophy is intrinsically linked to or fundamentally emerged as a consequence of subjective intellectuality. To produce philosophical knowledge in textual forms or as philosophical texts fundamentally requires the deploying of the individuality of the intellect and rational faculties to produce thoughts that are distinctly philosophical. When we gaze at the textuality of academic philosophy, particularly from the lens of subjective intellectuality, the many methods for doing philosophy that have emerged in the history of Western philosophy make more sense as they fit into this narrative of the individuality of reason, kaleidoscoping as it were different facets of subjective intellectuality. Philosophical methods such as the Cartesian method, the transcendental method, the dialectical method and the phenomenological method can be defined, and rightly so within the parameters of the subjective deployment of the intellect. The phenomenological method, for example, attempts to do philosophical investigations by first refining subjective consciousness or the intellect to get rid of all corrupting presuppositions and theoretical assumptions. The Husserlian phenomenological method, heavily informed by the Cartesian method, aims to aid a philosopher through the practice of epoche – the suspension of judgement of the external world – to focus purely on the structure and contents of his or her intellect, and uncover meanings of experiences purely as they present themselves to subjective consciousness. The aim of the phenomenological method is to attempt to guarantee that a direct and uncorrupted connection of the intellect to the object being investigated is possible, free from embodied, cultural, political and positioned distractions. Perhaps, one method that doesn't fit very nicely within this narrative of subjective intellectuality is the Socratic method because of its commitment to intersubjectivity and dialogue in the process of doing philosophy. Interestingly though, there is a noticeable tendency in the scholarship on the Socratic method to present it as subjective intellectuality, where the main features of the method, systematic questioning, inductive reasoning and the possibility of universal definitions are attributed to Socrates alone as if in the many dialogues, he alone asked the questions and drew the inferences (Overholser 1993; Benson 2010). Thus, methods of philosophy have often been developed and narrated to fit the idea of subjective intellectuality in the production of philosophical knowledge in textual forms.

The challenge that transhumanism, particularly in the form of artificial intelligence, poses to human subjective intellectuality, be it in philosophy or other disciplines, is that it promises to offer – and perhaps, it is already offering – non-human, high-tech subjective intellectuality. The idea is that artificial intelligence produces or has the potential to produce superintelligent results that beat the intellectual functioning of the human. Thus, if we accept that it takes human subjective intellectuality to produce philosophical knowledge and texts, then, the transhumanist argument is that artificial subjective intellectuality has the superintelligence to produce better philosophical knowledge and better texts. It is, to put it succinctly, the undermining and trivialization of the human intellect. We witness already today in academia, the dread of, and anxiety over, artificial intelligence, as if threatening our very means of being academic and scholarly, the subjective intellect. Of course, if subjective intellectuality is all we have as humans in entering into enquiries, there are good reasons to be worried and anxious about artificial intelligence. Perhaps, it is important to remember here that the challenge to the human intellect and the questioning of its reliability and dependability is not due solely to transhumanism but there has been a healthy suspicion of subjective intellectuality in postmodern thought, which in itself is foundational to transhumanism. Friedrich Nietzsche, for example, gives us much to think about the insignificant, dubious and cunning nature of the human intellect, particularly within the contexts of the broader human and non-human ecosystem of being in his seminal essay, 'On Truth and Lies in a Nonmoral Sense' (1873). In his opening lines, Nietzsche writes that:

> Once upon a time, in some out of the way corner of that universe which is dispersed into numberless twinkling solar systems, there was a star upon which clever beasts invented knowing. That was the most arrogant and mendacious minute of 'world history,' but nevertheless, it was only a minute. After nature had drawn a few breaths, the star cooled and congealed, and the clever beasts had to die. – One might invent such a fable, and yet he still would not have adequately illustrated how miserable, how shadowy and transient, how aimless and arbitrary the human intellect looks within nature. There were eternities during which it did not exist. And when it is all over with the human intellect, nothing will have happened. For this intellect has no additional mission which would lead it beyond human life. Rather, it is human, and only its possessor and begetter takes it so solemnly – as though the world's axis turned within it. But if we could communicate with the gnat, we would learn that he likewise flies through the air with the same solemnity, that he feels the flying centre of the universe within himself.

Perhaps, then, our anxiety about the human intellect in the wake of transhuman technologies is simply because of our overrating of it in the first place.

Trans-textuality, then, is to put it simply, the transhumanization of textuality. It consists of the deployment of non-human intellectuality, and in this particular case, artificial intelligence, in the production of knowledge in textual forms. There is an increasing interest in the publishing community for enhancing texts in whole or in part with artificial intelligence. Some publishers have gone as far as publishing books and articles wholly generated by artificial intelligence. By trans-textuality, then, I do not mean the co-opting of non-textual forms, such as oral narratives or the use of videos in enhancing the accessibility of texts, which is also quite common today (many today, for example, would prefer audiobooks and video books to the actual reading of texts). This, it seems to me, will best be described as forms of collaborative textuality where textual and non-textual forms are collaboratively enlisted to achieve specific goals. Trans-textuality does not also indicate post-textuality since it is not a move away from texts or a rejection of all forms of textuality. Post-textuality is not an ontologically imaginable mode of being human since humans always, by the very nature of their being, script and write. What is perhaps imaginable is the coming-to-end of regimes of textuality (to borrow the Foucauldian concept of regimes) and the beginning of new regimes. Trans-textuality understood as textuality transcending human subjective intelligence ought also to fundamentally include producing texts by not depending solely on the human intellect but also on the ecosystem of thought of the non-human, an ecocentric intellectuality and intelligibility, something we seldom do because of the anthropocentric nature of thought (Nietzsche 1873). Transhumanity fused with ecocentric intellectuality would provide robust and rich exploration of trans-textual possibilities today, but our focus at least in this context at this moment, is primarily on the implications of transhuman trans-textuality for the production of philosophical knowledge today.

The anxiety around trans-textuality is the crisis of relevance it presents for human intellect and the sustenance of the dominant human intellectual tradition. In a trans-textual age, there are several reasons for a legitimate concern for a crisis of relevance for textuality as we currently experience it. First is the dehumanization of thought and the undermining of human creativity. The substantial detaching of human consciousness and intellectuality from the textual production process reduces the production of texts to skilful assemblage and curation of what is already available, which is what artificial intelligence seems to offer. But texts, much like oral and symbolic forms of knowledge, require not just intellectual but collaborative creativity that is embodied and positioned – a point we will come back to. Such painstaking, careful and deliberate relational and collaborative crafting and creativity could be lost to trans-textuality. Second is the problem of epistemic laziness. Trans-textuality is effectively capable of creating an epistemically lazy community of selves. Epistemic laziness in this sense is not simply the lack of epistemic interest or lack of curiosity that some humans showcase in understanding their experience or the experience of others not like themselves (Jarczewski 2024), one that Immanuel Kant aptly captures in his Lecture, 'An Answer to the Question: What is Enlightenment?', thereby recommending the *sapere aude* epistemic disposition (1784). It involves, in the trans-textual sense, a lack of interest in exercising one's curiosity in knowing and understanding justified on the basis that the superintelligent tech-other already does such epistemic services for us. We are now confronted more than ever before with students and colleagues being comfortable with using artificial intelligence to generate text. This does not only promote epistemic laziness but, by implication, stifles the development of one's own understanding and the collaboration with others in the pursuit of knowledge and understanding. A third concern is the fostering of the coloniality of (philosophical) knowledge. If transhuman technologies are defined by specific power and capitalist structures, if the trans-textuality of philosophical knowledge is shaped in specific ways that rely essentially on the dominant Eurocentric textual heritage that has been fed to the intellectuality of the artificial subject, then, the trans-textual output will not necessarily deviate from the already colonized episteme of philosophy that marginalizes and excludes non-Western philosophical heritages, including non-textual repositories. Thus, when, for example, I ask a generative artificial intelligence chatbot to generate a text on 'The problem of knowledge in philosophy and the major theories proposed' – and this is an actual experiment that I have done – it immediately in a matter of seconds provides an extensive and detailed presentation of the Western textual history of the problem because that is what comes immediately to its consciousness. It explains the classical justified-true-belief approach, empiricism, rationalism, constructivism and reliabilism, including core Western thinkers that have postulated these perspectives, as well as the strengths and weaknesses of these views. That is the philosophical heritage it knows, one that excludes other traditions from its global history. It would take a very specific set of prompts for it to generate African, Indian or Asian perspectives on the question of knowledge.

How can we cope with the crisis of relevance that transhumanism poses to human creativity, understanding, and, more specifically, in our context, the capacity to perform and do philosophy without necessarily rejecting transhumanism completely? The answer, I believe, already stares us in the face. As we have highlighted at the opening of this book and discussed severally in relation to African ways of philosophizing, what we have as humans to deploy in performing philosophy is not only the subjective intellectuality of each individual philosopher. Beyond this, we have and can deploy intersubjective and ecocentric intellectuality in ways that are collaborative and relational. Our philosophizing is shaped not merely by our intellect but by our embodied and positioned realities and experiences, and we are capable of performing philosophy in ways that are non-textual. In what follows, we explore these possibilities more fully from African philosophical contexts.

Afro-communitarianism as Method toward Ecocentric Intellectuality

A central and cardinal feature of the performance of African philosophy that stands out seamlessly in the preceding chapters is a deep commitment to communality, both as an existential and moral ontology (Eze 2008). For example, we discussed in Chapter two how oral philosophy, such as names, proverbs and adages is used to present and transmit the communal and relational nature of existence, and in Chapter three, we examined how arts and symbols showcase commitment to a communitarian philosophy. We have discussed all through the preceding chapters concepts such as Ubuntu, *Ukama* and *Akomen*, and symbols such as the *Boa Me Na Me Mmoa Wo* (help me and let me help you) symbol and the *Bese Saka* (bunch or bag of kola nuts) symbol drawn from different African cultures to capture the idea and need for building relationships. As we discussed in the last chapter, the textuality of African philosophy relies heavily on these non-textual repositories of communal philosophy in African traditions in doing philosophy, which explains why the most defended overarching philosophy of sub-Saharan African peoples today in the recent textual literature is Afro-communitarian philosophy (Eze 2008). Hence, Afro-communitarian philosophy, African communal philosophy or African communitarian philosophy, however it is framed, is the backbone of the philosophical enterprise of African peoples. What emerges distinctly and clearly from this philosophical outlook is a noticeable shift from doing philosophy based essentially on subjective intellectuality and the kind of methods that it produces to doing philosophy in ways that emphasize intersubjective intellectuality, ecocentric intellectuality, and the relevance of embodiment and positionality. As distinct from subjective intellectuality, intersubjective intellectuality construes intellectual exercises, including the capacity for reasoning, understanding, cognizing, making sound judgements and solving problems, not purely as self-contained abilities and processes but as shared and co-created abilities and processes. To understand a phenomenon or an experience, to understand and resolve a problem, and to produce or revise meaning and thought in ways that prioritize intersubjective intellectuality, is to assume and defend the following: (i) a subjective self-contained intellectual process is deficient and less productive than an intersubjective and collective intellectual process; (ii) an intersubjective intellectual process produces richer and more robust reasoning and perspectives by drawing on varied individual mental capacities and on group mind and agency; and (iii) a person's intellectual capacity is nourished and developed within the context of the communal and interpersonal, and vice versa. Intersubjective intellectuality is further emphasized with the intensely felt presence of ecocentric intellectuality in African traditions. By ecocentric intellectuality, I mean the extension of intellectual capacity beyond the human to the non-human (both spiritual and material), an acknowledgement of the ecosystem of thought to which the human person is only a constituent part. To be sure, as Nietzsche expresses it above, acknowledging how insignificant the human intellect is in the broader scheme of things ought to produce intellectual humility for humans, knowing that we are always learning from and knowing through the intelligibility of the non-human. Our reasoning and understanding constantly depends on what the non-human, such as the trees, weather, air, migrating birds, our pets, and our inherited genes and energies, make intelligible to us about the past, present and future. There is a strong awareness of this in the philosophical systems of African peoples, a deeply embedded yearning of not only learning, knowing and understanding from fellow humans but as significantly from non-human beings and forces, such as the ancestors, deities and divinities, trees and animals.

The value for intersubjective and ecocentric intellectuality may perhaps explain the nature of, necessity for, and reliance on deliberative systems and practices in African cultures. A common example popularized in existing literature is what is often called the palaver model, although the choice of the word 'palaver' may be misleading and could distort the deliberative practice being denoted in African traditions. As Mukanda Mulemfo explains it (1996), palaver can be defined as a traditional meeting or gathering of the kinship group or the whole community, where talks and discussions are held, as means of deliberation and reconciliation (solving conflicts and differences, setting aside transgressions); organizing happy or sad events (e.g. marriages or funerals); or the healing of some diseases, with the goal of rebuilding or re-establishing order, security and protection in the community. In a palaver – as a meeting or a big gathering – the community involves itself in bad, sad or happy situations in which people find themselves. Conflicts and transgressions were often the subject of a big gathering of the whole community, firstly to seek out and identify the guilty person; and secondly to re-incorporate the person into the group. Palaver is therefore an old method to heal various diseases (psychological, social, mental or physical, individual or corporate), a reconciling and constructive method of dealing with a variety of situations in Africa (social, religious, economic, philosophical and political). Palaver is a communal language expression that concerns itself with the search for solutions to actual situations. The search for solutions is done in a holistic way. The striking characteristic of this practice is that food, traditional beer and dance demonstrate the community's joy at either the person's re-integration, the patient's recovery or the re-establishment of harmonious relationships in a particular group of people, a wedding ceremony, birth, a heated dispute and so on. This showcases the performative nature of palaver, weaving together orality and artistic performances. It also means that the community could be convened for a palaver for various purposes. The Congolese philosopher, Bénézet Bujo, provides a detailed analysis of the palaver model in his book, *Foundations of an African Ethic* (2001). As Ogonna Nwainya (2023) explains, Bujo examines how, for Africans, words possess such a tremendous power that they can create or destroy a community depending on how they are used. His model of the palaver essentially runs on the proper use of words, without which the palaver community is ruined, if not dead. Bujo describes the palaver as a space for open communication by which persons are integrated into the life and expectations of their communities. This space can be physical, as when community members gather under the ancestral tree or at the grave of a deceased family member, but more importantly, it is also a psychological and social space for open communication. The intersubjective intellectuality of the palaver model of deliberation is thus obvious as community members come together to reason matters, understand and learn as a community in line with the communitarian outlook already embedded in the tradition. As Fidèle Ingiyimbere (2024: 288) puts it:

> The palaver is foremost a way of life because it is rooted in a communal social, epistemological, and metaphysical philosophy that resonates with African cultures. Indeed, in most African cultures, individual persons find their meaning of life in their communal belonging. Such communal belonging is the site of rights and duties towards one another. Exiting one's community would mean alienating both rights and duties, and so is the meaning of one's existence. In that regard, even learning is communal ... people gather for discussing matters of the community because they deeply believe that knowledge is transmitted through dialogue. One finds the same belief in Burundian culture,

where it is said that *'Ubwenge burarahurwa'*, that is, knowledge is fetched from the neighbour, the same way one fetches fire from others. Still in Burundian culture, other proverbs go, *'Akanyoni katagurutse ntikamenya iyo bweze'*; *'Umutwe w'umwe wifasha gusara ntiwifasha gusaba'*... The first proverb means that one has to move from his or her place, in order to increase his or her knowledge, in the same way a bird has to move to different places to find food. Knowledge is considered as food for the spirit. The second proverb means that a single head cannot achieve anything good; it has to cooperate with others.

The ecocentric intellectuality of palaver is seen in the fact that not all participants are physically present but are felt and heard. Some participants are, by their nature, not visible but felt. Bujo (2001) explains, for example, that one could not possibly conceive of such coming together for discourse without the Supreme Being and ancestors as an integral part of the process. More so, the relevance of the ecosystem for such deliberations is again evident in the importance given to the place, time and setting in which the deliberations would take place: meeting under the tree, meeting outdoors in the cool of the evening as we saw in the case of *akota* in Chapter two as an example of palaver deliberative practices, the breaking of kola nuts as a symbol of life, good health and hospitality before a deliberation begins in some West African traditions, suspending the status of participants to emphasize equality and common ontological heritage as we see in, for instance, the no-standing rule setting in the kgotia public sphere of discourse and deliberation common among the Tswana people of Botswana, the conversations held by healers with trees and other non-human beings, specifically during a healing palaver (Bujo 2001; Scheid 2011), and similar affirmation of the non-human permeate deliberations across sub-Saharan African traditions.

Afro-communitarian philosophy thus produces or at least implies collaborative philosophy as a method for doing philosophy. Collaborative philosophy is, in a nutshell, doing philosophy intersubjectively and ecocentrically. This would mean that philosophy done this way acknowledges and is responsive to the multi-layered levels of collaborative, co-creative and ecologically-aware possibilities for philosophizing. Interestingly, collaborative spaces for the curating of thought in African communities were quite inclusive. Admittedly, some communal spaces could exhibit an ontology of exclusion (Imafidon 2024), patriarchal opportunism (Imafidon 2018), and a narrow and restrictive conception of community (Imafidon 2021), but this is not always or even often the case. I have discussed elsewhere (Imafidon 2018, 2021, 2024) how within African traditions communitarian philosophy as practice could produce in some contexts these challenges of excluding beings not ontically or normatively fitting within the community from forms of communal participation (an ontology of exclusion), excluding females from actively accessing specific groups (a form of patriarchal opportunism), and presenting quite a narrow sense of who is or ought to be part of the community. However, in terms of collaborative and deliberative practices for the production and analysis of thought and discourse, these challenges become blurred either because the group provides some legitimate but yet questionable reasons for exclusion of certain beings, or everyone has access to the deliberative group as long as they have interest in being part of it. I do not intend to elaborate on these challenges further here as my aim is to focus on identifying and analysing the key features that emerge from the disposition to do philosophy in a co-creative and collaborative way. There are several interwoven nuances that collaboration as a method or process of doing philosophy can result in. In what follows, I weave these possibilities around three key features or defining principles of collaborative philosophy as a method of philosophy.

Relationality, Fluidity and Difference

When we think about the fundamental claims of Afro-communitarian philosophy that we have been discussing and from which we discern the method of collaborative philosophy, relationality as a key defining feature and principle is quite obvious. Not so obvious, though, are two other cardinal features that I have often termed elsewhere as fluidity (Imafidon 2025a; 2025b) and difference [Imafidon 2022; 2023b; 2025b). In this section, I will pay attention to the three features with the primary aim of exploring how they present themselves in the collaborative method of philosophy. Relationality in a nutshell emphasizes the primacy and fundament of active relationships among human and non-human in pursuing and earning personhood, building community and producing knowledge. There is no point labouring the clarification of relationality further as it has emerged several times in our conversations so far. But the point to be drawn from it, in terms of philosophizing, is the obvious shift to, and prioritization of, intersubjective intellectuality over subjective intellectuality. Cognition, for example, in this sense, is relational and community-centred. Relational or communo-cognition (Imafidon 2023) does not deny individual cognitive capacities but emphasizes how individuals must bring such into dialogue with others. This is because processes of knowing and related cognitive functions, such as learning and remembering, are by the very nature of our ontological disposition best attained through a collaborative process and the deployment of group agency. More so, the subjectivity and alleged autonomy of our intellectuality and cognition fail to acknowledge, as intersubjective intellectuality does, how communities and their institutions and structures significantly impact and shape how, why and what we think, learn, remember, forget, defend or refute (the Foucauldian ideas of governmentality, discourse, power and the regimes of truth) and the importance of, and power in, collectively building, rebuilding, constructing and deconstructing such institutions and structures. In African traditions, there is a strong emphasis on individual minds cooperating, co-depending and interacting together to grasp and interpret realities and experiences. The African experience of relationality thus reverses the Cartesian dictum of 'I am because I think' to 'I am because we are' or, more aptly put in this context, I philosophize efficiently because we philosophize together.

Relationality also signifies a relational hermeneutics. There are two key senses of speaking about philosophical hermeneutics. First, and a more delimited and specific understanding is that philosophical hermeneutics is a paradigm or a European philosophical movement concerned with the metaphilosophical question of the essence of interpretation and the development of efficient methods of interpretation of texts and lived experiences. Anyone familiar with this tradition in European philosophy will no doubt be familiar with the many German and French names that dominate this tradition. To be sure, this first sense, as rich as the European tradition of it is, emits a problematic coloniality since it assumes that such concerns have existed only in European philosophy. I will avoid going into any elaborate or even skeletal critique of the coloniality of thought here in order to sustain the flow of thought. There are now, I believe, sufficient resources to ascertain that similar hermeneutical concerns existed all over the world, such as the Asian hermeneutical encounter with the classical i-Ching (Book of Change) and Shijing (Book of Songs) (Gu 2005). The second and much broader sense is the understanding of philosophy as an interpretive exercise. Philosophy as a mode of enquiry is the quest to find fundamental and general principles that help us understand and interpret our world, experiences, inherited texts and histories in the pursuit of meaning, and develop systematic and sophisticated arguments for and against specific principles. In line with subjective intellectuality, both senses dominantly present interpretation and understanding as a solitary encounter of the interpreter (e.g. the author) with the interpreted (e.g. the text). Hermeneutical concepts such as Dilthey's *verstehen*, Heidegger's unconcealment, and Gadamer's historical consciousness and the fusion of horizons are replete with such assumptions. What relationality offers as an alternative in line with the intersubjective intellectuality that it advocates is that individual interpretations are not sufficient but can be enriched through collective interpretations. In other words, a collective hermeneutical encounter provides a more robust understanding and interpretation of a phenomenon, experience or text. By relational hermeneutics, I mean, therefore, that the meaning of a text, phenomenon or experience is ideally sought by encompassing different perspectives of interpreters, which nourishes the interpretive process much more than a singular perspective would.

There are fluid ways of being, knowing and learning that defile rigidity, linearity and epistemic hierarchies in African communitarian philosophy. Communitarian concepts such as Ubuntu and Ukama imply that humans and non-humans are always in a fluid state of being. My choice of fluidity as a concept to provide linguistic care for the experience that I have in mind here as embedded in communitarian philosophy seems productive and useful as fluidity captures the exact ontological idea that a being in an African community of selves can take up new forms of being or status of personhood and at the same time retain an enduring identity. Thus, the status of being and personhood are not static and unchanging. Although maintaining an enduring identity, I can over a period of time, such as a life course, be a child, an adult, an elder, an elder acting like a child, an ancestor and other forms of being. During this life course, I can at the same time be a student and a teacher, a king and yet a participant in a deliberation where such status is suspended, a healer and a patient, a wise experienced elder and yet inexperienced in several aspects of life and so on. Being able to move and navigate almost seamlessly between phases of being and status of personhood at the same time and over a given period of time, and effectively perform the expected functions in such states and phases result from two enduring but yet fluid interconnected ontological conditions: the life force that a being possesses at a given period of time, and the relational mode of being, which partly defines one's life force. Thus, my life force in my state of being human will become much stronger and active when I become an ancestor. Becoming an ancestor and earning a higher life force depend largely on my relational mode as a human in building and sustaining a community. Also, at a human level of existence, my life force will dwindle or rekindle, and my personhood will be defined based on my relationship with other beings in the community and the extent to which it allows or prevents others from thriving and flourishing. The fluidity of being, knowing and learning, therefore, is always interwoven with temporality, finitude and relationality, since to be fluid invariably means being several things at different times and/or being able to take up different forms of being at the same time, based on one's active pursuit of relationships.

A third significant implication of African communitarian philosophy is the validation of ontological difference, the idea that to be is to be different. When we claim, as does Ubuntu, that a person is a person through other persons or, that a being is a being through other beings, we are claiming that a being is never on its own sufficient and complete as the being needs other beings to be complete and attain meaning and fulfilment, since other beings like the self have something different to contribute, an ontological status, a perspective, an idea, an embodied experience and so on. The goal of relationality then is to bring into communion the multifaceted ontological differences and uniqueness to create a co-dependent community where the lack of one is complemented by the have, surplus and expertise of the other. The idea of relationality as embedded in Ubuntu philosophy is, at least in principle, the recognition that each being, human or non-human, is ontically and fluidly different and needs to collaborate and blend such different modes of being and relationality together for the flourishing of communities. Ontological difference, understood in the sense just described, challenges the disembodiment and de-positionality of subjective intellectuality that presents the intellect as a tool that produces the same results and conclusions for everyone following the same logical process. Ontological difference acknowledges that because of our different ontological and embodied make-up and constructed realities as well as differences in our positionality of thought, how we think and learn about the same experience may differ, and that there is strength in such difference, such as reaching a more robust perspective. For example, as a person with albinism, my intellectualization of the human experience of the sun may be quite different from a typical Briton's ecstatic cognition of it, say, during British summer, even though we occupy the same place, London. As a person with albinism, my thinking of how to understand the rise in temperature and ultraviolet radiation during summer will revolve around fear of, and distancing myself from, the sun. But the typical Briton's understanding will revolve around euphoria and an embracing encounter with the sun. Clearly, our allegedly subjective intellectuality of the sun is fundamentally defined by our embodied experiences of it – the severe health-threatening implications for me as a person with albinism and the increased joy of association, summer dressing and a bit of tanning for the typical Briton. But the beauty of this difference is that in taking intersubjectivity and embodiment seriously in cognition, our interpretation of the sun is richer and more detailed.

Having examined and explicated these three key features of Afro-communitarianism, I turn now to examine some real implications they could have for philosophy (and indeed the humanities) today if we take them seriously.

Collaborative Research and Pedagogies

The current research and pedagogical realities that dominate mainstream academic philosophy today, fit, of course, very nicely into the subjective intellectuality framework we have examined above, including how that translates to individual authorship and the prioritization of textuality. The dominant academic research output remains texts, originality and novelty of a philosopher's ideas are individualized, and dominant student assessments remain written assessments. Again, we have discussed already how what is threatened in our age of transhuman, trans-textual realities and possibilities is not so much the very acts of knowing and learning – these continually unfold and can be achieved in several ways – but human subjective intellectuality in doing so, which the transhuman age promises to be good at and to get better at without recourse to the human. Gaining, learning and teaching the expertise to script philosophy is important. It is a fundamental, aesthetic and curating skill that requires painstaking and dedicated practice to develop, and as we have been discussing, because subjective embodiment and positionality feeds into knowledge production, including in textual forms – features that are largely lacking in transhuman technologies – transhumanity may never succeed in completely detaching the human from the knowledge production in textual forms. The challenge, I believe, is not so much in the importance of scripting or, more broadly, subjective intellectuality, but in the privileging of it over intersubjective intellectuality. Although subjective intellectuality and textuality no doubt have their place in philosophy, what Afro-communitarianism and its method of collaborative philosophy (with its key features of relationality, fluidity and difference) bring to our attention is the need to equally value the collaborative nature of philosophizing and to consciously train ourselves and our students not just as individual thinkers but as collaborators. Relationality, fluidity and difference provide useful insights on how to do so.

Relationality as discussed above reminds us in part not simply of the ontological reality that we are beings-with-others, but more significantly that we are beings that must form, pursue and sustain active relationships with others. Today, there is a growing awareness in academic philosophy of traditions of philosophy other than the Western tradition, which has dominated the discipline since the Enlightenment period. In line with relationality, the awareness is, on its own, not sufficient. We must actively pursue building relationships among philosophical traditions by exploring all the multifaceted layers of possible relationships, such as exploring how different philosophical traditions respond to shared thematic concerns in philosophy, recognizing and drawing resource from the variety of textual and non-textual repositories of philosophy in different traditions, and utilizing both written, oral and creative assessments to help learners not to simply be skilled subjective scripting intellectuals but skilled in creative ways as well. If we are to take seriously the idea behind the dictum 'a person is a person through other persons' and the implied dictum 'I am because we are', then academic philosophical practices would acknowledge and foreground among others that philosophy in the true sense of a global human enquiry is philosophy through the collaboration of the many traditions of philosophy, and that a philosopher becomes a philosopher through other philosophers. These assertions, particularly the latter, bring back to mind the imperative of co-creative spaces of production and output akin to the palaver deliberative spaces we explored above. Relationality encourages us to weave into our pedagogical and research practices as well as open up more dialogical and conversational spaces and forums for promoting knowing and learning in ways that are collective and shared. African communitarian philosophy thus provides the tools to rethink assessments and research outputs, for example, as it encourages co-creative, team-produced outputs that are either textual or non-textual.

The idea of fluidity is also relevant in reimagining research and pedagogies in ways that are collaborative. Fluidity acknowledges that a philosopher is always at the same time a learner and a knower, a teacher and a student, a knowledge producer and a discerner. It instils humility into the learning and knowing process. There are many times I have worked in a class teaching students, and I leave the classroom much more enlightened than I entered, struck with new ideas and perspectives that form the foundation for new research, or question the convictions I had before walking into that classroom. In essence, I am not merely a teacher as I walked into that space of learning, but a learner, and my students have collaboratively instructed me while at the same time learning from me. By implication, then, fluidity as a fundamental ingredient of collaborative philosophy disrupts educational and epistemic hierarchies. This fluid nature of instructing and learning is what often fascinates me about the Socratic method. Socrates often entered into a dialogue with the conviction that he was not the knower but the one who purges out what is known by the interlocutors. More so, his visit and consultation of the oracle of Delphi indicate his recognition of the non-human dimension of wisdom. In a sense, everyone already knows something, and everyone needs to learn something. Beyond disrupting educational and epistemic hierarchies, the idea of fluidity also disrupts linearity and rigidity in philosophy. A key point to draw from fluidity is that how we philosophize, how we know, learn and understand philosophy, is significantly impacted by our individual will, energy, commitment and force as well as the force and energies of the communities we interact with. They are not shaped solely by our subjective intellectual capabilities but also importantly by active and evolving commitments and relationships, re-emphasizing the relevance of embodiment and positionality. These forces, energies and relationships are obviously not with the human alone but also with the non-human – the tree, the atmosphere, energies from past generations, our pets and so on – and these also have epistemic competence that we can rely on.

The principle of difference encourages us to acknowledge and include different philosophical perspectives. It recognizes how varied embodiment, corporeality and positionality nourish the intellect, producing varied perspectives and reasoning. Difference as a principle of relationality acknowledges and prioritizes the corporeality of thought and the geography of reason. Taking difference seriously has immediate implications for research and pedagogical practices. These include taking seriously the need to draw on the resources from different traditions on thematic and disciplinary matters, and being keen to provide learners, which, in line with the fluid nature of learning, includes ourselves, with diverse philosophical perspectives that cut across bodies and places. This comes out quite nicely when we, for example, discussed the concept of truth in Chapter two from a variety of perspectives. More so, the principle of difference takes seriously the capabilities of learners and knowers as well as the different avenues and platforms of learning. Strategies for learning and knowing philosophy, as well as strategies for philosophizing for the one may not be quite what works for the other. And as a humble learner who understands and works within the fluid and relational nature of being, knowing and acting, each one would work within his or her capacity as learners and knowers. Such epistemic differences again validate collaboration since when the one collaborates with the other, they bring on board their strengths and their weaknesses, producing richer, more robust and more reliable perspectives. The recognition of difference in the capability of learners and knowers is, perhaps, why African traditions have embedded within them a philosophy for children. African philosophy for children employs humour-filled storytelling, epics, songs and simple riddles to engage children with philosophical issues, such as moral truths and epistemic claims, while reserving complex parables, proverbs, riddles and adages for adults and the elderly. Difference therefore calls our attention to the need to avoid the god's eye perspectives and approaches in doing philosophy, valuing the diversity in our global philosophical heritage.

On Polemics and Enigmatics

Some points need to be made, I believe, about dominant attitudinal dispositions in the doing of philosophy and in the production and revision of thought, and how such attitudinal dispositions shape the thought produced. The intellectual, including the philosophical tradition of the West, has dominantly been shaped by a polemical attitudinal disposition. Polemics as a way of producing thought is argumentation characterized often by hostile dissent, contentious rhetoric and a strong, quite emotional defence of one's perspective against opposing perspectives, done in ways that are meant to radically undermine such opposing viewpoints. Philosophical debates and argumentation thrive on polemics. It is a foundational pillar of deliberative practices and although defensive, aggressive and hostile in disposition, provides fertile ground for the obligation to clarify and defend positions and ideologies and aggressively challenge dominant narratives. As Serge Moscovici (1979: 55) puts it, 'Polemics is the supreme method in the sciences. It is easy to understand why. Explaining the nature of things, and being right in the world of ideas, those are the sole foundations of any discovery. Without the first one, there is no knowledge; without the second, no researcher will be obstinate enough to go on when, indifferent to his questions, reality keeps its answers in abeyance, and scientific opinion, remaining blind and deaf to evidence, invites him to give up with legitimate and well-formed arguments, so he will doubt his own senses and his own thinking.' Thus, the value of polemics lies in its usefulness for the subject to validate and legitimate his or her intellectuality. The rage must continue until my voice is heard and my point taken. Dissent, aggressiveness and hostility are good as they keep the deliberation going, assert identities and perspectives, and help the producer of thought to maintain ruggedness and rigidity. Philosophical polemics in particular serve not only to challenge specific thinkers but also to sharpen the contours of philosophical problems and delineate new intellectual pathways. From Plato's critique of the Sophists (in the Protagoras and Gorgias, for example), Descartes's hostility toward the Scholastics and Marx's polemical attack on the young Hegelians, polemics is replete in Western philosophy. Perhaps, this work itself is in many ways a polemical one, although I may not be the best judge of this as to whether it is radical and hostile enough to fit into this genre of thought.

In the more dominant sub-Saharan African attitudinal disposition to collaborative thought production and revision, I encounter an outlook quite different from polemics, one I believe is best captured with the concept of enigmatics. To have an enigmatic disposition as an individual or a group in the process of philosophizing involves at least two things: First, it involves entering into the performance of philosophy, knowing from the onset that the thematic concerns of philosophy are in themselves difficult to understand, explicate or interpret. If you recall, one of the examples on the philosophy of existence that I drew from my heritage (the Esan tradition) in Chapter two is the concept '*Aigunyibhin*', which translates as 'no one masters or can fully comprehend existence'. Existence, then, is an enigmatic for philosophers, the same way being, knowing, identity, the mind, destiny, freedom and other themes are. The end goal of such epistemic awareness is not to deter philosophizing but to keep in mind that the performance of philosophy does not result in infallible, sacrosanct, and absolute answers and clarity, but may actually produce thoughts that are curated in ways that repeatedly demand more clarity and hence, more deliberation. Philosophy in this sense is essentially submerged in a fluid aura of mystery, confusion, difficulty, vagueness and suspicion, always demanding clarity, aptness, and improvement of interpretation and understanding. Second, the enigmatics of philosophy, particularly as I can discern from African contexts, also consists of skilfully and tactfully curating current interpretations and understandings in ways and forms that are complex, obscure and cryptic but yet alluring, aesthetically appealing and even comic. If you have ever been in a public sphere in an indigenous African community where deliberations are going on about religious, political or philosophical matters, it would be one of the most elating, humorous and enlightening moments of your life. The exchange of riddles, parables, proverbs and the like, accompanied by interpretations, possible interpretations and critiques of interpretations, as well as the accompanying short stories, rites, songs, formulations of new cryptic lines and artistic performances, all taking place at the same within an atmosphere that pendulously and seamlessly swings between seriousness and laughter, presents not a polemic disposition but an enigmatic one. It seems to me, then, that it is the enigmatic nature of deliberative practices and spaces (as discussed above) observed by non-indigenous researchers in African communities that necessitated the conceptualization of such spaces and practices as palaver, literally meaning an unnecessarily elaborate, unduly complicated and even unproductive procedure. Admittedly, for a foreigner in the land who lacked knowledge of the contents and meanings of enigmatic sayings, and whose attitude was fundamentally to polemically defend strongly held truths, such deliberative spaces would be unproductive and unnecessarily elaborate and complex. In the words of Fidèle Ingiyimbere (2024: 288):

> While widespread all over Africa, the name palaver used to have a negative connotation. The word palaver is from the Spanish word Palabra and was used to pejoratively designate the African gatherings in specific place to discuss matters of ultimate importance for the community. As they usually take a long time, the first Spanish who witnessed them dubbed them a palaver to mean interminable discussions with idle ends. Even today in some languages, such as French, palabra carries that negative connotation of long and idle discussions without practical outcome. Yet, many scholars . . . recognize

that the practice was important for deciding the destiny of the community and constituted a public forum for debating and exchanging on important matters [pertaining] to the public good. Moreover, if the word palaver evokes those negative connotations, it is not the case when used in African languages.

Thus, the foreigner required a healthy dose of intellectual humility, openness and humble learning to access this new way of thinking together and deliberating. Consensus, agreement and producing new knowledge were not always the goal in enigmatic philosophy. In some cases, edification and building relationships were sufficient. And it is because of the complex and multifaceted forms of knowledge woven into an enigmatic discourse, what I consider a better phrasing than palaver, that allows for the much-needed collaboration to happen. An individual could not possibly introduce all of the knowledge forms into the deliberative space. It requires participation from many, and the more participants in a discourse, the richer the deliberation becomes, not just in its enigmatic essence but in its edifying and meaning-producing nature.

Polemics and enigmatics are both relevant for the performance of philosophy. In reality, philosophizing in enigmatic ways would always include some hints of polemics. The blending of both, I believe, is crucial and imperative if we are to develop a collaborative spirit in philosophy and embrace more fully, inclusive and humble ways of knowing and learning in research and pedagogies. For example, polemics stirs up conflict (Amossy 2021), and the enigmatics of deliberation are often geared toward strengthening bonds and forging reconciliation. The one is needed just as much as the other.

We have attempted in this chapter to explore a more in-depth and detailed analysis of the sort of methodological commitments that permeate and emerge from the doing of philosophy in African traditions. African philosophy is rich in intersubjective intellectuality and collaborative practices, which can be harnessed in the evolution of the global tradition of philosophy to complement the dominant disposition toward subjective individuality and independence of thought. As we have seen, the intersubjective and collaborative methodological disposition is heavily felt in the enigma of deliberative practices in public spheres of discourse and learning, which again complements and provides a fine balance to the polemics of thought. Beyond the constructed thick borders of academic philosophy, the methodological commitments examined above are imperative for broader spaces of learning and the curating of thought into always unfinished forms of knowledge, particularly in a postcolonial and transhuman age where collaborative, inclusive practices, and the acknowledgement of fluidity and differences in learning and knowing are paramount. What is perhaps interesting and fundamental to keep in mind here is the shift from a politically and legally motivated clamour for collaboration, inclusivity and recognition of diversity in formal settings of learning and research today, to achieving these by zooming our gaze on a more primoradial ontological necessity and the implied moral obligation to do so that African communitarian philosophy offers (Imafidon 2014). It is in the very nature of our being, human or non-human, our onticness, to be in and pursue relationships, which implies acting toward this nature by building communities. The self-fulfilment, self-identity, meaningful existence and flourishing of a being (either as entity or process) fundamentally depends on this ontic and epistemic awareness and the resultant moral action of communing and relating. Doing and promoting inclusivity, collaboration and diversity today cannot be sufficiently attained by following rules and learning guidelines but by re-centring our very ontological selves, our deeply seated ontic ways of being, knowing, learning and acting (Allan 2003).

The foregoing provides access to understanding the telos of why the methodological dispositions in African philosophy are crafted and shaped the way they are. The methods themselves guarantee the foregrounding, building and sustenance of community as well as the edification of the self who participates in the collective, fulfilling individual personhood and meaningfulness. There is a fundamental blueprint here, I believe, for thinking about the heated and valid debates today on the telos of pedagogical and research designs in neoliberal, capitalist societies. On the one hand, the knowledge as capital model that has been quite successfully pushed by capitalist neoliberal systems emphasizes that pedagogical and research designs should prioritize economic realities, practical skills for surviving economic realities, alignment with funding models and global competitions of knowing and learning. This, for example, explains the student debt and STEM priority funding models where knowing and learning are investments now for guaranteed materiality in the future. These, of course, have serious implications for academia. 'Recent studies have shown how capitalist reforms have strengthened functional hierarchy, centralized power and increased the unequal distribution of resources at universities ... Researchers have also investigated how academic excellence, competition, and performance measurement systems have not only negatively affected academic freedom and autonomy but also academics via bullying, stress, loss of meaning or precarious work conditions (Jensen and Zawadzki 2024: 1215).' On the other hand, many academics have legitimately argued for and defended the imperative of research and pedagogical designs that sustain the pursuit of truth and knowledge for its own sake and the intrinsic value of knowledge and wisdom rather than for materiality. In philosophy circles, for example, this would mean prioritizing philosophical theory and learning in ways that intrinsically value abstract thought with no immediate worry about practice or materiality. African communitarian philosophy, with its methodological dispositions, it seems to me, provides a framework to reimagine a fine balance between both sides of the debate, one that is both validating and critical of the different perspectives. To put it briefly, as I do not intend to substantiate this exercise of reimagination here, to know and to learn have the intrinsic value of edifying and enlightening the self, but also the extrinsic and relational value of building communities. To be sure, building communities is not synonymous with feeding neoliberal and capitalist expectations and might very well be a critique of such. Similarly, edifying and enlightening the self is not done by widening gaps between the knower or learner and the community but by building bridges. It follows then that the ultimate telos of research and pedagogical practices must be framed around the confluence of theory and practice. What is theory and what is practice in this sense would always remain fluid, varied and nourished by embodied and positioned experiences, and would need fleshing out in specific contexts of learning and knowing. African methodological commitments provide the framework to reimagine the theory-practice relationship in academic spaces.

6

Contemporaneities and Futures: On Street Philosophy

As I began and continued in the preceding pages, this intellectual, embodied and positioned journey of curating the doing of African philosophy, I have never forgotten at any point of this process of scripting that you, dear reader, have been an integral part of this journey. I have often written as if in a live conversation with friends genuinely interested in the questions and discourses that I have engaged with. More so, while I deploy my subjectivity in this scripting process, I am certainly aware that the writing process is still very much an intersubjective and collaborative one, since it comes into being fundamentally on the basis that one scripts this way because of the potential to be read, and in achieving this scripting, the author draws in several ways from the understanding and knowledges of others. If not anything else, it is this awareness of the intersubjective and collaborative nature of interpreting, understanding and knowledge production that is foregrounded in African philosophical practices and has consistently been emphasized throughout the pages of this book. As it was made quite clear early on in this book, doing philosophy is not synonymous with the features of textuality and individual authorship. Although these are important, for example, in crafting this book, it is imperative that we do not, on the basis of them, take for granted intersubjectivity, collective authorship and the collaborative spirit behind the production, refining and flourishing of philosophy. Our discussions and explorations of the orality, symbolism, textuality and trans-textual possibilities of African philosophy make abundantly clear how, in African contexts, indigenous (largely non-textual) philosophical practices and the more contemporary (textual) academic philosophical practices, in many ways shaped by the colonial/post-colonial experience, rely heavily on the intersubjective and collaborative spirit of philosophizing. As examined in Chapter four, the curation of a heavily textual repository of African philosophy in recent times, while partly connected with the demands of the whitening of non-Western philosophical traditions, is still not achievable if done in isolation from the non-textual, collectively shared and preserved repositories of philosophy of African peoples. African philosophers today rely heavily on such non-textual, collectively authored repositories in curating a textual heritage. But one must take this last point with caution to ensure that the contemporary curation of a largely textual heritage does not distract us or suffocate the many ways in which the non-textual and collective approach to doing philosophy continues to flourish in the contemporary as well as the futuristic possibilities that are on the horizon. It is in this sense that I speak about contemporaneities and futures where the former signals the sustenance of collective authorship and non-textuality/disruptive textuality in contemporary times, simultaneously with the craze for texts in academic spaces, and the latter represents the possibilities, intensely collaborative, that lie ahead of us. A vibrant example of these realities and possibilities, I believe, is what I call street philosophy.

The street has always been a vibrant, intensely rich and productive space, site and locus for social life, cohesion, action, concept-making, resistance, assimilation and creativity. Street life, street music, street art, street theatre, street food and other street-related concepts have for long been fertile resources for social and humanistic studies, such as in urban sociology, hospitality and tourism, development studies, literature and art studies. But an often ignored and underexplored street-related concept is street philosophy, which consists essentially of philosophical ideas emerging from, and collectively achieved in the street, about such matters as the understanding of existence, being, knowledge, morality, beauty, selfhood and resistance. In what ways is the street a sustained locus today of philosophical activities that dominate deliberative spaces in indigenous African communities, such as conversations, reflections, critique, deconstruction, construction of normativity, formulation of concepts and ideas about being, knowing, acting, valuing or simply existing? What intersections, if any, are there between street philosophy and academic philosophy? How might the street become a fertile ground for thinking about philosophy futures? To be sure, connections and intersections between the street and philosophy would at best be blurred if we continue to put on our star-gazing lenses in our academic skyscrapers and maintain the radical binary between academic philosophy, thought to be solely produced by the subjective intellectuality of the individuated self and the collaborative philosophy collectively achieved by and in cultures, traditions, lifeworld, communities and in this particular case, the streets. As we discussed extensively in the preceding chapter, academic philosophy construed essentially from the standpoint of subjective intellectuality not only pretends to remove academic philosophy from the situatedness, horizons and concreteness of its activities, but denies the importance of our lively communities and lived experiences for academic philosophy. In what follows, then, in this chapter, and relying heavily on the Nigerian streets that I am most familiar with, I elaborate on what I mean by street philosophy as a contemporaneity of African philosophy and examine some of its defining features, such as non-textuality and disruptive textuality, collaborative practices, the aesthetics of knowledge and the humour of deliberation. I then examine specific thematic concerns of this street philosophy, such as the existentiality of suffering and the critique of suffering, and the philosophy of migration. These would seamlessly lead to reimagining the futures of doing philosophy in Africa and beyond in ways that collapse the radical setting apart of mainstream academic philosophy from philosophy produced in unconventional academic spaces, such as in the streets or pubs.

Acknowledging Contemporaneity: Philosophy in the Streets

The streets are epistemic sites booming with ideas, concepts, debates, principles, argumentations and methods, including those we can rightly refer to as philosophical, maintaining a pursuit for the fundamental nature of things and lived experiences, a fondness for wisdom and a rigour of deliberation. Perhaps, it is we in academia who believe we no longer belong to the streets – the streets are for our academically unpolished selves – but to ivory towers that we and ones like us in the past have laboured and continue to labour to build and renovate. The streets, it seems to us, have nothing to offer us as philosophers, and letting the streets into our ivory towers will bring nothing but ruin and destruction to what we have laboured hard to build. But if we take a moment to come down from our ivory towers and gaze away from the stars into the streets, there is much we would find to learn and engage with. For example, *The Guardian* (24 December 2024) recently published a piece on street philosophy in China, focusing on the concepts of *neijuan, tangping and runxue*, which are used to express a pessimistic existentialist philosophy that represents and reflects hopelessness, meaninglessness and unhealthy competitiveness amid China's economy. *Neijuan* is the Chinese term for involution, literally meaning 'rolling inwards', to capture the reality of many young people that no matter how hard they work, progress is illusive and impossible. Young people, often called Gen Z, use this concept collaboratively to express the feeling and push the argument of existential meaninglessness that no matter how hard they work, meaning and reward is no longer guaranteed as it was for past generations. *Neijuan* thus tallies with *tangping*, which means to lie flat and choose to do nothing instead of hustling pointlessly, and *runxue*, which signals emigrating en masse to escape the meaninglessness. Chinese existentialist philosophy no doubt loses if it fails to pay close attention to these concepts emerging from, and their use in, the streets. Bearing this example in mind, there are specific features of street philosophy that are discernible and these features will be useful in conceptualizing street philosophy further and exploring its realities in Africa.

The instance of street philosophy just described is characterized by the value and power of collaboration, collective authorship and anonymity, formulation of new concepts, disruptive textuality, and the reliance on both physical and virtual spaces of deliberation. Street philosophy, the concepts it creates and its criticism of lifeworld, gains relevance because the creators and critics acknowledge and value the power of relational collaboration. Social media users, bloggers, music artists, graffiti artists and other kinds of artists and writers collaborate by drawing on their skills and expertise in curating, critiquing, constructing and deconstructing meanings. It is this power of collaboration and the ideological and existential change it can result in that Chinese leaders are worried about in relation to *neijuan*. As Amy Hawkins (2024) writes, 'Is China worried about *neijuan*? Yes. China's leaders have made it clear that they don't want the idea of *neijuan* to catch on more than it already has. In December, top economic policymakers gathered for the annual Central Economic Work Conference, which sets the national economic agenda. According to the readout of the closed-door meeting, the cadres pledged to rectify involutionary competition.' Closely linked to the collaborative nature of street philosophy, and perhaps a consequence of it, is anonymous and collective authorship. There are hardly any specifically named individuals as authors to be held responsible for the ideas and criticisms that emerge from the street. Group agency is affirmed and acknowledged in the context of street philosophy because of the elevation of intersubjective intellectuality and collective epistemic will in the doing of philosophy on the streets. Also, formulating new concepts, dictums, slogans, adages and the like to capture the nuances of human experiences in contemporary times and their fundamental ontology thrives in street philosophy. For example, concepts such as *runxue* in China and Sapa and Japa in Nigeria are effective in defining the ontology of global migration in contemporary times. More so, disruptive textuality thrives in the context of street philosophy. By disruptive textuality, I mean scripting and writing in ways that are radically different and have the possibility of interrupting, questioning, challenging, and even undermining conventional ways of scripting and writing. Disruptive textuality in street philosophy is defined by the nature of the text, where it is done and how it is done. Street writing and scripting can vary from short to long, anonymous to named, done virtually or on disruptive materials, such as tattooing on the body, or graffiti on walls, and cares less about formal rules of editing and publishing. But it remains effective in wielding political power and changing or revising meanings and narratives.

Although these features of street philosophy examined above are representative of the African experience as well, as we will discern shortly from the analysis of different facets of street philosophy in Nigerian communities, it seems to me that there are certain other defining features peculiar to the African contexts, features that have deep roots in indigeneity. Of particular interest and fascination to me are the heavy presence of humour, the sustenance of collaborative practices and the crafting of non-textuals in collaboration with the textual. It is fascinating and interesting to see how humour is effectively deployed to express matters of serious concern and engage in serious debates and deliberations in the Nigerian physical and digital streets. For when Nigerians use the word 'street', it goes beyond a geography or physical space to include attitudinal dispositions and shared solidarity that transcends the borders of a physical street to cross-border and digital spaces. You only need a little familiarity with Nigerian-made skits on social media, curated concepts and phrases in the Nigerian streets, to witness, for example, how the existentiality of suffering, moral dilemmas, discourses of migration, sexuality and education are heavily dosed with humour and laughter, signifying the enigmatic rather than polemic nature of the debates and issues. Street methods of philosophizing can in themselves be therapeutic and relieving rather than fuelling more intense feelings of hopelessness and meaninglessness. Street philosophy also effectively sustains existing deliberative spaces and develops new ones. If you spend some time quite regularly in a Nigerian pub, often called a beer parlour, you will soon find that you are immersed in a richly flavoured atmosphere of discourse and deliberation laced with laughter, jokes, arguments, fights, dancing, drinking and eating but yet with edification, understanding and interpretation. You would find the same in many other public spheres, such as marriages, funerals, naming ceremonies, and other parties and gatherings, as well as the sort of fluid gatherings with no fixed or stable interlocutors that happen at car parks, auto-repair shops, barbing saloons, market places and inside a public transport service. Of course, deliberative spaces and deliberative practices now transcend physical borders because of the availability of digital or virtual communities. Arguments and concepts emerging from these spaces and practices of deliberation feed directly into curating and crafting non-textual forms of knowledge, such as music, enigmatic sayings and films. Afrobeats, for example, is not only globally popular but is also an epistemic route into the street philosophies of African peoples. Afrobeats artists themselves acknowledge that they are made by the street and are repping the streets (Jatt, 2Face and Mode 9, 2011), and recognize the effectiveness of using music and art to posit street philosophy (Chike and Mohbad 2023). Chike and Mohbad, for example, sing about how (unlike books which you would require institutional access to) one has minimal choice as to the kind or content of music you listen to on the streets: 'Street orientation . . . Music does not require your permission to access your spirit; Anywhere you are, you will feel it' (translation from Nigerian Pidgin English is mine). To be sure, as you sell in the market, for example, and you here the blasting of music, which you do not choose, you feel the vibes and get the message. Afrobeats artists do not thus see themselves as vehicles for conveying street philosophy, but as equal, in fact, prominent participants in the streets, either popularizing concepts from the streets or crafting new ones.

Thus, street philosophy as a postcolonial site of collective authorship resembles in many ways the indigenous philosophical systems of African peoples we have been engaging with, and thus represents a contemporaneity of African philosophy. It sustains relationality, fluidity, collaborations, enigmatics, humour and deliberative practices that have been at, and remain in the heart of, indigenous African philosophy. It is a fertile ground for philosophical deliberations that academic African philosophers must take seriously. The sections that follow flesh out some specifics of street philosophy and its relevance for the present and future of African philosophy.

Japa, Sapa and the Philosophy of Migration

Migration is a highly debated topic today, perhaps because of growing increases in global migration indices. These debates have resulted in several social scientific theories on why migration, particularly international migration, happens. These theories include the gravity theory, the functionalist theory, the economic theory, the political theory, classical immigration theory, push and pull theory, and the human rights theory (Massey, et. al. 1993; Miller and Castles 1993; Haas 2021). For example, the functionalist theory describes migration as a positive phenomenon leading to prosperity, equality and productivity through bidirectional flow of resources, raising the question of whether there is always a bidirectional or even multi-directional flow when migration happens and failing to account for the politics of migration. The human rights theory sees migration as a fundamental human right, against the exclusionary 'blood and soil' perspective, but often proceeds on the basis of taken-for-granted assumptions as to who is human and who defines rights. The push and pull theory simply explains how push factors encourage people to leave a place, while pull factors encourage people to come to a place, but the push and pull factors are complex and complicated and would encompass a variety of factors. More broadly speaking, however, philosophical analysis of migration is rare. A philosophy of migration, it seems to me, would raise and ask fundamental questions about the very essence of migration, such as the ontological underpinnings, the epistemological framework, the ethical (axiological/aesthetic) principles and implications, and the logic of migration, say, within the context of power and identity. In philosophizing about immigration, I would, for instance, be interested in such questions as: How does migration come into being? What is the ontology of a here, a home, a place? What calls one's place into question, resulting in the yearning to be out-of-place and to occupy a different place? If the idea of being human is intrinsically interwoven with the idea of the earth as ontically a human place, what then is the logic and validity of the idea of a foreigner or the legitimacy of the idea of strangeness? How is a home made, sustained and disrupted, or what makes and disrupts one's home? What is the rationality, irrationality and embodiment of movement? To be sure, these are important questions, and the intellectual and embodied philosophical traditions can provide interesting perspectives to nourish our understanding of the concept of migration. In this section, I pay particular attention to what concepts forged in the Nigerian streets tell us about the existential ontology of migration.

The concept that has been curated in the Nigerian streets to express the essence of international migration or outmigration of Nigerians from Nigeria is Japa. Japa is a street-curated concept because although the word has Yoruba origins, what it connotes is primarily shaped by its use in the Nigerian street. As Okunade and Awosusi (2023: 2) explain it:

> Japa is a novel term used by Nigerians to describe the outmigration trend of Nigerians into Europe and other parts of the world. At a recent Youths in Business Forum, a French Ambassador curiously quizzed one of the Nigerian youths to understand the context and meaning of Japa, as popularly used in the country. In response, Peter Dingba, a Nigerian youth, averred that it is 'a word that describes the entrepreneurial spirit of Nigerians; in that same word, it means that Nigerians want to export their contents, gifts, skills, and products, including themselves'. This goes to say that Japa is a 'self-exportation' of Nigerians abroad . . . Japa means 'fleeing' beyond the shores of Nigeria. That is, deploying any migration strategy (regular or irregular) to escape from Nigeria's territory to other parts of the world. Although novel in literature, Japa is not a new development in Nigeria. As a concept, it explains not only the exodus of Nigerians through its international air borders (a phenomenon that attracted the terminology), but also the age-long practice of irregular migration, which seems to be ignored by the people and the concerned local actors.

Adegoke (2023: 4) adds rightly and aptly that:

> Japa is an urban Yoruba slang used mainly by young Nigerians to describe the recent emigration trends and patterns by those within that demographic category. It conatively means 'to quickly flee a

difficult situation', an apt depiction of the attitude of most Nigerians toward perceived bleak socioeconomic uncertainties prevalent in the country. The word itself is an informal expression used mainly by young people from the southwestern states of Nigeria. Japa is popular among millennials and post-millennials. It is a new form of migration distinct from the old patterns. In the past, Nigerian youths have been known to brave perilous terrains (e.g., deserts and oceans) to travel to Europe in search of better opportunities in the global north. Most of these were artisans, low-skilled young people on a quest for survival with a pocket of a few educated migrants, some of whom take the legal routes ... The Japa migration cohort is not limited to aspirational youths; it also consists of middle-aged adults who want to avoid the uncertainty of life ...

Thus, Japa in itself is an existentialist philosophy in many ways similar to the Chinese concept of *runxue* that we briefly examined above. To run swiftly as connoted by Japa implies an existentialist ontology that is characteristically defined by causality, agency, action, angst, anxiety, desperation and dread. In this sense, it implies a philosophy of a place, the sensing of danger, of hopelessness, of temporality and indeed of nothingness. Japa is a manifestation of the prevailing desperation to depart from Nigeria, a flight for survival. Japa as some Nigerian youths have described it, does not mean to migrate; it means to run for your life; it means relinquishing one's struggles and fleeing from overwhelming circumstances, a feeling of 'I'm done. I'm not doing this anymore. I am running away. I can't cope'. In this sense, it is fleeing that is important – the destination is secondary (Nwobodo 2024). Notwithstanding the nihilistic and pessimistic connotations of the concept, Japa also represents a projection, authenticity and finite transcendence in its immersion in a futuristic hope of becoming something from the state of, and other than, nothingness. Thus, what stands as the substratum of Japa and brings it into being is the existentiality and ample reality of suffering and the lack of opportunities for self-fulfillment, connoted with a similar street curated concept, *Sapa*. *Sapa* is used to connote situations of extreme material poverty, brokenness and hopelessness. I am often fascinated with the play with words in the streets to express the degree of *Sapa*, where as always, the street draws concepts from all facets of the post colony. *Sapa* Pro Max, borrows concepts from the Apple Company to indicate the severity of the poverty or hopelessness of someone, which then necessitates the pursuit of Japa or the embrace of hopelessness and the meaninglessness of life. In resorting to Japa, there are obvious epistemic assumptions about the destination that one emigrates to. Those who Japa seem to be convinced that where they flee to will be better than where they flee from. The deliberation and collective analysis of Japa in the streets, in forms including music, skits, discussions in physical and virtual spaces, and stand-up comedy are often meant to show that individuals who Japa are not often epistemically aware of their target destination and this results in *Yawa*, another Street/Yoruba concept meaning trouble, disaster or problem. Thus, those who Japa end up struggling even more to settle in and survive in their new locales and continue in some way to struggle with anxiety, depression and loss of meaning. Thus, the philosophy of migration as encapsulated in the concepts of Japa, *Sapa* and *Yawa* examines the existentiality of suffering that necessitates migration and remains with migrants, a situation where what used to be home does not feel like home and what is now home still emits strangeness and inhospitality. It reminds us of how migrants are often left unstable and unsettled.

'*School na Scam*': Critiquing Education

A popular dictum collectively curated in the Nigerian streets is '*School na scam*', a Nigerian Pidgin English way of saying: 'Education is fraud.' Here, there is a specific kind of education in mind, the formal Western education system, particularly university/tertiary education rather than, say, basic, technical and vocational education, or indigenous knowledge acquisition. Nigerian youths employ this dictum to express their frustration with the higher education system and its failure to guarantee a better and meaningful life, even though it requires a huge investment of time and money. To be sure, this is quite a shared feeling across the globe where higher education students feel they invest a lot of time and money to acquire degrees and knowledge but often end up without employment, struggling for a meaningful life. In a sense, there is little or no return for investing in higher education. Oliseneku and Jike (2023: 147) explain this dictum thus:

> The ... phrase captures the mindsets of many youths in Nigeria who see formal education as a wasted venture. As far as they are concerned, Nigerian schools are teaching things students may never need or use in life ... Unfortunately, the society keeps telling young people that the road to success in life lies in school, when they can actually see that most of their peers doing well early in life are school dropouts. And the ones that the society idolises do not even have degrees ... To them, people spend so many years in school and still come out to do things that do not really require any form of academic rigour to handle. For example, we have instances of graduates ending up as fashion designers, photographers, event planners, etc. That reflects sheer waste of time as these ones could have invested their energy in these vocations rather than waste their time studying what is not really relevant to their lives ... the lapses evident in education systems in Nigeria has to do with gaps in knowledge impartation that incorporate technical skill acquisition and human capacity development ... Their inability to find a job in government or private parastatals that require their services, make them almost jobless or non-functional. This situation has given room to many of them venturing into all manner of activities that are criminal in character.

The critique of higher education encapsulated in the dictum '*School na scam*' implies a number of arguments and questions that the collective producers of this knowledge, the Nigerian youths, have about higher education systems. What is the essence of education? How do neoliberal and capitalist systems shape the perception of education? To what extent are African education systems decolonized? To what extent is a capitalist-driven materialist ontology shaping the interpretation and understanding of education?

Concerning the essence of education, there has been a protracted debate as to how and why formal education systems, specifically in this case, higher education systems, come into being. Education broadly construed as ways of learning, teaching, instructing and enlightening is primordially ontic. However, carefully structured, systematic and organized systems of education, such as higher education systems, are fundamentally shaped and constructed by ideological commitments, power and tradition. Major theories in the philosophy of education offer differing but interrelated views on the fundamental essence of systematic education, often centring on the development of the individual and their relation to society. Essentialism, for example, holds that the essence of education is the transmission of core knowledge and cultural values necessary for responsible citizenship and intellectual competence. Progressivism, influenced by John Dewey, asserts that education should be student-centred, experiential, and aimed at cultivating critical thinking and problem-solving skills, where learning is a dynamic interaction with the environment. More recently, critical pedagogy, particularly as shaped by Paulo Freire (1970), understands education as a transformative act that challenges oppressive structures and empowers learners to become agents of social change. The essence of education, often conveyed in existing theories, then, emphasizes the need for education not to simply be about transmitting information but also about a profound process of human formation that shapes the person intellectually, morally, culturally and socially, and equips the person with critical skills and survival skills. The dictum '*School na scam*', it seems to me, is the collective expression of how knowledge for its own sake dominates higher education systems in Nigeria and consequently, the expression of the frustration that the knowledge pursued is irrelevant or not immediately and contextually relevant for the formation, transformation and survival of the self.

Also, the dictum has a strong neoliberal and capitalist foundation, aspects of which we examined in the preceding chapter. The frustration expressed in it emerges from the student experience in higher education today, which is fundamentally shaped by the intersecting forces of neoliberalism and capitalism, where education is presented as foremostly a market-driven investment rather than the edifying and critical development of the student. Under neoliberal ideology, higher education is commodified and marketed as a pathway to personal economic success, positioning students as consumers who are expected to make rational choices that will yield profitable returns in the form of secure employment, upward mobility and a meaningful life. This instrumentalist view reduces the value of education to its economic utility, marginalizing its critical, civic and emancipatory possibilities. In current capitalist economies characterized by precarious labour markets, wage stagnation and increasing automation, many graduates find themselves underemployed, burdened by debt and disillusioned by the unfulfilled promises of the educational system. The resulting frustration that education is a fraud stems not only from material disappointment but also from a sense of existential betrayal, as the narrative of education as a guarantor of future prosperity fails to align with the lived experiences of many graduates. This disjuncture and paradox underscore the need to critically interrogate the ideological assumptions underpinning contemporary education systems and to reimagine education beyond the logic of profit and market efficiency.

Again, 'School na scam' exposes the persistent coloniality of education in postcolonial African societies, where education is still fundamentally defined by leftover colonial structures and there are often far-fetched connections between what is taught and being enlightened about the lived experiences in African contexts. Despite political independence, many postcolonial African societies have inherited educational models designed to serve colonial administrative needs rather than to foster critical engagement with local realities. Curricula often prioritize Western knowledge systems, languages and values, marginalizing indigenous knowledge, African philosophical traditions and contextually relevant problem-solving approaches. As a result, there exists a troubling disconnect between what is taught in universities and the socio-cultural, economic and political realities faced by African populations. This epistemic dissonance limits the capacity of higher education to generate transformative knowledge that speaks to the continent's complex histories and contemporary challenges. Scholars have increasingly called for the decolonization of education, a reorientation that involves not only revising curricular content but also challenging the underlying assumptions about what constitutes valid knowledge, whose voices are heard, and how learning can meaningfully contribute to African self-understanding and development (wa Thiong'o 1986; Knaus, Mino and Seroto 2022; Uetela 2023). I received my education in philosophy (BA, MA and PhD) in Nigeria. The philosophy curriculum was and still remains fundamentally entwined with the curriculum inherited from Britain during colonization, and very little has changed. For example, the four-year undergraduate programme is primarily devoted to studying ancient Greek philosophy (first year), medieval philosophy (second year), early modern European philosophy (third year) and late modern/contemporary European philosophy (fourth year). It took a deep sense of rebellion and resistance to shift my attention from this dominantly Eurocentric understanding of philosophy to searching for an African understanding of philosophical themes and issues. Such rebellion and resistance were necessitated, I believe, by the hermeneutic void left from having a comprehensive understanding of European philosophy but yet struggling to make sense of how that knowledge translates to and fits within the realities of African peoples. Thus, the feeling of frustration because of the coloniality of knowledge and education in African places is real and could be checked through a commitment to decolonization, and there is still much to be done in this regard.

The widespread perception among Nigerian youths that education is a fraud, captured in the popular dictum 'School na scam', is also deeply rooted in a materialist ontology that increasingly defines social value and personal worth through materiality, consumerism and the showcasing of material wealth. In contemporary Nigeria, the criteria for a meaningful existence are often tethered to visible signs of wealth, such as luxurious homes and automobiles, the latest technological gadgets and designer fashion. The inability of many graduates to acquire these goods, despite having completed higher education and attained formal qualifications, fosters a profound sense of disillusionment with the educational system. This disaffection is further intensified by the observable reality that those who are visibly affluent and socially celebrated often lack formal higher education credentials, which undermines the narrative that education is the primary pathway to success. Multiple facets of the streets, such as Afrobeat music, popular art, everyday street discourse and political life, are actively deployed to reinforce this materialist existential ontology, embedding it within the collective consciousness and normalizing the equation of success with consumption. Even individuals who attain stable, respectable jobs through higher education experience pressure to acquire more conspicuous material assets to validate their social standing and existential fulfilment. This way of being is intrinsically linked to the broader neoliberal capitalist framework, which promotes competition, consumerism and individual achievement as the ultimate indicators of success, thereby relegating the intrinsic and social values of education to the margins. Perhaps the challenge of materiality in relation to higher education is primarily caused by the neoliberal and capitalist framing of higher education as guaranteeing material success. Higher education institutions present this problematic narrative of themselves in order to attract learners and sustain the business model of education, knowing fully well that the edification, enlightenment and instructions derived from them may not directly or immediately translate to, and is perhaps not intended in the first place to directly translate to, material success.

From the foregoing, we can therefore conclude that the collaborative, quite anonymous and collectively owned crafting and curating of relevant philosophical concepts to capture the essence of lived experiences that have dominated African philosophy has been sustained in contemporary times. Street philosophy is a sterling example of the contemporaneity of African philosophy that requires more attention, particularly from academic philosophers, considering what could be gleaned from it in terms of concepts, debates and practices.

Reimagining Futures

This text has been developed around the central theme of the doing of African philosophy, how philosophical enquiries have been performed, curated, preserved and transmitted in a longstanding and enduring African tradition. Core defining features of African philosophy and its rich and enduring tradition and heritage that we have examined include the equal and complementary relevance of textual and non-textual processes and repositories, intersubjective, ecocentric and embodied intellectuality, enigmatic sayings and attitudinal disposition, deliberative processes and practices, epistemic openness and humble learning. In terms of the thriving of non-textuality, we have examined how, for example, African philosophy fundamentally centres orality as a fundamental epistemic repository. Oral forms of knowledge such as proverbs, folk tales, songs, names and communal narratives, constitute a fundamental medium through which philosophical thought is articulated, transmitted and preserved. Orality in African traditions is not a secondary or less important source of philosophy but rather a distinct mode of philosophizing that is deeply rooted in lived communal experience and historical continuity, such that the search for, say, indigenous African thought on ethical and metaphysical themes and concepts, would need to take seriously the structure of oral language and communal practices. To engage authentically with African philosophy, then, we must attend closely to oral forms not only as vehicles of transmission but as epistemic sites where philosophical reasoning, moral values, and collective interpretations and understandings are negotiated and embodied. Ignoring orality risks distorting and erasing African philosophical traditions, and a further perpetuation of epistemic injustice. Similarly, we have seen that African symbols possess profound philosophical significance, functioning not merely as aesthetic or decorative elements as often globally perceived but as complex repositories of philosophical thoughts, including indigenous knowledge systems, ethical values, ontological commitments and metaphysical principles. Symbolic forms such as the Adinkra symbols of the Akan and the Nsibidi of the Igbos encode intricate philosophical ideas about existence, morality, time, community and non-human beings, such as the ancestors. These symbols are often embedded in ritual, oral performance, architecture and textile art, serving as visual metaphors that are ubiquitous in expressing communal wisdom. As such, to treat African symbols merely as artefacts or aesthetic motifs is to overlook their function as visual philosophy and dynamic tools of abstraction and conceptualization that are integral to African ways of knowing. Philosophical engagement with African traditions thus requires interpretive attentiveness to the symbols through which existential questions and ontological frameworks are communicated. African texts, while serving multifaceted purposes, such as resistance, defence, mirroring and performing of African philosophy, deliberately or non-deliberately rely on oral and symbolic repositories as subjects for interpretation, sources of wisdom and philosophical thought, and as sources of method. Thus, doing African philosophy in textual forms is always entangled with non-textual forms of philosophical knowledge.

My fascination with street philosophy that has necessitated paying some attention, no matter how briefly to it in this chapter stems from how it manages to effectively sustain the non-textual spirit of philosophizing that dominates indigenous African spaces in postcolonial, densely neoliberal and capitalist physical urban and virtual spaces, weaving it nicely with the textual in quite disruptive ways. Street philosophy testifies to the resilience and durability of a philosophical tradition, considering the attacks and denial that the tradition has been subjected to for ages. The African tradition of philosophy no doubt has displayed and continues to display the key features of a philosophical tradition, such as an enduring commitment to philosophizing, rugged resilience and durability, and epistemic openness and humility. If we take the core defining features of African philosophy cum its philosophical tradition that I have attempted to capture in the pages of this book seriously and deliberately, what future can we then imagine for African philosophy in relation to the continuous flourishing of itself and of global philosophy? To personalize the question – and to be sure, such personalization would vary from reader to reader, how can I, as an academic philosopher, for example, imagine and reimagine my disciplinary, pedagogical, research responsibilities and trajectories in African philosophy futures? To be sure, if there is anything that is abundantly clear in terms of what not to be doing in this regard, it is refraining from performing one tradition simply by mirroring another or trying tirelessly to resemble or become the other. Not doing so does not threaten learning from or comparing with the other, as learning and comparing do not result in a transfiguration into the other. If there is anything we learn from the feature of difference in the Afro-communitarian model of thought, it is that two things cannot be ontically the same and cannot be individually self-complete. These indicate that mirroring is counterproductive to our very nature of being, while still acknowledging the need and value for learning and interdependence. The cardinal goal of African philosophy in the future, I believe, is to become more authentically self in its relation with others, and in its contribution to the fulfilment of global philosophy. There are at least four interrelated things to do to achieve this cardinal objective of pursuing self-authenticity and contributing to developing the global philosophizing culture now and into the future: taking the multiple textual and non-textual repositories and processes of African philosophy seriously, prioritizing linguistic care, engaging with the many possibilities of collaborative philosophy, and strengthening the contextual (positional and embodied) core of philosophy curriculum and research in Africa.

Concerning the first, taking seriously textual and non-textual repositories and processes, the future of African philosophy must be grounded in a serious engagement with the interconnection between textual and non-textual repositories and approaches to doing philosophy, recognizing that written philosophical discourse cannot be authentically developed in isolation from the oral, symbolic and performative dimensions that have historically sustained African thought. This integrated approach is crucial for constructing an authentic self-image that is rigorous and robust in intellectual, embodied and cultural ways. The spirit of reducing African philosophy to purely textual forms that seems to possess contemporary academic spaces risks becoming a mere mirroring of Eurocentric standards of knowledge production and further obscuring and erasing the diverse modes of thought embedded in African lifeworlds. Therefore, current and future philosophical work must develop interpretive frameworks that acknowledge, respect and critically engage both textual and non-textual epistemologies, forging a self-understanding that is faithful to the depth, plurality and creativity of African philosophical traditions. Concerning the second, prioritizing linguistic care, particularly in relation to oral forms of knowledge, I imagine a future of African philosophy in which indigenous African concepts and principles are no longer dismissed as inferior or relegated to the margins under labels such as 'ethnophilosophy' or 'folk philosophy', but are instead recognized as legitimate and sophisticated modes of thought deserving of serious philosophical engagement. This future demands a commitment to conceptual decolonization, an intentional effort to dismantle colonial reading of African philosophical concepts, and the privileging of Western categories and languages over African ones. Central to this process is the practice of linguistic care as discussed in Chapter two, which consists of the thoughtful and respectful recovery, revitalization and unveiling of authentic meanings in African languages and their philosophical insights through a process that is surgical and intended to heal. African languages carry unique conceptual frameworks that are often distorted or lost when translated into colonial languages without critical and careful mediation. Prioritizing linguistic care, especially in relation to oral forms of knowledge, enables philosophers to engage more carefully with indigenous epistemologies, restoring the philosophical significance of proverbs, idioms, metaphors and names as sources of insight rather than mere cultural tags. Concerning the third, exploring the possibilities of collaborative philosophy, we have explored severally in this book, how African philosophy, particularly through its communitarian paradigms, such as Ubuntu, offers a valuable framework for reimagining the future of global philosophy through the lens of collaboration, interdependence and relationality. The emphasis on the interconnectedness of persons (human and non-human) and the co-creation of knowledge prioritizes intersubjective and ecocentric intellectuality. The communal, collaborative and relational orientation positions African philosophy to contribute meaningfully to a future in which philosophical enquiry is pursued through collaborative research networks, dialogical pedagogies and co-authored interpretations of philosophical themes across traditions. By foregrounding values of mutual respect, shared enquiry and epistemic humility, African philosophy can help foster a more inclusive global philosophical landscape where multiple perspectives are not only acknowledged but actively engaged with. Furthermore, embracing collaborative outputs, such as performances, visual art, oral storytelling and digital media can expand the boundaries of what counts as philosophical work, acknowledging the diverse modalities through which African thought has historically been expressed. In doing so, African philosophy can play a transformative role in shaping a global philosophical future that is more dialogical, pluralistic, mutually responsive and creatively nourished. Finally, in envisioning a future for African philosophy that is authentic and contextually relevant, there is an urgent need to revamp the heavily Eurocentric philosophy curricula and research agendas that continue to sustain the coloniality of philosophical knowledge within African academic institutions. These curricula and research designs that marginalize and erase African traditions and indigenous epistemologies are often rooted in the uncritical adoption of the Western philosophical canon, and they perpetuate the illusion that Western philosophy constitutes a universal system of thought. A genuinely decolonized, inclusive and collaborative curriculum does not imply the wholesale rejection of Western philosophy but rather its rightful repositioning as one among many philosophical traditions with particular historical and cultural origins. This recalibration opens space for the inclusion of African philosophical systems that engage with the lived realities, moral frameworks and existential questions relevant to African contexts. It also affirms the epistemic value of indigenous insights, oral traditions, symbolic systems, and community-based knowledge in addressing contemporary social, political and ethical issues. By reshaping philosophy curricula and research to reflect Africa's diverse philosophical heritage, and present-day and future concerns, academic institutions can cultivate a generation of philosophers who are both globally conversant and locally grounded enough to enter into philosophical enquiry in ways that acknowledge and serve African realities and futures.

I am well aware that the African philosophy futures that I envision here would be pursued even if partly within the complex terrain of the politics of knowledge, marked by entrenched systemic and institutional hierarchies, neoliberal academic structures and the enduring legacies of colonial epistemologies. These forces often work to marginalize non-Western modes of thought, commodify knowledge production and prioritize metrics of academic success that devalue collaborative, oral and community-based epistemologies. Although such realities pose significant obstacles to the decolonial and transformative aspirations of African philosophy discussed above and through the pages of this book, they do not constitute sufficient justification for inaction or resignation. Rather, they underscore the urgency and ethical imperative for African philosophers, scholars and students to actively commit to reimagining and restructuring the enterprise of philosophy. We have a moral and scholarly obligation to challenge epistemic injustice, to recover and revitalize indigenous intellectual and embodied resources, and to cultivate philosophies that speak meaningfully to African experiences and futures. This responsibility involves not only critique but also constructive engagement – building new curricula, research networks and platforms of expression that affirm the richness, plurality, and dignity of African and human thought. Doing African philosophy invariably involves, therefore, navigating these challenges while sustaining a narrative of authenticity. Perhaps, this entire book has been fundamentally an attempt to do so.

References

Adegoke, D. (2023), '"Japa": An Exploratory Study of the Roles of Social Media in an Out-Migration Trend in Nigeria', *Social Media and Society*, 19 October 2023: 1–11.

Adjei, S. K. and LeGall, Y. (2024), *Fifteen Colonial Thefts: A Guide to Looted African Heritage in Museums*, London: Pluto Press.

Ahonen P., et. al. (2020, 'Writing Resistance Together', *Gender Work Organization*, 27 (4): 447–70. https://doi.org/10.1111/gwao.12441.

Allan, J. (2003), 'Productive Pedagogies and the Challenge of Inclusion', *British Journal of Special Education*, 30 (4): 175–9.

Amossy, R. (2021), *In Defence of Polemics*, Cham: Springer.

Ansah, R. and Mensah, G. (2018), 'Gyekye's Moderate Communitarianism: A Case of Radical Communitarianism in Disguise', *Ujah Unizik Journal of Arts and Humanities*, 19 (2): 62–87.

Asante, D. and Archibald, T. (2023), 'Beyond Ubuntu: Nnoboa and Sankofa as Decolonizing and Indigenous Evaluation Epistemic Foundations from Ghana', *Journal of Multidisciplinary Evaluation*, 19 (44): 156–65.

Asante, M. K. (2000), *The Egyptian Philosophers: Ancient African Voices from Imhotep to Akhenaten*, Chicago: African American Images.

Benson, H. H. (2010), 'Socratic Method', in Donald Morrison (ed), *The Cambridge Companion to Socrates*, 179–200, Cambridge, Cambridge University Press.

Blocker, H. G. (1999), *World Philosophy: An East-West Comparative Introduction to Philosophy*, New Jersey: Prentice Hall.

Bodunrin, P. O. (1981), 'The Question of African Philosophy', *Philosophy* 56 (216): 161–79.

Bujo, B. (1998), *The Ethical Dimension of Community: The African Model and the Dialogue between North and South*, Nairobi: Paulines Publications.

Bujo, B. (2001), *Foundations of an African Ethic: Beyond the Universal Claims of Western Morality*, Nairobi: Paulines Publications.

Bunnin, N. and Yu, J. (2004), *The Blackwell Dictionary of Western Philosophy*, Malden MA: Blackwell Publishing.

Cabral, A. (1979), *Unity and Struggle: Speeches and Writings of Amilcar Cabral*, edited by Basil Davidson, New York: Monthly Review Press.

Césaire, A. (2000), *Discourse on Colonialism*, New York: Monthly Review Press.

Chiké and Mohbad. (2023), *Egwu*, Lagos: Pinkline Productions.
Chimakonam, J. O. (nd.) *History of African Philosophy*, Internet Encyclopedia of Philosophy, https://iep.utm.edu/history-of-african-philosophy/#H6.
Chinweizu, I. (1975), *The West and the Rest of Us: White Predators, Black Slavers and the African Elite*, New York: Vintage Books.
Clark, S. (1991), 'Discipline and Resistance: The Subjects of Writing and the Discourses of Instruction', *College Literature*, 18 (2): 119–34.
de Haas, H. (2021), 'A Theory of Migration: The Aspirations-Capabilities Framework', *Comparative Migration Studies*, 9 (8): 1–35.
Derrida, J. (1976), *Of Grammatology*, translated by G. C. Spivak, Baltimore: Johns Hopkins University Press.
Devereaux, M. (1990), 'Oppressive Texts, Resisting Readers and the Gendered Spectator: The New Aesthetics', *The Journal of Aesthetics and Art Criticism*, 48 (4): 337–47.
Diagne, S. B. (2004), 'Precolonial African Philosophy in Arabic', in Kwasi Wiredu (ed), *A Companion to African Philosophy*, 66–77, Malden MA: Blackwell Publishing.
Dzobo, N. K. (1992), 'African Symbols and Proverbs as Sources of Knowledge and Truth', in Kwasi Wiredu and Kwame Gyekye (eds), *Person and Community: Ghanaian Philosophical Studies I (Vol. 1)*, Washington DC: The Council for Research in Values and Philosophy.
Edelglass W. and Garfield, J. L. (2011), 'Introduction' to *The Oxford Handbook of World Philosophy*, Oxford: Oxford University Press.
Etieyibo, E. and Ikuenobe, P. (Eds.) (2020), *Menkiti on Community and Becoming a Person*, Lanham: Lexington Books.
Eze, E. C. (1997), *Race and the Enlightenment: A Reader*, Cambridge MA: Blackwell Publishing.
Eze, E. C. (1997), 'Introduction' to *Race and the Enlightenment*, edited by Emmanuel C. Eze, 1–9, Malden, MA: Blackwell Publishing.
Eze, M. O. (2008), 'What is African Communitarianism? Against Consensus as a Regulative Ideal', *South African Journal of Philosophy*, 27 (4): 386–99.
Fanon, F. (1961), *The Wretched of the Earth*, London: Penguin.
Fayemi, A. K. (2014), 'Oral Tradition in African Philosophical Discourse: A Critique of Sophie Oluwole's Account', *Sophia: An African Journal of Philosophy*, 15 (1): 101–12.
Flynn, E. A. (1996), Writing as Resistance, *Journal of Advanced Composition*, 16 (1): 171–6.
Freire, P. (1970), *Pedagogy of the Oppressed*, London: Continuum.

Freter, B. (2018), 'White Supremacy in Eurowestern Epistemologies: On the West's Responsibility for its Philosophical Heritage', *Synthesis Philosophica: Journal of the Croatian Philosophical Society*, 33 (1): 237–49.

Gadamer, H. (2004), *Truth and Method*, translated by Joel Weinsheimer and Donald G. Marshall, London: Bloomsbury Academic.

Goldman, A. (1999), *Knowledge in a Social World*, Oxford: Oxford University Press.

Goldman, E. (2018), Emojis and the Law, *Washington Law Review*, 93: 1227–91.

Gordon, L. R. (2011), 'Shifting the Geography of Reason in an Age of Disciplinary Decadence', *Transmodernity: Journal of Peripheral Cultural Production of the Luso-Hispanic World*, 1 (2): 96–104.

Gordon, L. R. (2018), 'Re-Imagining Liberations', *International Journal of Critical Diversity Studies*, 1 (1): 95–103.

Graness, A. (2022), 'The Status of Oral Traditions in the History of Philosophy: Methodological Considerations', *South African Journal of Philosophy*, 41 (2): 181–94.

Gu, M. D. (2005), *Chinese Theories of Reading and Writing: A Route to Hermeneutics and Open Poetics*, New York: State University of New York Press.

Gutema, B. and Verharen, C. C. (Eds.) (2013), *African Philosophy in Ethiopia: Ethiopian Philosophical Studies II with A Memorial of Claude Sumner*, Washington DC: The Council for Research in Values and Philosophy.

Gyekye, K. (1996), *African Cultural Values: An Introduction*, Accra: Sankofa Publishing Company.

Hallen, B. (2002), *A Short History of African Philosophy*, Indiana: Indiana University Press.

Hallen, B. (2006), *African Philosophy: The Analytic Approach*, Trenton, African World Press.

Hamminga, B. (2005), 'Epistemology from the African Point of View', in Bert Hamminga (ed.) *Knowledge Cultures: Comparative Western and African Epistemology*, Amsterdam: Rodopi.

Hawkins, A. (2024), 'What is neijuan, and why is China worried about it?' *The Guardian*, 24 December 2024, https://www.theguardian.com/world/2024/dec/24/what-is-neijuan-china-viral-buzzword-laptop-bicycle.

Hegel, G. W. F. (1956), *The Philosophy of History*, translated by J. H. Clarke, New York: Dover.

Hountondji, P. (1983), 'On African Philosophy', *Radical Philosophy*, 35: 20–5.

Huang, Y. (2006), 'Interpretation of the Other: A Cultural Hermeneutics', in Inwon Choue, Samuel Lee, and Pierre Sane (eds), *Inter-regional Philosophical Dialogues: Democracy and Social Justice in Asia and the Arab World*, 189–204, Korea: Korea National Commission of UNESCO.

Hung, R. (2018), *Education between Speech and Writing: Crossing the Boundaries of Dao and Deconstruction*, London: Routledge.

Ikuenobe, P. (2006), *Philosophical Perspectives on Communalism and Morality in African Traditions*, Lanham: Lexington Books.

Ikuenobe, P. (2018), 'Oral Tradition, Epistemic Dependence, and Knowledge in African Cultures', *Synthesis Philosophica*, 65 (1): 23–40.

Imafidon, E. (2012), 'The Concept of Person in an African Culture and its Implication for Social Order', *Lumina: Journal of Interdisciplinary Studies*, 23 (2): 78–96.

Imafidon, E. (2014), 'On the Ontological Foundation of a Social Ethics in African Tradition', in Elvis Imafidon & John A. I. Bewaji (eds), *Ontologized Ethics: New Essays in African Meta-Ethics*, 37–54, Lanham: Lexington Books.

Imafidon, E. (2018), 'Is the African Feminist Moral Epistemology of Care Fractured?' *Synthesis Philosophica: Journal of the Croatian Philosophical Society*, 47 (2): 165–78.

Imafidon, E. (2019), *African Philosophy and the Otherness of Albinism: White Skin, Black Race*, London: Routledge.

Imafidon, E. (2021), 'African Communitarian Philosophy of Personhood and Disability: The Asymmetry of Value and Power in Access to Healthcare', *International Journal of Critical Diversity Studies*, 4 (1): 46–57.

Imafidon, E. (2022), 'Beyond Continental and African Philosophies of Personhood, Healthcare and Difference', *Nursing Philosophy*, 23 (3): 1–9.

Imafidon, E. (2023a), 'Exploring the Theory of Communo-Cognition', in Peter A. Ikhane and Isaac E. Ukpokolo (eds), *African Epistemology: Essays on Being and Knowledge*, 48–60, London: Routledge.

Imafidon, E. (2023b), 'Difference and Exclusionism', in Uchenna Okeja (ed.), *Routledge Handbook of African Political Philosophy*, 138–50: London, Routledge.

Imafidon, E. (2024), 'Procreation, Legitimated Adultery, and Ancestorship: Exploring Issues of Systemic Patriarchy in African Cultures', in Dawn Llewellyn, Sian Hawthorne and Sonya Sharma (eds), *The Bloomsbury Handbook of Religion, Gender and Sexuality*, London: Bloomsbury Publishing, 363–78.

Imafidon, E. (2025a), 'The Non-Human in African Metaphysics', in Stephen Green (ed.), *Doing Metaphysics in a Diverse World: How We Make Sense of Things Across Cultures*, 259–70, London: Bloomsbury Academic.

Imafidon, E. (2025b), 'African Philosophy of Disability', in David Bolt (ed.), *The Oxford Research Encyclopaedia of Disability Studies*, New York: Oxford University Press, forthcoming.

Ingiyimbere, F. (2024), 'Public Reason Under the Tree: Rawls and the African Palaver', *Philosophy and Social Criticism*, 50 (2): 281–98.

Ivor, A. (2024), *A History of Manhyia Place Museum: Inaugural and Other Objects*, Tema, Ghana: Digi Books.

James, G. G. M. (2001), *Stolen Legacy: Greek Philosophy is Stolen Egyptian Philosophy*, Chicago: African American Images.

Janz, B. B. (2004), 'Philosophy as if Place Mattered: The Situation of African Philosophy', in Havi Carel and David Gamez (eds), *What Philosophy Is*, 103–15, London: Continuum.

Janz, B. B. (2009), *Philosophy in an African Place*, Lanham: Lexington Books.

Jarczewski, D. (2024), 'Exempting Oneself from Knowing Better. Epistemic Laziness and Conspiracy Theories', *Social Epistemology*, 1–13. https://doi.org/10.1080/02691728.2024.2438114.

Jensen T, Zawadzki M. (2024), 'Contextualizing Capitalism in Academia: How Capitalist and Feudalist Organizing Principles Reinforce Each Other at Polish Universities', *Organization*, 31 (8): 1214–36.

Kagame, A. (1966), *La Philosophie Bantu-Rwandaise l'Etre*, London: Johnson Reprint Co.

Kant I. (1784/1991), 'An Answer to the Question: What is Enlightenment?', in Hans Reiss (ed.) and H. B. Nisbet (trans.), *Kant: Political Writings*, 54–60, Cambridge: Cambridge University Press.

Kayange, G. M. (2021), *The Question of Being in Western and African Analytic Metaphysics: Comparative Metaphysics Using the Analytic Framework*, Cham: Springer.

Kiros, T. (2017), 'An Interpretive Introduction to Classical Ethiopian Philosophy', in Adeshina Afolayan and Toyin Falola (eds), *The Palgrave Handbook of African Philosophy*, 181–206, New York: Palgrave Macmillan.

Kissi, S. B., Fening, P. A., & Asante, E. A. (2019), 'The Philosophy of Adinkra Symbols in Asante Textiles, Jewellery and Other Art Forms', *Journal of Asian Scientific Research*, 9 (4): 29–39.

Knaus, C. B. Mino, T. & Seroto, J. (Eds.) (2022), *Decolonising African Higher Education: Practitioner Perspectives from Across the Continent*, London: Routledge.

Komo, L. B. (2017), 'The Hermeneutical Paradigm in African Philosophy: Genesis, Evolution and Issues', *Nokoko: Institute of African Studies*, 6: 81–106.

Kotei (2024), *Ga Samai (Ga Wisdom Symbol): Artistic Expressions of Ga Proverbs and Colourful Word Statements*, Vol. 2. Accra, Ghana: Unique Xpressions Limited

Kotei, R. A. (2023), *Ga Samai (Ga Wisdom Symbols): Artistic Expression of Ga Proverbs and Colourful Word Statements*, Ghana: Ghana Library Authority.

Kotevska, L. (2022), 'Writing Women into the History of Philosophy: Contextualism Re-Examined', *Journal of the History of Women Philosophers and Scientists*, 1: 23–47.

Kwame, S. 'Rethinking the History of African Philosophy', in Adeshina Afolayan and Toyin Falola (eds), *The Palgrave Handbook of African Philosophy*, 97–104, New York: Palgrave Macmillan.

Kwarteng, A. K. (2016), 'The Sankofa Bird and Reflection', *Journal of Applied Christian Leadership*, 10 (1): 61–9.

Lloyd, G. (1998), 'The "Maleness" of Reason', in Linda Martin Alcoff (ed.), *Epistemology: The Big Questions*, 387–91, Malden, Massachusetts: Blackwell Publishing.

Lyotard, J-F. (1984), *The Postmodern Condition: A Report on Knowledge*, Minneapolis: University of Minnesota Press.

Maqoma, W. P. (2020), 'In Defence of Communitarianism Philosophy: The Contribution of Moderate Communitarianism to the Formation of an African Identity', *Verbum et Ecclesia*, 41 (1): 1–8.

Masolo, D. A. (1994), *African Philosophy in Search of Identity*, Edinburgh: Edinburgh University Press.

Masolo, D. A. (2004), 'African Philosophers in the Greco-Roman Era', in Kwasi Wiredu (ed.) *A Companion to African Philosophy*, 50–65, Malden MA: Blackwell Publishing.

Massey, D. S., et. al. (1993), 'Theories of International Migration: A Review and Appraisal', *Population and Development Review*, 19 (3): 431–66.

Matusov, E and St. Julien, J. (2004), 'Print Literacy as Oppression: Cases of Bureaucratic, Colonial, and Totalitarian Literacies and their Implications for Schooling', *Text and Talk*, 24 (2):197–244.

Matt, J., 2Face and Mode9 (2011), *Stylee*, Jimmy Jatt Production.
Mbiti, J. S. (1969), *African Religions and Philosophy*, London: Heinemann Publishers.
Menkiti, A. (1984), 'Person and Community in African Traditional Thought', in Richard A. Wright (ed.), *African Philosophy: An Introduction*, New York: University of America Press.
Metz, T. (2007), 'Toward an African Moral Theory', *The Journal of Political Philosophy*, 15 (3): 321–41.
Metz, T. (2021), *A Relational Moral Theory: African Ethics in and Beyond the Continent*, Oxford: Oxford University Press.
Miller, M. J. & Castles, S. (2013), *The Age of Migration: International Population Movements in the Modern World*, New York: Guilford Press.
Molefe, M. (2018), 'Personhood and Rights in an African Tradition', *Politikon: South African Journal of Political Studies*, 45 (2): 1–15.
Molefe, M. (2019), *An African Philosophy of Personhood, Morality and Politics*, New York: Palgrave Macmillan.
Møller, V. S. (2002), *Philosophy without Women: The Birth of Sexism in Western Thought*, London: Continuum.
Moscovici, S. (1979), 'The Proper Use of Polemics', *Yale French Studies*, 58: 55–83.
Mudimbe, V. Y. (1983), 'African Philosophy as an Ideological Practice: The Case of French-Speaking Africa', *African Studies Review*, 26 (3/4): 133–54.
Mulemfo, M. M. (1996), 'Palaver as a Dimension of Communal Solidarity in Zaire: A Missiological Study on Transgression and Reconciliation', *Missionalia*, 24 (2): 129–47.
Mungwini, P. (2022), *African Philosophy: Emancipation and Practice*, London: Bloomsbury Academic.
Murove, M. F. (Ed.) (2010), *African Ethics: An Anthology for Comparative and Applied Ethics*, Pietermaritzburg: University of KwaZulu-Natal Press.
Ndofirepi, A. and Shanyanana-Amaambo, R. N. (2015), 'Rethinking ukama in the context of "Philosophy for Children" in Africa', *Research Papers in Education*, 31 (4): 1–14.
Nietzsche, F. (1873/2006), '*On Truth and Lies in a Nonmoral Sense*', In D. Breazeale (ed.) *Philosophy and Truth: Selections from Nietzsche's Notebooks of the Early 1870s*, 79–100, New Jersey: Humanities Press.
Nwainya, O. H. (2023), 'African Palaver Ethics, the Common Good, and Nonrecognition of Women', *Journal of the Society of Christian Ethics*, 43 (1): 189–202.

Nwobodo, R. E. E. (2024), 'Japa Pandemic: Battling for the Souls of Nigerian Youths', *International Journal of Social Sciences and Management Research*, 10 (4): 11–25.

Nyerere, J. K. (1968), *Ujamaa: Essays on Socialism*, London: Oxford University Press,

Obenga, T. (1992), *Ancient Egypt and Black Africa: A Student's Handbook for the Study of Ancient Egypt in Philosophy, Linguistics, and Gender Relations*, London: Karnak House.

Obiechina, E. (1993), 'Narrative Proverbs in the African Novel', *Research in African Literatures*, 24 (4): 123–40.

Ogude, J. (Ed.) (2018), *Ubuntu and Personhood*, Trenton: African World Press.

O'Hear, A. (2005), 'Tradition and Traditionalism', in Edward Craig (ed.), *The Shorter Routledge Encyclopedia of Philosophy*, London: Routledge.

Okeja, U. (Ed.) (2023), *Routledge Handbook of African Political Philosophy*, London: Routledge.

Okeja, U. (2022), *Deliberative Agency: A Study in Modern African Political Philosophy*, Indiana: Indiana University Press.

Okere, T. (1983), *African Philosophy: A Historico-hermeneutical Investigation of the Conditions of its Possibility*, New York: University Press of America.

Okrah, K. A. (2003), *Nyansapo (the Wisdom Knot): Toward an African Philosophy of Education*, New York: Routledge.

Okunade, S. K. and Awosusi, O. E. (2023), 'The Japa Syndrome and the Migration of Nigerians to the United Kingdom: An Empirical Analysis', *Comparative Migration Studies*, 11 (27): 1–18.

Oladipo, O. (2008), *Thinking about Philosophy: A General Guide*, Ibadan: Hope Publications.

Oliseneku, E. L. and Jike, V. T. (2023), '"Skul na scam" and the Interpretive Understanding of Nigerian Youths: A Study of Delta State', *Journal of Public Administration Research and Theory*, 7 (1): 146–60.

Oluwole, S. B. (1999), *Philosophy and Oral Traditions*, Nigeria: ARK Publications.

Ong, W. (1967), *The Presence of the Word: Some Prolegomena for Cultural and Religious History*, New Haven: Yale University Press.

Ong, W. J. (2012), *Orality and Literacy: The Technologizing of the Word*, 30th Anniversary Edition, London: Routledge.

Onwuatuegwu, I. N. (2022), 'A Philosophical Appraisal of Igbo Epistemic Metaphysical Notion of Truth', *Annals of Bioethics & Clinical Applications*, 5 (4): 2–4.

Onyewuenyi, I. C. (2005), *The African Origin of Greek Philosophy: An Exercise in Afrocentrism*, Nsukka: University of Nigeria Press.

Oruka, H. O. (1998), 'Four Trends in Current African Philosophy', in P. H. Coetzee and A. P. J. Roux (eds), *The African Philosophy Reader*, 141–6, London: Routledge.

Overholser, J. C. (1993), 'Elements of the Socratic Method: 1. Systematic Questioning', *Psychotherapy: Theory, Research, Practice, Training*, 30 (1): 67–74.

Oyeshile, O. A. (2006), 'The Individual-Community Relationship as an Issue in Social and Political Philosophy', in Olusegun Oladipo (ed.), *Core Issue in African Philosophy*, Ibadan: Hope Publications.

Park, P. K. J. (2013), *Africa, Asia, and the History of Philosophy: Racism in the Formation of the Philosophical Canon, 1780–830*, New York: State University of New York Press.

p'Bitek, O. (1976), 'Fr. Tempels' Bantu Philosophy', *Transition*, 50: 66–8.

Plato, (1997), *Plato: Complete Works*, edited by J. M. Cooper, Indiana: Hackett Publishing.

Quijano, A. (2000), 'Coloniality of Power, Eurocentrism, and Latin America', *Nepantla: Views from South*, 1 (3): 533–80.

Rettová, A. (2002), 'The Role of African Languages in African Philosophy', *Rue Descartes*, 36: 129–50.

Ricoeur, P. (1974), *The Conflict of Interpretations: Essays in Hermeneutics*, Illinois: Northwestern University Press.

Said, E. (1979), *Orientalism*, New York: Vintage Books.

Salemohamed, G. (1983), 'African Philosophy', *Philosophy*, 58 (226): 535–8.

Saussure, F. (1983), *Course in General Linguistics*, translated by R. Harris, London: Duckworth.

Scharfstein, B. (1998), *A Comparative History of World Philosophy: From the Upanishads to Kant*, New York: State University of New York Press.

Scharfstein, B. (2014), *The Nonsense of Kant and Lewis Carroll: Unexpected Essays on Philosophy, Art, Life, and Death*, Chicago: University of Chicago Press.

Scheid, A. F. (2011), 'Under the Palaver Tree: Community Ethics for Truth-Telling and Reconciliation', *Journal of the Society of Christian Ethics*, 31 (1): 17–36.

Serequeberhan, T. (1994), *The Hermeneutics of African Philosophy: Horizon and Discourse*, New York: Routledge.

Skitolsky, L. (2020), *Hip-hop as Philosophical Text and Testimony: Can I Get a Witness?*, Lanham: Lexington Books.

Slater, J. (2019), 'Sankofa – the Need to Turn Back to Move Forward: Addressing Reconstruction Challenges that Face Africa and South Africa Today', *Studia Historiae Ecclesiasticae*, 45 (1): 1–24.

Smith K. M. (2011), 'Female Voice and Feminist Text: Testimonio as a Form of Resistance in Latin America', *Florida Atlantic Comparative Studies Journal*, 12: 21–37.

Sogolo, G. S. (1990), 'Options in African Philosophy', *Philosophy*, 65 (251): 39–52.

Soyinka, W. (2020), *Beyond Aesthetics: Use, Abuse, and Dissonance in African Art Traditions*, Ibadan: Nigeria, Craft Books.

Strickland, L., & Wang, J. (2023), 'Racism and Eurocentrism in Histories of Philosophy', *Open Journal of Philosophy*, 13 (1): 76–96.

Sumner, C. (2004), 'The Light and the Shadow: Zera Yacob and Walda Heywat: Two Ethiopian Philosophers of the Seventeenth Century', in Kwasi Wiredu (ed.), *A Companion to African Philosophy*, 172–82, Malden MA: Blackwell Publishing.

Sumner, C. (1985), *Classical Ethiopian Philosophy*, Addis Ababa: Commercial Printing Press.

Táíwò, O. (2014), *Africa Must Be Modern: A Manifesto*, Indiana: Indiana University Press.

Táíwò, O. (2022), *Against Decolonisation: Taking African Agency Seriously*, London: C. Hurst and Company.

Tempels, P. (1945), *La Philosophie Bantoue*, Paris: Presence Afrcaine.

Tempels, P. (1952), *Bantu Philosophy*, Paris: Presence Africaine.

Tieku, A. K. (2022), *The Scrolls of Ashanti Proverbs*, Ghana: Unnamed Publisher.

Udoidem, S. I. (1987), 'Wiredu on How Not to Compare African Thought with Western Thought: A Commentary', *African Studies Review*, 30 (1): 101–4.

Uetela, P. J. (2023), *Higher Education and Decolonization in Africa*, New York: Springer.

Voltaire, (1901), *The Works of Voltaire. A Contemporary Version, Vol. IV*, translated by William F. Fleming, New York: E. R. DuMont.

wa Thiong'o, N. (1986), *Decolonising the Mind: The Politics of Language in African Literature*, Nairobi: Heinemann Educational Books.

Wainwright, L. (2024), 'African Art as Found Object', *Burlington Contemporary*, 10, https://doi.org/10.31452/bcj10.wainwright.african.art.

Wiredu, K. (1980), *Philosophy and an African Culture*, New York: Cambridge University Press.

Wiredu, K. (1987), 'The Concept of Mind with Particular Reference to the Language and Thought of the Akans', in Guttorm Fløistad (ed.), *Contemporary Philosophy: A New Survey*, 154–66, Dordrecht: Martinus Nijhoff Publishers.

Wiredu, K. (2002), 'Conceptual Decolonization as an Imperative in Contemporary African Philosophy: Some Personal Reflections', *Rue Descartes*, 36: 53–64.

Wiredu, K. (2004), 'Introduction: African Philosophy in Our Time', in Kwasi Wiredu (ed.), *A Companion to African Philosophy*, 1–27, Malden MA: Blackwell Publishing.

Wiredu, K. (2009), 'An Oral Philosophy of Personhood: Comments on Philosophy and Orality', *Research in African Literatures*, 40 (1): 8–18.

Index

ableist 3
abstraction 7, 182
academic community 20
academic conditions 17
academic curricula 45
academic dishonesty 30
academic excellence 163
academic freedom 163
academic futures 138
academic philosopher 183
academic philosophy 2, 14, 35, 54, 67, 110, 111, 138, 139, 154, 155, 162, 167
academic practice 21
academic production 118
academic regulations 30
academic research 154
adage 99, 102, 103, 105, 132
adages 13, 38, 51, 53, 60, 64, 75, 78, 79, 109, 138, 144, 158, 169
Adinkra 13, 36, 81, 82, 88–90, 94, 95, 97, 98, 100–105, 107, 181, 191
adinkra symbols 36, 81, 82, 88–90, 94, 97, 100–105, 181, 191
Adire 97, 99–101
adire symbols 97
aesthetic 13, 81–88, 99, 119, 127, 154, 172, 181, 182
aesthetic encounter 87
aesthetic fascination 81
aesthetic functions 99
aesthetic hermeneutics 84
aesthetic intentions 86
aesthetic interpretation 13, 82
aesthetic judgement 119, 127
aesthetic motifs 182
aesthetic narrative 13, 86
aesthetic objects 85, 86
aesthetic value 82, 83
African agency 120, 122, 196

African artefacts 82
African arts 13, 82–87, 90, 92, 107
African communitarian 70, 145, 152, 153, 156, 162, 163, 190
African diasporic 8–10
African epistemology 132, 189, 190
African ethics 132, 193
African experience 33, 45, 46, 112, 126, 133, 150, 170
African gatherings 160
African heritage 10, 187
African identity 192
African languages 38, 46, 47, 55–58, 60, 68, 70, 74, 161, 184, 195
African literatures 194, 197
African palaver 191, 193
African socialism 121
African spirituality 118
African symbols 82, 101, 105, 107, 181, 182, 188
Afrobeats 171
Afrocentrism 194
Afro-communitarian 15, 145, 148, 149, 183
Afro-communitarianism 14, 132, 144, 154, 155
afterlife 92
agbon 73
Agbonkhale 73
agency 1, 15, 27, 28, 31, 33, 39, 43, 62–66, 91, 93, 96, 98, 99, 101, 120, 122, 138, 145, 150, 169, 174, 194, 196
Aguyaa 101
ahistoricization 111, 119
Aigunyibhin 59, 159
Akan 32, 36, 39, 82, 98, 101, 102, 105, 124, 181
Akan adage 105

Akan philosophy 101
Akomen 76, 144
akota 55–58, 148
akugbe 76
albinism 153, 154, 190
alphabets 36
ancestors 91–93, 146, 148, 182
ancestral 91–93, 104, 147
ancestral arts 93
ancestral knowledge 104
ancestral shrine 91
ancestral tree 147
angst 174
anthropocentric 142
anti-colonial 121
anxiety 11, 140–42, 174, 175
art 5, 10, 19, 52, 81, 83, 87, 89, 117, 119, 166, 171, 180, 182, 185, 188, 191, 195, 196
artefacts 38, 82, 83, 92, 94, 182
Asante 69, 90, 93, 94, 97, 104, 112, 113, 187, 191
Asante proverb 69
Asante stools 93
Asante textiles 191
Asante tradition 97
atuu 93
aural 52, 53
authenticity 11, 49, 122, 129, 174, 186
author 8, 30, 33, 67, 84, 111, 112, 151, 165, 199
autonomy 76, 78, 96–99, 101, 128, 150, 163
axiological 113, 172
Aya 98

Baluba 123
Bantu 34, 123–25, 195, 196
Bantu philosophy 34, 123–25, 195, 196
beings-with-others 155
beliefs 21, 28, 64, 68, 95, 103, 128
bi-dimensional community 94
binary 167
bird 104, 114, 148, 192

blackness 47
black people 44
black race 44, 190
bodies 2, 3, 5, 13, 36, 77, 81, 92, 94, 106, 157
bodily experiences 3
Botswana 148
breathe 118
bronzes 13, 83
brotherhood 76

Cartesian cogito 3
Cartesian dictum 150
Cartesian method 139
carvings 13, 81
categorical imperative 22, 119
categories 11, 27, 40, 41, 125, 130, 184
causal explanations 93
causality 45, 174
ceremonial dancing 88
ceremonies 60, 64, 77, 90, 171
checkered symbol 105
christening rites 59
Christianity 124, 125
co-authored 185
co-created 145
co-creation 87, 89, 91, 92, 185
co-creative learning 88
co-creative outputs 87
co-creative spaces 156
co-dependency 28, 76
co-dwelling 71
co-existence 97
cogito 3, 22, 27
cognition 29, 30, 65, 103, 119, 138, 150, 153, 154
cognitive abilities 66
cognitive empire 32
cognitive functions 44, 150
cognitive process 29
cognitive system 86
co-learning 46
collaboration 30, 31, 38, 53, 89, 100, 104, 109, 134, 135, 138, 143, 149, 155, 157, 161, 162, 168–70, 185

Index

collaborative creativity 142
collaborative curriculum 185
collaborative deliberations 56
collaborative episteme 128
collaborative learning 104, 106
collaborative method 150
collaborative methods 9
collaborative outputs 185
collaborative pedagogies 138
collaborative philosophy 138, 148, 149, 155, 156, 167, 183, 184
collaborative practices 133, 134, 137, 161, 167, 170
collaborative processes 38
collaborative research 154, 185
collaborative spaces 9, 149
collaborative spirit 138, 161, 165, 166
collaborative strategies 49, 137
collaborative textuality 141
collective agency 15, 28, 39, 43
collective cognition 103
collective consciousness 180
collective episteme 32
collective intentionality 65
collective interpretations 151, 181
collective resistance 118
collective wellbeing 97
collective will 96
colonial categories 125
colonial encounter 82, 85
colonial epistemologies 186
colonialism 26, 120, 121, 187
colonial languages 184
colonial mentality 72
colonial reading 184
colonial structures 178
colonial thefts 187
comic 16, 160
coming-to-be 77
community-based knowledge 186
communo-cognition 29, 150, 190
conceptual decolonisation 56
conceptual decolonization 56, 184, 197
constructed gap 90

constructed narrative 36, 81
constructed realities 153
continuity 42, 43, 106, 181
cooperation 28, 100, 107
co-producers 62
corporeality 3, 157
cosmic forces 91, 93
crescent 93
crossroads 99
curating philosophy 87
curators 86, 111
custom 7, 69

Dame-Dame 105, 106
death 72, 94, 95, 118, 129, 195
de-centring 38
decoloniality 86
decolonization 56, 120, 122, 130, 179, 184, 196, 197
deconstruction 15, 38, 166, 190
de-embodied 4, 5
defence 14, 23, 42, 69, 83, 110, 123, 125, 126, 131, 134, 158, 182, 187, 192
deflationary theory 68
dehumanity 138
dehumanizing logics 121
deities 92, 146
deity 74
delegitimating 12
deliberative disposition 60
deliberative practices 15, 148, 149, 158, 160, 162, 171
deliberative processes 48, 181
deliberative spaces 156, 160, 166, 170, 171
deliberative systems 146
democracy 122, 132, 190
democratic practices 107
de-positionality 153
de-positioned 4, 5
destiny 72, 82, 90, 92, 100, 130, 132, 159, 161
dialogue 30, 38, 49, 69, 103, 140, 147, 150, 156, 187

Dibia 95
dictum 73, 132, 150, 155, 175–77, 179
dignity 101, 119, 186
dilemma 60, 81
disability 132, 133, 190, 191
disciplinary anxiety 11
disciplinary decadence 189
diseased 93
disembodied metrics 118
disembodiment 3, 67, 153
disinterestedness 58
disruptive materials 170
disruptive textuality 15, 166–69
diversity 15, 39, 68, 97, 98, 107, 158, 162, 189, 190
divination 99
divinities 146
documentation 116
Dogon 93
doing philosophy 1–3, 6–10, 12, 14, 17, 19, 20, 28, 33, 37, 39, 42, 45, 47, 55, 63, 68, 111, 126, 127, 129, 133, 137–40, 144, 145, 148, 149, 158, 165–67, 183
dread 140, 174
drum 52
drumming 95
duties 78, 101, 147
Dwennimmen 103, 106

ecocentric intellectuality 142, 144–46, 148
eco-friendly 66
ecologically-aware 149
ecology 130
ecosystem 77, 97, 141, 142, 145, 148
effervescence 69
Egypt 25, 111–13, 115, 116, 194
elders 53, 63, 64
emancipation 98, 131, 193
emancipatory possibilities 178
embodied experiences 3, 154
embodied intellectuality 181
embodied performance 95
embodied thought 101
embodiment 3, 63, 93, 99, 107, 145, 154, 157, 173
emojis 107, 189
empiricism 143
emu 69
emuata 68, 69
energies 146, 157
energy 91, 93–95, 112, 121, 157, 176
enigma 162
enigmatic approach 15
enigmatic deliberation 138
enigmatic discourse 161
enigmatic disposition 159
enigmatic essence 161
enigmatic philosophy 161
enigmatic processes 138
enigmatics 15, 49, 60, 158–61, 171
enigmatic sayings 55, 60, 160, 171, 181
enlightenment 27, 44, 45, 60, 119–22, 143, 155, 180, 188, 191
entity 162
environment 64, 78, 97, 127, 177
ephemeral 37
epics 60, 158
episteme 32, 78, 86, 128, 143
epistemic agency 28, 65, 66
epistemic awareness 159, 162
epistemic burden 69
epistemic canon 28, 78
epistemic collaboration 89
epistemic colonization 5, 39
epistemic commitment 48, 49
epistemic communities 65
epistemic competence 104, 105, 157
epistemic dependence 63, 65, 190
epistemic heritages 28, 30, 31
epistemic hierarchies 152, 156
epistemic humility 48, 49, 88, 103, 105, 185
epistemic injustice 33, 41, 111, 112, 126, 181, 186
epistemic laziness 142, 143, 191
epistemic openness 181, 182
epistemic reliability 61–63

epistemic repositories 37, 62, 81, 83, 87, 132
epistemic responsibilities 65, 70
epistemic responsibility 62, 63
epistemic sites 167, 181
epistemic trust 63, 66
epistemologies 7, 120, 184–86, 189
equality 4, 39, 148, 172
Esan 2, 68, 91, 93, 159
essence 2, 11, 69, 73, 74, 76, 129, 134, 151, 156, 161, 172, 173, 176, 177, 180
ethical commitments 7, 60
Ethiopia 112, 115, 116, 189
ethnophilosophical approach 63
ethnophilosophy 11, 127, 129, 184
Eurocentrism 112, 195, 196
evanescent 63
Ewe 89
existence 2, 6, 12, 14, 16, 21–24, 32, 34, 35, 52, 56, 59, 63, 67, 71–78, 93, 95, 98, 110, 115, 123–25, 131, 144, 147, 152, 159, 162, 166, 167, 179, 182
existentialism 71
existentialist philosophy 2, 168, 174
existentiality 109, 167, 170, 174, 175
extrasensory perception 92, 95
Eyin 99
eziokwu 70, 71

facticity 71, 98
fallibility 49
falsehood 69, 123
familial 60, 91
family 10, 76, 91–93, 101, 147
fashion 176, 180
fatalism 130
feminine 4
femininity 133
fern leaf 98
fertile ground 158, 167, 171
festivals 90, 93
figurines 92, 99
fluid gatherings 171

fluidity 15, 49, 110, 138, 149, 150, 152, 155, 156, 162, 171
folklores 38, 75
folktales 54
forces 91–93, 95, 99, 106, 124, 146, 157, 177, 186
forehead 95
freedom 3, 71–73, 76, 78, 96–101, 109, 118, 130, 132, 159, 163
funerals 77, 146, 170
Funtunfunefu 100
futures 15, 16, 49, 121, 134, 137, 138, 165–67, 181, 183, 186

Ga 13, 70, 97–99, 101, 192
galleries 81, 83
Ganda 124
gatekeepers 35, 110, 111, 117
gender 118, 133, 187, 190, 194
generations 18, 43, 52, 62, 78, 91, 117, 134, 157, 168
genetic fallacy 7
genetic ontology 77
geography 3, 7–9, 127, 130, 157, 170, 189
Ghana 13, 25, 70, 82, 88, 103, 115, 187, 191, 192, 196
global heritage 48, 134
global history 117, 134, 143
global migration 169, 172
global philosophy 16, 182–84
go-back-and-get-it 104, 106
good 2, 21–24, 53, 59, 64, 65, 70, 71, 88, 125, 139, 140, 148, 154, 159, 161, 193
graffiti 169, 170
graphocentric-phonocentric 5, 12, 17, 37
Greek philosophy 31, 32, 179, 191, 194
group agency 33, 62–66, 150, 169
group authorship 32
group knowledge 28, 31
group philosophy 31, 33
gye nyame 94

harmonious relationships 147
harmony 61, 91, 96, 98, 101
head 91, 104, 121, 148
healer 95, 152
healing 58, 61, 66, 77, 90, 95, 146, 148
healthcare 60, 190
hegemon 34, 35
Hençkwꟻmç 99
hermeneutic encounter 83, 84
hermeneutic gaze 107
hermeneutics 82, 84–87, 150, 151, 189, 190, 195
hermeneutic void 179
hierarchies 44, 152, 156, 186
hieroglyphics 36, 113
historical consciousness 84, 151
historicity 78, 130
histories 9, 79, 111, 115, 151, 179, 196
holism-individualism 28, 31
hopelessness 168, 170, 174, 175
hospitality 78, 100, 148, 166
hostility 2, 159
human existence 71–73
human experience 41, 52, 74, 137, 153
human intellect 140–42, 145
humanism 96, 107, 121
human rights 130, 172
humble learning 103, 161, 181
humour 15, 167, 170, 171
humour-filled storytelling 158
Hwehwemudua 105, 106

i-Ching 151
identity 1, 8–12, 14–18, 43, 45, 56, 71, 88–91, 96, 109–11, 114, 119, 120, 122, 130–33, 152, 159, 172, 192
idioms 184
Ifa 81, 99
Igbo 59, 69, 71, 73, 82, 95, 124, 194
ignorance 105, 106
Igueben 55, 68
Ikpabonelimin 93
illiteracy 46
image 11, 12, 17, 68, 130

immigration 172
immortality 22, 113
inclusion 39, 48, 109, 112, 185, 187
inclusive practices 162
inclusive repositories 33
indigenous African philosophy 61, 88, 92, 171
indigenous epistemologies 184, 185
indigenous knowledge 54, 175, 178, 181
indigenous knowledge systems 54, 181
individual agency 33, 43, 96, 98, 99, 101
individual authorship 12, 17, 26–28, 31, 32, 37, 39, 43, 85, 128, 137, 139, 154, 165
individual-community debate 96
individual-community relationship 96, 195
individuality 74, 76, 78, 96–101, 107, 109, 130, 139, 162
individual rights 96, 101
infallibility 2
inhospitality 175
injustice 33, 41, 111, 112, 126, 181, 186
institutional access 171
institutional hierarchies 186
institutional power 29
intellectual abilities 118
intellectual agility 105
intellectual competence 105, 177
intellectual group 42
intellectual humility 30, 33, 102–4, 145, 161
intellectual process 145
intellectual tradition 3, 23, 26, 142
interconnectedness 61, 92, 96, 105, 106, 185
interconnected thinking 105
interculturality 132
interdependence 61, 97, 100, 104, 183, 185
interlocutors 30, 69, 76, 156, 171

interpersonal relationships 94
interrelatedness 76
intersubjective intellectuality 14, 16, 144, 145, 147, 150, 151, 155, 161, 169, 185
intersubjective thought 109
intersubjectivity 60, 140, 154, 165
intertextuality 34–36
intratextuality 34
irrationality 173

Japa 169, 172–75, 187, 193, 194
jewellery 90, 92, 191
justice 114, 132, 133, 190
justificatory theories 44
justified-true-belief 143

kalam 44
kaleidoscoping 139
kente 89
kgotia public sphere 148
kinetic knowledge 51
kinship 146
knot 102, 104, 106, 194
knowers 48, 62, 103, 157
Kokuromotie 104, 106
kola 77, 78, 100, 144, 148
Kyemfere 103, 106

labelling 12, 17, 40, 41, 72, 94
Lagos 89, 188
language 3, 9, 13, 28, 30, 31, 37, 38, 46, 47, 55–58, 62, 63, 67, 68, 71, 78, 87, 125, 130, 133, 146, 181, 196, 197
legitimacy 12, 19, 20, 54, 61, 70, 75, 121, 172
liberation 86, 120, 121, 130
liberative hermeneutics 86
libertarians 19
liberties 96, 128
liberty 97
life-giving force 78
lifeworld 167, 169
linguistic power 59
linguistic burden 56

linguistic care 57–59, 61, 64, 68, 70, 72, 74, 152, 183, 184
linguistic convenience 68
linguistic mentality 56
linguistic predicament 56
linguistic schemes 69
literacy 5, 12, 17, 26, 43, 46, 47, 192, 194
literate 44, 46
literature 35, 54, 63, 68, 75, 76, 118, 145, 146, 166, 173, 188, 196
lived experiences 2, 6, 9, 22, 65, 72, 75, 87, 90, 134, 151, 167, 168, 178, 180
lived philosophy 55, 90
lived realities 74, 185
locales 10, 175
logic 11, 27, 44, 83, 113, 118, 172, 178
logical positivist 7
logical thinking 33
logograms 36
luba katanga 125
lyrics 52

mainstream academia 1, 3, 12, 54, 137
mainstream academic philosophy 2, 14, 54, 67, 111, 154, 167
maleness 3, 4, 192
marginalization 5, 38, 39, 110, 119–21, 126
masculinity 4
materialist ontology 176, 179
materiality 10, 34, 35, 62, 63, 81, 163, 167, 179, 180
maxim 70, 76
Ma'at 116
meaningfulness 78, 162
meaninglessness 22, 168, 170, 175
memory 10, 37
mental capacities 145
mental categories 27
meta-philosophical 126, 127
metaphors 60, 114, 182, 184
metaphysics 7, 40, 119, 133, 191
method 7, 14, 17, 21, 23, 30, 49, 84, 137, 139, 140, 144, 146, 148–50, 155, 156, 158, 182, 187, 189, 195

migration 16, 167, 169, 170, 172–75, 188, 192–94
mind 6, 36, 38, 40, 49, 58, 66, 85, 88, 93, 98, 102, 109, 121, 128, 129, 131–33, 139, 145, 152, 156, 159, 162, 168, 175, 196, 197
mirroring 14, 32, 110, 127–33, 182–84
misinterpretation 106, 107
misrecognition 39
moderate communitarianism 76, 96, 97, 187, 192
morality 13, 105, 166, 182, 187, 190, 193
mother 77, 93
motifs 13, 51, 52, 81, 89, 99, 182
museums 81, 83, 187
music 10, 13, 53, 55, 60, 75, 79, 88, 90, 166, 169, 171, 175, 180
myths 114

names 13, 41, 51, 55, 58–60, 64, 71–75, 78, 94, 120, 144, 151, 181, 184
naming 12, 17, 26, 40, 41, 58, 59, 77, 170
naming-owning 5
narratives 33, 44, 60, 64, 75, 85, 110, 119, 122, 127, 141, 158, 170, 181
Ndidi-Amaka 59
ndu 73
Ndubuisi 73
Nduka 73
Ndukwe 73, 74
neijuan 168, 169, 189
neo-colonization 43, 45
neoliberal ideology 178
Nigerian 15, 54, 125, 126, 167, 170, 171, 173–76, 179, 193, 194
nka bi 98
Nkyinkyim 98
non-existence 12, 44, 112, 123
non-human 2, 66, 75–78, 92, 106, 135, 140–42, 145, 146, 148, 153, 156, 157, 162, 182, 191
non-physical 95, 99
non-recognition 39, 118

non-textual forms 37, 38, 48, 51, 85, 86, 141, 142, 171, 182
non-textuality 14, 51, 109, 132, 166, 167, 181
non-textual repositories 35, 37, 49, 51, 72, 134, 135, 143, 144, 155, 183
nothingness 174
Nsibidi 81, 82, 181

obligation 102, 121, 158, 162, 186
Odu ifa 81
okwu 70, 71
ontic 5, 6, 13, 117, 138, 162, 177
onticness 71, 162
ontological commitments 9, 92, 94, 109, 181
ontological difference 153
ontological disposition 150
ontological embodiment 63
ontological primacy 96, 100
ontologies 7, 9, 31, 107, 125, 130
ontology 7, 8, 40, 41, 65, 71, 77, 91, 99, 113, 122, 144, 149, 169, 172–74, 176, 179, 180
openness 102, 103, 105, 161, 181, 182
opportunism 149
oral forms 37, 47, 52–55, 61, 62, 64, 67, 78, 79, 81, 181, 184
oralizing relationality 74, 75
oral knowledge 63, 64
oral performance 182
oral philosophy 52–55, 58, 60, 65, 79, 97, 144, 197
oral repositories 52, 53, 55, 61, 75, 78, 132
oral traditions 52, 54, 61, 63, 64, 67, 185, 189, 194
orita meta 99
Oromo 116
ota 55
other-regarding duties 101
out-of-place 172

paganistic interpretations 84
paintings 51

palaver 15, 146–48, 156, 160, 161, 191, 193, 195
parables 53, 75, 138, 158, 160
paradigm 151, 192
patience 59, 102
patriarchal opportunism 149
patriarchy 4, 36, 91, 117, 118, 190
pedagogical ethics 15
pedagogical practices 157, 164
pedagogical system 63, 64
pedagogy 15, 45, 46, 106, 177, 188
perception 7, 29, 56, 85, 92, 95, 176, 179
performative action 1
performative philosophy 91
performativity 1, 12, 109, 110, 116, 127, 137
performing philosophy 9, 19, 49, 52, 54, 92, 144
performing resistance 117, 121
personhood 13, 38, 56, 76, 78, 90, 97, 122, 129, 132, 150, 152, 162, 190, 193, 194, 197
phenomenon 145, 151, 172, 173
philosophical canon 19, 185, 195
philosophical commitments 10, 60
philosophical community 19, 23
philosophical concepts 5, 51, 56–58, 61, 72, 133, 135, 180, 184
philosophical discourse 46, 72, 99, 183, 188
philosophical heritage 32, 143, 158, 186, 189
philosophical practices 155, 165
philosophical systems 7, 55, 123, 124, 146, 171, 185
philosophical texts 34, 46, 75, 113, 133, 137, 139
philosophy-in-practice 89
phonocentrism 37
planetary bodies 94, 106
plurality 184, 186
poems 52
polemical 49, 158, 159
polemics 15, 158, 159, 161, 162, 187, 193
positionality 6, 145, 153, 154, 157

post-textuality 142
prayers 77, 91
pre-judgements 84, 85
proverbs 13, 38, 51–54, 57, 60, 61, 64, 66, 75, 78, 79, 87, 88, 109, 128, 138, 144, 148, 158, 160, 181, 184, 188, 192, 194, 196

racial hierarchies 44
racialization 4
racism 4, 10, 19, 112, 117, 119, 120, 126, 195, 196
radical communitarianism 96, 187
ram's horn 103
rationalism 143
rationality 3–5, 11, 24, 65, 77, 173
reality 30, 38, 47, 52, 53, 65, 67, 68, 71, 77, 88, 92, 155, 158, 161, 168, 174, 180
rebellion 179
rebirth 77
reciprocity 100, 101
reconciliation 61, 146, 161, 193, 195
refusal-to-read activism 117
reimagining futures 16, 181
reimagining identity 10
relational cognition 30, 138
relational collaboration 169
relational ethics 78
relational factuality 77
relational hermeneutics 150, 151
relationality 13, 15, 28, 49, 52, 60, 67, 74–78, 82, 96, 101, 106, 109, 138, 149–51, 153, 155–57, 171, 185
relational ontology 8, 122
relational perception 29
relational philosophy 75, 76
relational values 76
relationships 2, 61, 72, 76, 94, 101, 133, 144, 147, 150, 153, 155, 157, 161, 162
repositories 5, 13–15, 33, 35, 37–40, 49, 51–53, 55, 59–63, 65, 70, 72, 74, 75, 78, 81–83, 85, 87, 106, 107, 109, 131, 132, 134, 135, 137, 143, 144, 155, 166, 181–83

research designs 163, 185
research networks 185, 186
resilience 98, 182
resistance 14, 59, 83, 110, 115–19, 121–23, 131, 134, 166, 179, 182, 187, 188, 196
riddles 13, 53, 60, 61, 64, 158, 160
rights 78, 96, 101, 130, 147, 172, 193
rigidity 152, 156, 159
rigour 105, 128, 168, 176
rituals 64, 91
runxue 168, 169, 174

sage 11, 32, 127, 129
Sankofa 104, 106, 187, 189, 192, 196
Sapa 169, 172, 174, 175
scientific method 7, 23
script 36, 88, 142, 154
scripting resistance 134
sculptures 38, 51, 81, 84, 90
self 10–12, 27, 29, 34, 39, 47, 69, 85, 98, 101, 129–31, 153, 162–64, 167, 177, 183
self-authenticity 10, 12, 183
self-contained properties 27
self-fulfilment 85, 162, 183
selfhood 101, 166
self-identity 19, 162
sexuality 170, 190
shared destinies 100
shared experiences 9–11
Shijing 151
silencing 45, 84
similitude-dissimilitude exercise 127
skits 170, 175
slavery 10, 43, 120
slogans 53, 169
socialism 121, 130, 194
solidarity 28, 29, 85, 100, 101, 170, 193
speech 13, 37, 38, 52, 54, 71, 75, 102, 190
spider web 98, 105
spirals 89
spiritual artefacts 83
spirituality 74, 118, 119
storytelling 13, 38, 51, 55, 60, 79, 89, 158, 185
strangeness 173, 175
street philosophy 15, 165–71, 180, 182
street writing 169
subaltern cultures 46
subjective consciousness 139
subjective embodiment 154
subjective experience 27
subjective individuality 162
subjective intellectuality 3, 5, 14, 139, 140, 144, 145, 150, 151, 153–55, 167
subjectivity 10, 120, 150, 165
sub-Saharan 8, 9, 13, 16, 33, 53, 67, 72, 74, 75, 78, 81, 88, 93, 111, 132, 145, 148, 159
substance 69, 134
suffering 16, 72, 130, 167, 170, 174, 175
survival 72, 75, 78, 96–98, 100, 174, 177
symbol 84, 88, 89, 93–95, 97–107, 132, 144, 148
symbolism 13, 15, 37, 71, 81, 82, 88, 89, 97, 134, 165
systemic patriarchy 190
systemic prejudices 117

tablets 36
tales 181
tattooing 170
team-produced outputs 156
tech-other 143
temporality 152, 174
textiles 51, 81, 88, 92, 100, 191
textuality 12–15, 17, 26, 33–37, 39, 61, 62, 67, 81, 85, 88, 109, 110, 116–18, 120, 121, 128, 133–35, 137–39, 141, 142, 144, 154, 155, 165–69
theory-practice relationship 164
togetherness 70, 77, 100
topophilic affinity 2

topophobic hostility 2
tradition-modernity debate 18
transcendence 4, 13, 46, 82, 92, 174
transdisciplinarity 89, 91
transgenerationality 43, 52, 61, 65, 89
transhuman age 14, 138, 154, 162
transhuman possibilities 138
transhuman realities 138
transhuman technologies 141, 143, 155
transhuman trans-textuality 142
translation 31, 56, 62, 69, 71, 117, 171
trans-textual age 135, 142
trans-textuality 14, 137–39, 141–43
trans-textual possibilities 142, 165
trans-textual realities 139, 154
trauma 133
truth 13, 38, 39, 41, 52, 56, 67–71, 73, 78, 84, 88, 104, 105, 109, 129, 132, 138, 141, 150, 157, 163, 188, 189, 193, 194
twisted symbol 97

Ubuntu 76, 132, 144, 152, 153, 184, 187, 194
ubwenge burarahurwa 148
Uhu 68
uhu-ebhon 68, 69
Ujamaa 121, 194
Ukama 76, 132, 144, 152, 193
umuntu ngumuntu ngabantu 76
unconcealment 151
unity 42, 89, 100, 107, 121, 187
unity-in-diversity 100
universality 2, 41
universities 22, 37, 128, 129, 163, 178, 191

Unu 73
Unuagbon 58, 59, 73
unveiling 184
utterance 66
utu uhu-ebhon 68

vagueness 69, 159
validation 70, 103–5, 153
validity 75, 94, 172
vernacular illiterate languages 46
vernacularization 46
violence 42, 43, 72, 84, 119–21, 133
virtue 38, 39, 56, 103

weaving 101, 147, 182
West–Africa 82
whiteness 5, 12, 17, 26, 43–45, 47
whitening 45, 46, 166
wisdom 1, 2, 6, 7, 9, 18, 19, 24, 25, 32, 36, 38, 40, 41, 46, 48, 49, 57, 61, 63, 67, 81, 92, 98, 101–6, 124, 156, 163, 168, 182, 192, 194
women 36, 77, 192, 193
wood 36, 91
wooden figures 93
writing 13, 14, 31, 32, 37, 38, 40, 46, 52, 54, 57, 60, 75, 81, 82, 86, 112, 116–19, 128, 133, 138, 165, 169, 187–90, 192

xenophobia 133

Yawa 175
Yetunde 77
Yoruba 31, 33, 36, 39, 74, 97, 99, 111, 124, 173, 175

Zulu 39, 76, 81, 124